Providing
Reference Services
for Archives *&* Manuscripts

ARCHIVAL
FUNDAMENTALS
SERIES II

Managing Archival and Manuscript Repositories
by MICHAEL J. KURTZ

Arranging and Describing Archives and Manuscripts
by KATHLEEN D. ROE

Selecting and Appraising Archives and Manuscripts
by FRANK BOLES

Providing Reference Services for Archives and Manuscripts
by MARY JO PUGH

Preserving Archives and Manuscripts
by MARY LYNN RITZENTHALER

Understanding Archives and Manuscripts
by JAMES M. O'TOOLE & RICHARD J. COX

A Glossary of Archival and Records Terminology
by RICHARD PEARCE-MOSES

Providing
Reference Services
for Archives *&* Manuscripts

MARY JO PUGH

SOCIETY OF
American
Archivists

CHICAGO

The Society of American Archivists
www.archivists.org

©2005 by the Society of American Archivists.
All Rights Reserved.

Library of Congress Cataloging-in-Publication Data
Pugh, Mary Jo.
  Providing reference services for archives and manuscripts / Mary Jo Pugh.
      p. cm. -- (Archival fundamentals series. II)
  Includes bibliographical references (p.) and index.
  ISBN 1-931666-12-1
    1. Archives--Reference services. I. Society of American Archivists.
  II. Title. III. Series.

CD971.P84 2005
025.5'2—dc22

                          2005049037

Graphic design by Matt Dufek, dufekdesign@yahoo.com.
Fonts: Minion (text and footnotes); Meta (secondary text and captions).

To

Robert M. Warner

Teacher, Mentor, Exemplar

TABLE *of* CONTENTS

PREFACE TO THE ARCHIVAL FUNDAMENTALS SERIES II • xi
ACKNOWLEDGMENTS • xv

1 LOOKING BACKWARD, LOOKING FORWARD • 1
Technology and Archives • 1
Professional Changes • 5

2 REFERENCE SERVICES IN ARCHIVES • 9
What Are Archives? • 9
Why Keep Archives? • 16
How Has the Use of Archives Changed through Time? • 19
Access to Archives • 22
What Are the Dimensions of Reference Services
in Archives? • 24
Promoting the Use of Archives • 29
Ethics of Reference Services • 29
Goals of this Book • 30

3 IDENTIFYING USES AND USERS OF ARCHIVES • 33
The Continuing Usefulness of Records • 34
The Uses of Archives • 36
Understanding Individual Needs • 40
Identifying Vocational User Groups: Using Archives
for "Profit" • 43
Identifying Avocational User Groups: Using Archives
for "Fun" • 57
Information Seeking • 61
Archives and the Economics of Information • 72
Conclusion • 73

4 Providing Intellectual Access to Archives • 75

Arrangement • 76

Description • 83

Providing Information about Repositories • 92

Providing Information about Holdings • 97

Providing Information from Holdings • 103

Providing Information about Records Creators • 106

Providing Referrals • 108

Conclusion • 109

5 The Reference Process • 111

Reference Interaction in the Repository • 112

Reference Interaction with Remote Users • 132

Reference Services on the Web • 138

Outreach • 143

6 Determining Access Policies • 149

Defining Access and its Relationship to Reference Services • 149

Access Concepts • 151

Laws Affecting Access to Information • 155

Donor Restrictions • 158

Ethical Norms • 159

Restrictions • 160

Elements of a Repository Access Policy • 162

Conclusion • 173

7 Providing Physical Access to Archives • 175

Reference Facilities • 176

Security • 180

Preservation • 185

Public Hours • 187

Directions • 187

Policy and Procedure Statements for Users • 188

Registration and Identification • 189

Personal Belongings in the Reading Room • 197

Managing Materials in the Reading Room • 199

General Rules for Handling Records • 202

Taking Information from Records • 203

Forms • 204

Automation of Registration and Retrieval Procedures • 204

Electronic Records • 205

Conclusion • 207

8   PROVIDING INFORMATION FROM ARCHIVES:
    COPIES AND LOANS • 209

Copying Documents • 210

Copyright • 225

Publishing Documents • 239

Providing Access to Digital Surrogates of Documents • 240

Loan Policies and Procedures • 242

Conclusion • 246

9   MANAGING REFERENCE SERVICES AND EVALUATING
    THE USE OF ARCHIVES • 249

Organizing Reference Services • 249

Managing Reference Services • 254

Measuring and Evaluating the Use of Archives • 258

Understanding the Value of Use • 266

User Studies • 268

10 BIBLIOGRAPHIC ESSAY • 271

General Works on Reference Services in Archives • 272

On-line Works for Reference Services in Archives • 275

Related Organizations • 276

Keeping Up • 277

Understanding the Creation of Records and Archives • 278

Users of Archives • 279

Information Seeking • 290

Reference Process • 291

Access • 299

Administration of Reference Services • 306

Education of Reference Archivists • 311

Evaluation of Reference Services • 311

Ethics • 312

Appendices

    1: ALA-SAA Joint Statement on Access to Original Materials in Libraries, Archives, and Manuscript Repositories • 313

    2: Statement on the Reproduction of Manuscripts and Archives for Reference Service • 316

    3: Checklist for Access Policies and Reference Services • 318

    4: Reference Procedures Manual—Suggested Contents • 323

    5: Standards for Reference Archivists—Behaviors Associated with Good Reference Service • 327

    6: Standards for Reference Archivists—Knowledge Associated with Good Reference Service • 331

Notes • 335

Index • 357

Preface to the
ARCHIVAL FUNDAMENTALS SERIES II

There was a time when individuals entering the archival profession could read a few texts, peruse some journals, attend a workshop and institute or two, and walk away with a sense that they grasped the field's knowledge and discipline. This was an inadequate perception, of course, but it was true that the publications—basic or advanced, practical or theoretical—were modest in number.

The archival world has changed considerably since these more quiet times. A rich monographic research literature is developing. Scholars from far outside the field are examining the "archive" and the "record." Archives, archivists, records, and records managers are in the daily news as cases appear testing government and corporate accountability, organizational and societal memory, and the nature of documentary evidence—all challenging basic archival work and knowledge.

The new edition of the Archival Fundamentals Series (AFS II) is intended to provide the basic foundation for modern archival practice and theory. The original preface (written by Mary Jo Pugh in her capacity as the series editor) to the first editions, which were published in the early to mid-1990s by the Society of American Archivists (SAA), argued that the seven volumes "have been conceived and written to be a foundation for modern archival theory and practice" and aimed at "archivists, general practitioners and specialists alike, who are performing a wide range of archival duties in all types of archival and manuscript repositories." It is hard to state the purpose of the new AFS editions better.

There are some differences, both subtle and obvious, in the new volumes. The new editions are more open-ended than earlier versions, extending back to the Basic Manual Series published a quarter-of-a-century ago by SAA, reflecting evolving viewpoints about archival theory and practice. Even more important a difference is the broader and deeper context of archival publishing AFS volumes reside in. Mary Jo Pugh, in her introduction of just a decade ago, noted that the AFS titles are companions to "more specialized manuals also available from SAA." Now, SAA has four other series (some just underway), including *Archival Classics* (featuring reprints or new collections of older publications with pivotal importance to the profession), *Archival Readers* (both collections of new and previously published essays intended to supplement the descriptions of foundational theory and practice of the AFS II volumes), *International Archival Studies Readers* (both collections of new and previously published essays intended to provide glimpses of archival work and knowledge outside of North America), and *Archival Cases and Case Studies* (examining archival work in a variety of institutional types and with a variety of media). Added to SAA's own publications is a vast sea of new titles pouring from the presses of other professional associations and trade, professional, and university publishers.

Both the earlier *Basic Manual* series and the *Archival Fundamentals* series provide benchmarks in the development of archival knowledge and work. One can trace changing ideas and practices about archival reference services by reading the 1977, 1992, and 2005 volumes dedicated to this subject in the respective SAA manual series. One also expects to find in this volume current standards and consensus about this aspect of archival work. One also expects now, of course, that some may disagree with aspects of the current presentation, and may point to the growing research and case study literature being generated by the archival profession.

Many people participated in the production of the various volumes constituting the *Archival Fundamentals Series II*. The profession owes its gratitude not only to the authors, but to various chairs and members of the SAA Publications Board; Miriam Meislik, Photo Editor for the series; the SAA Executive Directors, Susan Fox and Nancy P. Beaumont; and especially to Teresa Brinati, SAA Director of Publishing, whose good humor, organization, and steady commitment to a quality product helped keep the publishing of these and other SAA volumes on track.

RICHARD J. COX
Publications Editor
Society of American Archivists

Acknowledgments

I am grateful to the Society of American Archivists for asking me to revise this book and for their patience as I did so. Teresa Brinati again was thoughtful and supportive. Miriam Meislik, Matt Dufek, and Amy Hosa added photographs and figures. Meg Moss, copy editor, was thorough and helpful. I am particularly grateful to readers of the drafts. Elizabeth Yakel provided rigorous, yet always constructive criticism. Kathy Marquis provided a helpful view from the field. William Maher read and edited the section on copyright not once but twice, a gift indeed. These and the anonymous readers pushed me to make this a better book. What results is my responsibility.

Students at the University of California Berkeley taught me by their questions. The staff of San Francisco Maritime National Historical Park taught me by their example, especially the archivists in the Historic Documents Department, Lisbit Bailey, S. Taylor Horton, Sara Diamond, and Erica Toland. Diane Vogt–O'Connor, formerly Chief Archivist of the National Park Service, provided opportunities for professional growth.

I am also grateful to the 1997 Research Fellowship Program for the Study of Modern Archives administered by the Bentley Historical Library, University of Michigan, and funded by the Andrew W. Mellon Foundation, the National Endowment for the Humanities, and the University of Michigan. This month away from daily work surrounded by the resources of the University of Michigan recharged my intellectual batteries and started me thinking about the relationship of information seeking and reference services in archives. I am sustained

by the continuing friendship and support from colleagues, both for-
mer and current, of the Bentley Historical Library at the University of
Michigan, especially directors Robert M. Warner and Francis X.
Blouin, assistant director Bill Wallach, and reference archivists Nancy
Bartlett and Kathy Marquis.

Tom, Katie, and Christopher McCort have nurtured me through
these years with patience and love.

SONNET

As barren fields in wintertime are lined

With broken stalks and ears of corn long spent,

So records are the stubble of mankind—

They have no life, and give no nourishment.

They are the words and numbers of the past,

The dry, misshapen kernels in the bran,

Like chaff stripped from the germ, they cannot last—

Yet you do let them feed the mind of Man.

Then hearty, golden grains these records be:

They are the sustenance of History.

—Thomas Michael McCort, 1982

CHAPTER 1

Looking Backward, Looking Forward

The first edition of *Providing Reference Services for Archives and Manuscripts* was published in 1992. This revision seeks to create a model for understanding the legacy from the archival institutions we inherit and for assessing how new developments extend and change it. It also seeks to assist reference archivists in managing accelerating change, keeping the best of past practice, while becoming integral to the knowledge organizations of which archives are a part.

Technology and Archives

Archives at the millennium face a paradigm shift comparable to the invention of the printing press five centuries ago, perhaps even comparable to the invention of writing itself five millennia ago. To update this manual in 2004 is to reflect on a decade of transformations, resulting from revolutionary changes in tools for creating and managing records.

First is the exponential increase in the availability and power of computers, driven by the development of faster, smaller, and cheaper electronic devices. Recent decades have proved the validity of Moore's law that silicon chips double in capacity every eighteen months. End-user computing has become almost ubiquitous in the developed world. No longer does a researcher have to depend on a technician to program a main frame computer to analyze data. Almost every

The monitor displays the hull lines of the *Eppleton Hall,* produced by the Historic American Engineering Record in 1996 using computer-rectified photogrammetry. On the right are photographs of the hull and a copy of the hand-measured and hand-drawn midship section used to build the vessel c. 1914. In 1996, the drawings had to be mailed on floppy disks from Washington to San Francisco. San Francisco Maritime NHP 98-02-10-09.

researcher has desktop access to extended power of computation, whether for writing, manipulation of data, storage of data, statistical analysis, graphic presentation, project management, or communication through increasingly powerful, yet more user-friendly, software applications for word processing, spreadsheets, or databases. Many people have laptop computers that can go almost anywhere. More recently people have ready access to scanners and digital cameras to create digital records, store them, and transmit them. Because more and more forms of communication are digital, they can be shared and integrated in powerful new ways. Text, sound, and images now converge in digital formats, which can be searched, manipulated, copied, and transmitted by one person. The first edition of this book was composed on the first generation of personal computers. It used 5 ¼ inch floppy disks for storage and for transmission—through the postal service.

Connectivity of computers is the second revolution in the past decade, the advent of telecommunications tools for communicating across time and space. The World Wide Web was launched in 1993–1994, shortly after publication of the first edition. The Internet, particularly the interface provided by the World Wide Web, is a watershed in human communications, with profound implications for providing reference services. The Web has doubled in size every six months since 1993. In 1996, some 61 million users had access to the Internet; by 1998 an estimated 147 million users; and by 2000 some 320 million users.[1]

These tools greatly expand archivists' ability to provide intellectual access, especially information about repositories and holdings. A quantum leap in the last decade has taken archivists from participation in national bibliographic networks available only in subscribing libraries, such as RLIN and OCLC, to finding aids encoded in a standard structure developed in a matter of years and served on-line through the World Wide Web to unknown users around the world.

Networks enable archives to provide direct access to information in electronic form, whether through intranets within organizations or through the Internet to the world. They also allow archives to provide access to digital surrogates of analog documents. Records in electronic form can be copied, and the copies reorganized, reformatted, and transmitted without altering the original record. The availability of optical disks, CD-ROM, and other storage media make it possible to store, retrieve, and use archival information in a wide variety of settings off-site. Information can be downloaded into personal computers, searched, manipulated, and sent on, without ever taking physical form. Increasing speed and ease of dissemination parallel the massive increase in the volume of information in archives in recent decades—and in the raised expectations of our users.

The decade also witnessed revolutionary changes in reference services. The archival system is no longer predicated on interaction between the user and the archivist. Researchers can directly access finding aids and increasingly locate documents on-line. Remote inquiries come through e-mail, often from "accidental users," and are increasing exponentially.

Information-seeking behaviors are changing rapidly as information is increasingly "born digital," recorded in electronic forms, especially in networked environments. A search engine on the World Wide Web may yield a list of archival repositories or archival holdings, available to the public in ways undreamed of a decade ago, but it will list them among hundreds, or thousands, or tens of thousands of sites. Understanding the information needs and research methods of significant users of archives is even more important now as archivists compete for the attention of users on the Internet among a universe of clamoring pop-up ads and banner ads. "Attention is a scare resource— perhaps the most precious scarce resource there is. . . . What information we select to attend to, and how intently, is still the most important question about learning."[2]

Perhaps a greater concern is the new popular illusion that all information is available on-line, especially when this illusion is coupled with the normal consequence of the Principle of Least Effort, to be discussed in chapter 3. This combination militates against searching for information that is not on-line. Changing researcher expectations mean that archivists will have to develop innovative ways to connect with them. Although archivists are increasingly linked to users via telecommunication networks, personal networks remain the most important means by which users find archival repositories. Archivists must connect with those personal networks so that archives will be on the mental maps of users. Users must think of archives as an information resource.

Most users are unprepared for the complexities of using archives; they will still depend on archivists. Even experienced users may rely on reference archivists to provide road maps through the forest of citations produced by on-line search services. Determining a search strategy for approaching archival materials and providing the context for understanding them remain important reference services. New "chat" services, collaborative references tools, and video interfaces may bring users in personal touch with reference staff in new ways.

The accelerating pace of technological change exacerbates our concerns for the issues for legal access. In an age when information about individuals is collected, stored, and linked, little individual privacy may remain. Ensuring the proper use of such personal information will become even more critical as the reach and power of these tools increase. The uses of copyrighted information becomes more complex and more salient in a network environment.

Harnessing these tools to administer the research room more effectively is underway. Automated registration of users and the retrieval and control of materials in use are now available. Much of the routine information now collected on forms can be automated through the use of light pens and bar codes. Collecting this information in electronic form may make if easier to analyze. Sophisticated ongoing analysis of data about use of archives can be employed to improve reference services.

Reference service may be redefined in ways yet unseen. Reference archivists may be called upon to provide information rather than records. They may design user interfaces for and refer to electronic databases that remain in the physical custody of the creating agency. They need to be present at the creation of information systems rather than the last to know of them.

Reference archivists, like all archivists, have begun to realize the vital necessity for advocacy and for educating records creators, records users, and the general public about the value of archives. Reference archivists shape the image of their repository. But more, they can improve archives' accessibility and value by making the collective memory of an organization readily usable by current staff, by studying the dissemination of information from archives, by analyzing the common characteristics of information-seeking behavior of major user groups to improve finding aids, and by reaching out to potential users.

Professional Changes

This revision also provides an opportunity to reflect on the dramatic changes in a professional lifetime. I was only the second reference archivist at the Michigan Historical Collections, or MHC, known to us as "The Collections." It is now the Bentley Historical Library. When I joined the staff, the institution was about thirty years old, solidly part of the historical manuscripts tradition. The primary access tool was a card catalog in the reading room. The 3 x 5 inch catalog cards provided brief descriptions of collections, with added entry cards and subject entry cards interfiled in one alphabet. For larger collections, the card referred to a "contents list," a list of box titles or file-unit titles. Like a table of contents, it was filed in the first box of the collection. In the early 1970s, after lugging innumerable first boxes from the basement storage area to the reading room so that user after user could examine a contents list and determine that a collection was not needed, we finally saw the obvious solution and placed the contents lists in the reading room.

For researchers outside the library, the first *Guide to Manuscripts in the Michigan Historical Collections of the University of Michigan* was published in 1963 and was still in use when I joined the staff. The entries from this guide were sent as the first report to NUCMC (National Union Catalog of Manuscript Collections), and collections were added to NUCMC on an irregular schedule. The second *Guide to Manuscripts in the Bentley Historical Library* was published in 1976, by herculean effort on the part of professional staff and typist. In the late 1980s, these brief collection-level descriptions were converted to electronic form and exported to RLIN. In the 1990s, the contents lists were converted to the EAD format and placed on the World Wide Web available to anyone in the world.

I will not forget one of my earliest experiences as reference archivist. In my first days on the job, a researcher asked for the Alexander Winchell Collection. From the catalog card, I figured out that it had a contents list. I knew that the list was in the first box of the collection in Room 100 in the basement. I was quite pleased with myself when I found the fixed location guide, determined the location of the collection, and retrieved it. The researcher set to work through the dozen boxes. Toward the end of the week, on my way to something else, I realized with dismay that the collection included hundreds of bound volumes, which lined the bookcases in the reading room, a separate contents list filed with them. I tentatively brought the list to the researcher, who said scathingly, "It would have been nice to have seen this earlier in the week!" I can now see the collection-level description and the full text of the finding aid, brought to national standards for description, from my computer in my California study, as can any researcher with comparable equipment anywhere in the world.

When I began my professional career, researchers took notes in pencil or with a typewriter. They could request photographic, microfilm, or photostatic copies, all made by outside labs at some expense. The only photocopy machine was in the dean's office upstairs. Today, researchers request permission to copy documents with digital cameras or scanners. Repositories provide access to documents on-line: through on-line publications, exhibits, or images embedded in finding aids.

Whatever the future brings, the joint quest of users and archivists to find patterns in the past that have meaning for the present will persist. Reference archivists share with users an enthusiasm for historical research because they feel the need to understand the past, both to make sense of the present and to plan for the future. Archival research is "shared by archivist and user alike, both bending their skills toward wrestling knowledge from information and wisdom from knowledge in this troubled world."[3] Recorded memory is vital to cultural continuity. "It is a hallmark of human societies that they seek to preserve a memory of the past, and have always done so. Indeed, keeping and using the past is central to our concept of human cultures and civilization."[4]

Reference archivists contribute to individual growth and understanding, to the solution of practical social problems, to scholarly research, and to cultural continuity. They empower individuals and groups by helping them to link their past and future. Reference work calls for ingenuity and perseverance. It depends on the virtues of patience, attentiveness, understanding, and sympathy. At its best, reference work brings forth the meaningful association of information and insights that result in new understanding of the human condition. Reference archivists breathe a second life into records and do indeed "let them feed the mind of Man."

CHAPTER 2

Reference Services in Archives

Archives are tools; like all tools, they are kept to be used. They allow people to communicate information and evidence through time. Archival and manuscript repositories identify and preserve records of continuing usefulness. Most importantly, they make them available for use. Reference services in archival and manuscript repositories assist users, and potential users, in using archival holdings and locating information they need.

What Are Archives?

Although the general public has some understanding of libraries, many people do not immediately understand the word "archives." All archivists are familiar with the problem of telling new acquaintances what archives are. Elizabeth Yakel found a considerable "degree of uncertainty among college educated people about what archives are."[5] Archivists note that newspaper references to archives are often preceded by the words *musty* and *dusty.* The words *documents, records, archives, historical records,* and *historical manuscripts* are often used interchangeably. Understanding is further complicated because archives are found in institutions variously called archives, libraries, records centers, historical libraries, historical societies, museums, manuscript collections, special collections, and even rare book rooms.

The practice among computer specialists to use the word *archive* as a verb further complicates matters. Even in this sense, it is variously used to mean storing something off-site, or storing something off the network. On many Web sites, the word is used to mean collections of earlier editions of newspapers or articles. As we will see, however, these words can be used to make distinctions that are useful.

Document

Some 5,000 years ago, people began to create documents to communicate through space and time. David M. Levy, in an extended thought-provoking meditation, defines documents as "quite simply,

An example of early communication and recordkeeping. Sumerian Rectangular Cuneiform Tablet, Ur, Third Dynasty, ca. 2050 BCE. Baked tablet inscribed with an administrative record concerning 39 personnel.
Photograph and description courtesy Howard Nowes Ancient Art.

talking things. They are bits of the material world—clay, stone, animal skin, plant fiber, sand—that we've imbued with the ability to speak. . . ." More graphically, he says that "Writing is the act of breathing our breath into the dust of the earth."[6] Levy notes that "Documents are exactly those artifacts to which we delegate the task of speaking for us. Each kind of document, each genre, is specialized to do a certain kind of job—to carry a certain kind of information and to operate within a particular realm of human activity."[7]

Recording technologies have proliferated since writing was first embedded in clay tablets with a stylus. Documents may be textual, graphic, photographic, audio, video, or electronic. Levy notes that modern documents "speak through text and sound, through still and moving images—the same basic communicative repertoire we had before computers appeared on the scene."[8] The rapid convergence of recording technologies into digital forms is, of course, the dominant fact of the last two decades. The importance of documents is demonstrated by the way people seek to invent or improve recording technologies. People find these "talking objects" useful and invest effort and expense to produce them and keep them.

Record

A document created or kept in the course of practical activity is a *record*. Actions create records. As people order, direct, design, build, report, inform, communicate, instruct, plan, evaluate, advertise, apply, announce, authorize, request, compensate, contract, or otherwise do their jobs, they create records. The title of a record often reflects the action that creates it, such as *report, order, request, plan,* or *permit*. All records are utilitarian, created in the course of practical activities. Records provide evidence of the actions that created them.

> Records systems consist of three elements: communication patterns, recording technologies, and documents.

Records can be thought of as "the working files of working folks." Both individuals and organizations create, receive, and keep records. Records systems consist of three elements: communication patterns, recording technologies, and documents.

Personal Records

First let us consider personal records. The public can understand archival concepts better if they are related to personal collections. People save legal papers to prove citizenship or ownership. Most people keep documents such as birth certificates, social security cards, tax records, deeds, insurance policies, bank statements, or stock certificates as evidence of their actions, obligations, and rights. People also create records when they use recording technologies to create documents to communicate to others or to capture memories of important events. People use such documents as calendars, address books, or diaries to remember obligations, information, or actions. Nearly all families keep photographs of weddings and birthday parties, trips to the beach, and other ceremonies and events that tie the family together. Many keep school papers and school photographs of their children. Increasingly, families also create and keep audio recordings and videotapes of family events. When they are separated, family members communicate through cards, letters, or e-mail.

Manuscript repositories, or collecting repositories, collect such personal papers because the activities of the individuals who generated them contain evidence or information of interest to others. Manuscript repositories also collect the records of organizations that do not maintain their own archives. Such records of individuals, families, or organizations collected because of their usefulness to others are called *historical manuscripts*.

Organizational Records

Second, consider the organization and use of information in a complex modern institution, where the relationship of communication patterns, recording technologies, and documents is clearer than it is among personal papers. In the course of their work, staff members receive and send information, some of which is captured in documents, both analog and digital. Most documents are not static; they are used to send information from one person or office to another in the organization and beyond. Some documents, such as rules and directives, flow downward through the organization to communicate orders and instruction. Others, such as reports, flow upward to give managers information needed to control money, labor, and materials. Still other documents, such as memoranda, communicate laterally to coordinate activities and share information needed by more than one department. Today, records systems are increasingly called information systems or even knowledge systems.[9]

Activities in modern organizations generate *organizational records* that collect in files maintained where the information is needed in the course of daily business. The filing systems of individuals and departments reflect the activities that generate them. Office files contain incoming documents, copies of outgoing documents, and documents created and retained in the office, such as notes, calendars, and minutes. The filing structure is the primary mode of retrieval. Twentieth-century recording technologies, such as electrostatic copying, have increased the likelihood that copies will be found in many locations, but the aggregation of documents in any one location will be unique, reflecting the activities carried out at that location.

Archives

In its narrowest sense, the word *archives* means the records of organizations, created or accumulated in the course of daily activities, and saved by the organization because they are useful for continuing administration. Although archives are retained by the organization that created them, they may also be useful for researchers outside the organization. Today, the word *archives* is often used to refer to both organizational records and historical manuscripts. In the broadest sense, *archives* are *all* records of continuing usefulness created in the course of daily activity, whether organizational or personal. Archives are kept so that people can find information or evidence necessary to ongoing work. Archives are also kept so that the information they contain can be reused by others. As archivists, we are interested in records both as the evidence of actions taken and for the information they contain. In this book, the word *archives* will generally be used in the broader sense, except in those cases where significant differences between the use of organizational archives and historical manuscripts exist. See figure 2-1.

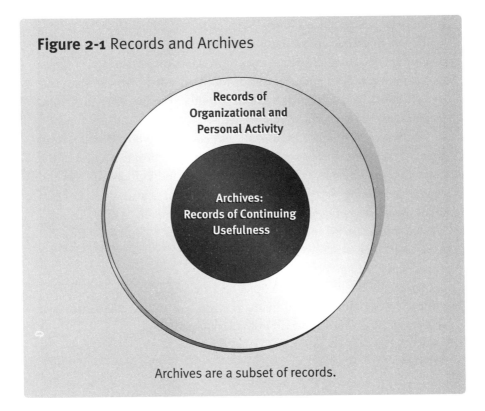

Figure 2-1 Records and Archives

Records of
Organizational and
Personal Activity

Archives:
Records of Continuing
Usefulness

Archives are a subset of records.

The word *archives* derives from the Latin word *arca*, a place to keep things, such as a box or chest. We still use the word *ark* in this way, when we speak of the Ark of the Covenant, or Noah's Ark.[10] The earliest archives were boxes or chests of documents. The first documents kept were probably created as aids to memory, such as lists and accounts. Early archives also contain incoming communications, that is, documents received, such as orders and letters.

Early archives rarely contain copies of outgoing documents. The only way to make copies was to do so by hand, so retained copies are not exact facsimiles of communications as they were sent. Some two hundred years ago, however, people invented mechanical means to capture copies of documents sent. The letterpress made copies of handwritten documents in the nineteenth century; carbon paper made copies of typewritten documents in the early twentieth century. Both of these methods required the copy to be made at the time of creation. With the advent of the photocopier in the mid-twentieth century, however, exact copies could be made easily at any time. Today, many documents are written and sent in electronic form. They may be retained in electronic form, with printers used to create paper copies for study, convenience, or retention.[11]

To complicate definitions further, the English language also uses the word *archives* to refer to the building that houses records of continuing usefulness and to the agency charged with responsibility for identifying, preserving, and using them. In the United States, to confuse matters more, the words *library* or *historical library* are often used for archival agencies or buildings. For example, the archival agencies called "presidential libraries" are actually units of the National Archives. They hold both the personal papers of the president and others in his administration as well as the records created by the Office of the President. The Bentley Historical Library at the University of Michigan holds *archives* and *historical manuscripts* created by organizations and individuals in the state of Michigan and the *archives* of its parent institution, the University of Michigan. The Bancroft Library at the University of California similarly holds archives and historical manuscripts collected from all western states, as well as the archives of the University of California. The reader must be alert to context to ascertain the intended meaning of the word "archives."[12]

It is further useful to distinguish between *archives* and *libraries*. Archival agencies differ from libraries in the materials they hold. In general, libraries collect published documents that are deliberately created in large numbers and widely disseminated to inform, educate, entertain, or delight a wide audience. Individual items are self-contained and self-explanatory. In contrast, archives preserve documents created to communicate to a defined audience, often a particular individual, for a specific purpose. Archival documents result from the activity they record, and can be best understood in the context of other documents created by the same activity over time. These unique aggregations of records, created as the by-product of daily activity, are saved for future use, both by their creators and by later researchers.[13]

Thus, it is not the form of materials, whether published or unpublished, that distinguishes libraries and archives. Rather the difference stems from the purpose and the process by which the documents are created and maintained. Archival materials consist of a wide variety of forms, many requiring special conditions of use. They typically comprise correspondence, diaries, case files, memoranda, circulars, and other unpublished textual records. Modern archives also include photographs, films, videos, sound recordings, and electronic records. They may also contain documents published in the course of organizational activity, such as reports, directories, posters, or advertisements. Manuscript repositories often include collections of published material that support the research topics in the repository's collecting domain.

Although their holdings differ, libraries and archives share common activities and a common mission. Both select, preserve, organize, and make available information in documentary form, whether in textual, audiovisual, or electronic formats. The mission of both libraries and archives is to preserve our collective memory and to make accumulated knowledge available for present and future use. The relationship of the forms of documentation is illustrated in figure 2-2.[14]

Museums also share this mission by collecting artifacts. Documents are artifacts, but as information-bearing objects, they differ from most of the artifacts usually collected by museums. Levy suggests that documents are a special class of artifacts, significantly different from other museum collections, "documents are representational artifacts."[15] In the National Park Service, archives are managed as part of the museum collection. Historical societies often collect both artifacts and historical manuscripts. Some, such as the Wisconsin Historical Society, also serve as the archives for both state government and local governments.

Why Keep Archives?

Because actions create documents captured in records systems, records continue to provide *evidence* of the actions that created them, long after the actions are completed. Records also provide *information* about the people, events, and objects that were the subject of the actions. American census records are created by the constitutionally mandated act of counting people for apportioning representation in Congress, but it is the information about the people counted that has continuing usefulness for family historians.[16]

Figure 2-2 Information Family Tree

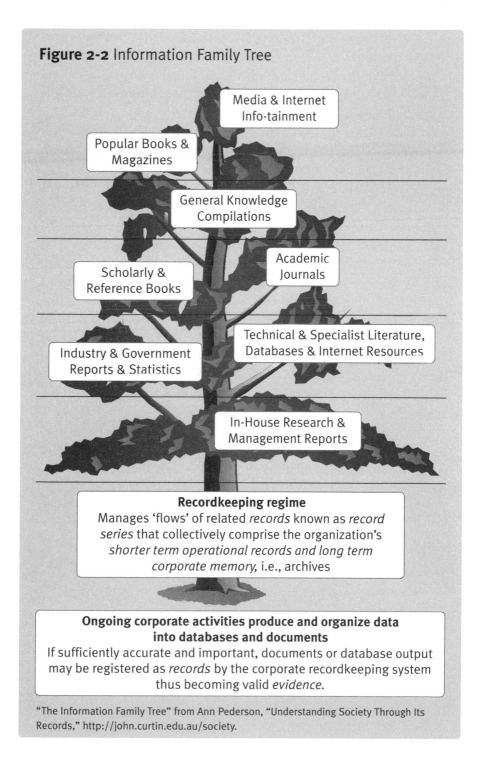

Media & Internet Info-tainment

Popular Books & Magazines

General Knowledge Compilations

Scholarly & Reference Books

Academic Journals

Technical & Specialist Literature, Databases & Internet Resources

Industry & Government Reports & Statistics

In-House Research & Management Reports

Recordkeeping regime
Manages 'flows' of related *records* known as *record series* that collectively comprise the organization's *shorter term operational records and long term corporate memory,* i.e., archives

Ongoing corporate activities produce and organize data into databases and documents
If sufficiently accurate and important, documents or database output may be registered as *records* by the corporate recordkeeping system thus becoming valid *evidence.*

"The Information Family Tree" from Ann Pederson, "Understanding Society Through Its Records," http://john.curtin.edu.au/society.

With the passage of time, employees leave or retire, but the organization continues. With good records management, records documenting significant actions with continuing consequences are transferred to organizational archives so that later information seekers, whether organizational successors or others seeking evidence of past actions, can find them. The mission of the archival profession is to identify records that have continuing usefulness, preserve them, and make the information in them accessible through time.

The use of archives depends, in part, on the mission of the parent organization. The three most common rationales for maintaining archives are administrative use, public accountability, and research. Many corporate entities, such as businesses, churches, voluntary associations, universities, and museums, establish institutional archives to care for their records. Such organizational archives are kept primarily to meet the long-term administrative, legal, or fiscal needs of the institution itself. If an activity continues, the need for access to records continues. If an activity is useful, the records resulting from it are useful. When such an organization keeps its records because of their continuing usefulness for its ongoing business, *administrative use* is the primary rationale, and reference services are provided first to the creators of the records and their successors.

Governmental archives have an additional responsibility for *public use*. As a "cornerstone of democracy," public archives provide for government accountability by preserving records that enable citizens to monitor the conduct of the people's business and the performance of their official servants. As James Madison stated in 1822,

> A popular Government without popular information or the means of acquiring it, is but a Prologue to a Farce or a Tragedy or perhaps both. Knowledge will forever govern ignorance, and a people who mean to be their own Governors, must arm themselves with the power knowledge gives.[17]

Public archives also preserve records confirming individual rights and benefits. The National Archives "ensures, for the citizen and the public servant, for the President and for the Congress and the Courts, ready access to essential evidence." Reference services in public archives, therefore, serve all citizens.[18]

Research by users outside the originating organization is another rationale for keeping archives and the primary rationale for preserving historical manuscripts. Since manuscript repositories collect the papers of individuals and the records of outside organizations expressly because they provide evidence for historical research, providing reference services to researchers has a higher priority in this type of repository.

While the mission of the parent institution guides priorities for reference services, the cultural value of archives as the memory of civilization transcends the current uses of records in the organizations that create or preserve them. When considering the needs of users, archivists balance these enduring cultural values against the immediate practical needs of the organizations that pay to preserve records. These short-term and long-term values may conflict as archivists provide access and reference services for the primary user groups—as identified by the mission of the parent institution—and also seek to meet the cultural needs of the larger society.

How Has the Use of Archives Changed through Time?

Access policies and reference services in an archival or manuscript repository can be best understood by knowing the repository's history and appreciating its relationship to the historical development of the uses of archives. Administrative use was the first use of archives. By and large, governments were the first organizations to create and keep records. Until the French Revolution, governmental archives were used almost exclusively by sovereigns and their servants. The archives of institutions such as universities and churches were also used only by their administrators.

During the French Revolution, the public recognized the value of government archives. The new French government declared that its archives were the property of the people, who are the source of sovereignty in a democratic society. The records of government, therefore, are public records and must be accessible to the people. Other western nations also adopted the concept of public access to public records. In the United States, this principle, often called the *public archives tradition,* was enunciated from the beginning of settlement. Records, such as land records and tax records, were kept in public courthouses and made accessible to all, although archival agencies expressly charged to preserve archives developed slowly. Interest in public archives gained momentum only at the end of the nineteenth century with the development of an identifiable historical profession and with reformers' interest in better management of governmental activities. The first true state archives was founded in Alabama in 1901; the National Archives was founded in 1934.[19]

Modern manuscript repositories are descendants of the libraries of medieval monasteries and universities, which, before the invention of the printing press, copied and collected literary and scholarly texts for research. In the nineteenth century, university libraries, manuscript libraries, and historical societies also began to collect unpublished records created in the course of private activity, such as personal and family letters, diaries, drafts of literary productions, notes, and the like. In the United States, collecting and preserving historical records centered at first in private historical societies, founded by gentlemen scholars who collected the manuscripts of the great men and great families of the eastern seaboard. In the mid-nineteenth century, publicly funded historical societies in the Midwest began to collect the manuscripts and reminiscences of early settlers and pioneer families. In addition to collecting papers of prominent individuals and families for historical and genealogical research, historical societies also edited and published significant manuscripts. Manuscript libraries, administered by scholars for the use of scholars, first provided access only to members of the society or to researchers with academic affiliations. The narrow elitism of this research-based *historical manuscripts tradition* persisted well into the twentieth century, but now most repositories are open to all.[20]

These differing institutional purposes and histories gave rise to a confusing welter of institutional policies for access to archival materials and divergent views of the appropriate and permissible uses of archives and manuscripts. Private archives and scholarly research libraries tended to limit access, in the first case, to administrators of the creating institution and, in the second, to recognized scholars. In contrast, governmental archives and publicly funded historical societies opened access more broadly.

During the last half of the twentieth century, however, access opened to the broader public. Freedom of information laws, open meeting laws, and sunshine laws provided wider access to information in the public sphere generally, and this sense of the public's right to know expanded to archives. Simultaneously, American society attempted to reduce prejudice based on race, class, and education that limited access to its cultural institutions.

The archives of private organizations, especially businesses, make notable exceptions. Modern businesses generate masses of records to manage their own activities, and governmental agencies demand that businesses produce and keep masses of records to regulate them. American society has become more litigious. For these reasons, many businesses keep only the records required by law, and only for the period required by law. They use records management programs to pare their records to the minimum. Few records are kept in archives, and access is restricted to staff and a few others. There are notable exceptions; and a number of large corporations have arranged for their older records to be managed, often as large manuscript collections, by collecting repositories.

In the twenty-first century, government may also follow private organizations and restrict access. For example, the United States government, in response to the events of 11 September 2001, expanded its limitations on access to government information. It is too early to assess the full implications of these events, but all archivists must monitor limitations on access and provide an intelligent dissenting voice as necessary.

In general, the archival profession has moved from a custodial role, in which the archivist's primary duty was to protect repository collections by limiting use, to a more activist role promoting the wider use of archives. The predominance of the public archives tradition, the development of national guides and national standards, and the promotion of professional standards by funding agencies such as the National Historical Publications and Records Commission and the National Endowment for the Humanities have strengthened the trend toward wider access. The Society of American Archivists has also taken an important role in melding these divergent institutional traditions into a professional whole and in setting professional models for reference services, access policies, professional ethics, and outreach activities.

The change in professional culture causes occasional conflict between traditional practices and new attitudes. Today, most archivists emphasize service to a broad public, and they seek to develop new constituencies to support archival programs. Archivists' attention to reference services and user education reflects a desire both to enlarge constituencies and to respond to their needs. It also acknowledges the reality that these constituencies influence continued funding and growth for many archives.

Access to Archives

To use archives, users need intellectual, legal, and physical access to them.

Intellectual Access

In the broadest sense, access refers to the process of identifying and locating records likely to contain information useful for solving problems. Access in this sense is *intellectual* access, provided both through the arrangement and description of records discussed in chapter 4 and through reference assistance discussed in chapter 5.

Legal Access

In a narrower, *legal* sense, access can mean the authority or permission to use archives. Records created initially for personal or internal use may contain private or confidential information that should not be disseminated immediately. Legal and ethical issues may condition the use of archives: most importantly, privacy, confidentiality, and freedom of information. Archivists strive to provide fair, equitable access to records in their care, but they must also protect information affecting creators or third parties until it is no longer sensitive. These concepts will be discussed in chapter 6.

Physical Access

Access may also mean *physical* access, the opportunity to examine documents, which will be the subject of chapter 7. Repositories provide physical access by maintaining regular and sufficient hours of operation and by providing space to study records. While meeting these needs of current researchers, archivists must also consider those of future users by protecting archives from theft or abuse and from wear and tear.

Physical access may also be provided through copies and loans, the subject of chapter 8. Copying raises questions of technology, preservation, and copyright. Today, access to documents may also be provided

---

Figure 2-3 Fundamental Elements of Archival
Reference Services

- Intellectual Elements
  - Arrangement
  - Description
  - Reference Services
- Human Dimension: Interpersonal Elements
- Administrative Elements

Figure 2-4 Reference Services in Archives

Reference services in archives provide:

- Information about the repository
- Information about holdings
- Information from holdings
- Information about records creators
- Referrals to other repositories or resources
- Information about laws and ethics regarding the use of information
- Instruction in using records
- Education about the research process
- Physical access to holdings
- Copies, permissions, and loans from holdings

through digital surrogates disseminated electronically through the Internet or other means.

What Are the Dimensions of Reference Services in Archives?

Reference services, broadly conceived, are the activities by which archivists bring users and records together to meet user needs. As listed in figure 2-3, they encompass a wide variety of activities and call upon intellectual, administrative, and interpersonal skills. Reference services assist users in person in the research room, or remotely by telephone, mail, fax, or electronic mail systems. Public programs both inside and outside the repository also provide reference services. On the Internet, reference services assist users who discover them there. In a small repository, these intellectual, interpersonal, and administrative activities may be the responsibility of one person; in a large repository, several professional staff members as well as paraprofessional and clerical staff may share them. See figure 2-4.

> Reference services, broadly conceived, are the activities by which archivists bring users and records together to meet user needs.

Bruce Dearstyne argues that the term *reference services* is "too narrow and too reactive." He believes that the term suggests that services begin only when a user approaches the repository. He argues that archivists should focus on *researcher services,* a more active function, in which staff members encourage research use, actively assist users, and evaluate use to improve it. Although this book uses the customary term, like Dearstyne, it argues for a full program of public services engaging all aspects of interaction with users and potential users. Dearstyne's argument is usefully captured in figure 2-5.[21]

Intellectual Dimensions of Reference Services

Facilitating research, undertaking research, and educating users are three important intellectual components of reference service in archives.

FACILITATING RESEARCH

To facilitate research, reference archivists help users find records that meet their information needs. Users bring a wide variety of inquiries to archives, and archivists help them refine their questions and organize search strategies. Although finding aids are increasingly standardized, most repositories have inherited a wide variety of finding aids that are yet to be integrated into a repository-wide system meeting national standards. Such diversity of finding aids often requires the

Figure 2-5 What's in a Name?

Research Services	or	Reference Services
User Orientated		*Custodial Orientated*

• *Researcher* services is the common term.	• *Reference* is the common term.
• Use is the main rationale for archival work.	• Use is one of several rationales.
• Information on users is essential for progam planning.	• Information on users is interesting but of secondary importance for program planning.
• Systematic gathering and analysis of user information.	• Researchers are merely counted.
• Marketing is a priority.	• Marketing is secondary.
• Promoting use, researcher services are regarded as program priorities.	• Promoting use, researcher services are secondary to appraisal and other functions.
• Subject indexing fosters retrieval.	• Reliance on provenance as a means of retrieval.
• Finding aids and services are geared to users' needs.	• Reference is mainly educating users to appreciate records, contexts, how the repository works.

Bruce Dearstyne, *Managing Historical Records Programs: A Guide for Historical Agencies* (Lanham, Md.: Scarecrow Press, 2000): 105.

mediation of archivists before users can understand them. Most users also need information about repository rules and procedures and information about legal and physical access to archival materials.

Once likely records are identified, researchers often request assistance in using them. Because archives are the products of activities, understanding them requires knowledge of the organizations and individuals that created them. Archivists and users must understand the historical context, organizational communication patterns, and recording technologies that produced the records to understand and evaluate the information they contain. Archival arrangement according to provenance, though critical to understanding organizational context, is unfamiliar to many users and may present initial difficulties for users outside the organization or even for later users from the organization.

Facilitating research requires continuing interaction between archivist and user throughout the research project and may not be completed until the last question regarding copyright or citation is answered. In addition to using records and descriptive tools within the repository, reference archivists often facilitate research by referring researchers to other sources beyond the repository.

Undertaking Research

Undertaking research is a second important intellectual role. Reference archivists undertake research themselves to learn about the parent organization and the history of records creators, to understand the functions and forms of records, to place the finding aids and records in context, to locate information in the records for others who cannot do so themselves, and to evaluate records or information for users.[22] Reference archivists also undertake systematic analysis of the use of their holdings both to improve them and promote them.

Educating Users

Educating users is an essential part of reference work, a third significant intellectual function of the reference archivist. Instructing users in the research room is an important part of daily work. Few users have experience with primary sources, and most are unprepared for the complexity of archival sources, finding aids, and archival practice. Most have no experience integrating and understanding the undigested mass of information so often found in primary sources. Although every schoolchild learns how to use library classification and catalogs, many archives users have never encountered archival arrangement and archival finding aids. They need instruction to understand primary sources and the finding aids that describe them. Archivists must impart an understanding of archival theory and practice beyond the repository, to provide "a better intellectual framework for understanding both the organizational principles behind archival records as well as the multiplicity, interconnectedness, and appropriate selection of one type of access tool over another."[23]

Beyond daily teaching in the research room, reference archivists often find education in a broader sense part of their role. Since reference archivists encourage the use of records, educational programs grow naturally from reference functions. Public programs such as orientation sessions, workshops, handouts, or introductory slide, video, or on-line presentations extend the ability of the reference archivist to help users to be more efficient in exploiting archives. Increasingly, these educational programs are presented through a repository's Web site.

Human Dimensions of Reference Services

Because archival reference service can be very personal, good communication between users and archivists is critical. Archivists and users may have very different expectations about the reference interaction. Discrepancies in expectations may cause confusion, disappointment, or failure to use archival holdings effectively. For example, users and archivists may differ in their expectations of the conditions under which archival materials are to be used. In some repositories users must apply in advance for admission. Expecting archives to be like libraries, users may feel rebuffed if they cannot be accommodated without an appointment. Because archives must ensure the integrity of unique materials, most require users to submit to rigorous security provisions; users who prefer to be left alone may find archival registration and security procedures intrusive or annoying. Archivists must remember that if they are not careful, the first message they give to users is "We think you are a thief," or "We think you are not worthy of using these materials."

Users and archivists may also have different expectations about the appropriate role of the archivist and the amount of time required to locate needed information. Most archivists expect to provide instruction in using finding aids and guidance to records likely to contain needed information, but many users expect archivists to furnish information directly. Usually archivists have neither the time nor the resources to do so.

Policies and priorities must be clearly and convincingly communicated; they must also be reviewed regularly to recognize changing publics, user needs, and technologies. Inherited finding aids, architectural barriers, and procedures that work well enough for experienced users may need to be revised to meet the needs of current users.

Archivists strive to make every user feel welcome and to treat all users fairly. Research in archives requires an effective partnership between archivists and users. Sensitivity, clarity, and a genuine spirit of public service are needed to ensure successful interpersonal relationships in archival reference services.

Administrative Components of Reference Services

Administering the daily tasks of reference services, or managing the staff providing them, may be the most time-consuming aspect of archival reference services. Among the many administrative tasks required for the smooth operation of reference services are receiving, identifying, registering, and orienting users; locating and retrieving materials; and supervising copying and loans.

The daily practice of reference services must be grounded in administrative policy. Identifying appropriate policies and efficient procedures and ensuring fair and equitable treatment of all users are important managerial tasks for reference archivists. Further, reference archivists advocate user needs in repository planning and relay user information to other repository staff.

Promoting the Use of Archives

Outreach and advocacy touch many aspects of archival management, such as funding, donor relations, and acquisitions, but they are integral to the work of reference archivists, who educate users and potential users about the value and use of archives and encourage wider use of them. Archivists sometimes have reservations about promoting the wider use of their repositories because of limited physical facilities and staff resources. Although greater numbers of users may increase the workload for the staff, the repository can use the demands of increased numbers to argue for greater support from resource allocators. Users are also resources for the repository. Users help identify records of enduring value and work to preserve them. Many users volunteer for time-consuming but significant tasks such as preparing materials for microfilming or indexing records. Users can also contribute significantly to outreach activities that make archival resources better known.

Promotion of archives ties in closely to the future of reference services. Without strong constituencies to advocate increased resources, funding for archives likely will remain low. Identifying the products and services that archives provide to their parent institution and to other user constituencies, thinking creatively about the costs and venues for providing them, and publicizing them aggressively are necessary to sustain the archival mission in the developing information economy.[24]

Ethics of Reference Services

Because the success of reference services turns on negotiating a series of balances, its ethical dimensions assume considerable importance. Archivists respond to inquiries and promote the use of their holdings. While making records available for use as widely as possible, archivists protect the legitimate needs of the creators of records and the privacy rights of third parties identified in them. Even when information from holdings cannot be supplied, repositories provide information about themselves and their holdings. Archivists strive to supply all documents of interest to a researcher, although meeting this obligation may be difficult, given the arrangement and descriptive practices of most repositories. Reference archivists respect the confidentiality of the reference interview and divulge the details of users' research only with permission. Careful formulation of policies and training of staff are needed to ensure fair and equitable access and service for all researchers.[25]

Goals of this Book

This book describes policies and procedures for reference services that represent a commonly accepted professional standard. It describes the wide variety of users and potential users of archives and advocates for user-centered policies and procedures. It discusses the relationship of access tools and reference services. In administering reference services, policy must come first; procedures should reflect established policies. Any reference program must be flexible enough to accommodate itself to the unique characteristics of its particular archives. Each repository will need to adapt these general policies and procedures to its own conditions and to codify them in a repository procedures manual.

Traditionally, reference archivists directed traffic through the intersection of users, finding aids, repository staff, and records. Mediation by reference archivists is changing rapidly as more and more resources are published on the Internet. Nonetheless, reference archivists still balance and integrate the intellectual, interpersonal, and administrative elements of reference services to meet the needs of users, protect records, and promote the most effective use of repository resources.

What cannot be codified either in this manual or in a repository manual is the joy of reference work. It can bring great personal satisfaction. The excitement of the hunt for information is followed by the satisfaction of the find. Reference archivists feel personal accomplishment in locating or directing users to information or records that could not be found without the reference archivist's knowledge and skills and find satisfaction in helping others. Reference archivists satisfy their own curiosity about historical events as they assist others. They apply their historical knowledge and build their own research skills. The amazing variety of questions from users stimulates intellectual growth; answering one question raises yet new questions. The serendipity of research, the unexpected discovery of new sources and insights, frequently entertains and delights.

CHAPTER 3

Identifying Uses and Users of Archives

Many people use archives, both directly and indirectly, because the information found in them is useful outside the repository. Archives can be put to a variety of uses that result in a variety of products. Archivists need to understand both current users and potential users. Most archivists agree that archival records are not used to the extent that the information and evidence they contain might warrant. As we will see in chapter 9, archivists can conduct research to discover the information needs of potential users and design reference and public programs to meet them.

When providing reference services, reference archivists seek to understand every user's particular information need by learning their research purpose, intended uses of archival information, type of questions, degree of experience, preparation, and constraints. When planning reference programs, public services, and outreach programs, repositories need to identify user communities and analyze their needs. This chapter begins by discussing the users of archives as they might be seen from the reference desk. It concludes by discussing information seeking in archives by looking at archives as they might be seen from the user's point of view.

The Continuing Usefulness of Records

As noted in chapter 2, records are kept because of their continuing usefulness, either to their creators or to others. T. R. Schellenberg, one of the first generation of American archivists at the National Archives, shaped the discussion of these ideas. His concepts, outlined in figure 3-1, provide useful insights into how people use records.

Primary Uses of Records

Organizations and individuals create records initially to carry out administrative, fiscal, economic, social, legal, or other activities. Schellenberg calls these the "primary values" of the records. These values may continue as long as the organization continues. Architectural records are created to build structures and they are needed for as long as the structure is maintained. For example, an architectural drawing provides information about the electrical system in a building. The primary value of many records, however, may be exhausted within years, months, days, or even hours. Such records are scheduled for routine destruction. For example, grocery lists can be discarded as soon as groceries have been purchased.

Figure 3-1 Uses of Archives

The Continuing Usefulness of Records
- Primary Uses of Records
- Secondary Uses of Records
  - *Informational value*
  - *Evidential value*
  - *Intrinsic value*
- Direct and Indirect Users of Archives
  - *Direct users*
  - *Indirect users*

Secondary Uses of Records

Some records, however, can be used by a wide variety of users beyond the organization, and Schellenberg calls these the "secondary values" of records. He further distinguishes informational value, evidential value, and intrinsic value.

INFORMATIONAL VALUE

Informational value is the most straightforward. It describes the value of the information that records contain about people, events, objects, or places. In the course of daily activities, records creators capture information about the objects of their activities or the places in which they occur.

EVIDENTIAL VALUE

Evidential value refers to value of the information (or evidence) that records provide about their creators, their activities, or the actions that generated the records. Information in archives gains much of its value from its context. Archives may reveal patterns of action and document accountability. For example, that a report is in the files of the recipient indicates that the report was sent and received; a copy of a response to it in the same file indicates that it was read. Thus, file contents and filing structures can be as important for documenting the flow of information as for retrieving information itself. Some readers might remember the famous question, "What did he know and when did he know it?" The evidence in archives may provide an answer.

INTRINSIC VALUE

Intrinsic value describes the value that records have as artifacts—as symbols, or tangible links to the past. The Declaration of Independence has been reproduced many times, but the original document still awes citizens viewing it in the National Archives. Some years ago, one of the twenty-three known examples of the first printed Declaration sold for $1.5 million; what price could be put on the handwritten original document?[26] Similarly, families treasure family photographs or a Bible with handwritten entries of baptisms, marriages, and burials of their ancestors, for these are tangible links to a personal past. While the economic value of these items may not be high, their intrinsic value makes them priceless to the family.

Records and Archives

Schellenberg expanded his distinction between primary and secondary values into a distinction between records and archives, a more problematic concept. According to Schellenberg, archives were those records whose primary values had been exhausted, that is, archives were records useful only for researchers other than their creators. In practice, this was a fatal distinction. Because archives were seen as records whose primary use had been exhausted, they were used only by secondary users. Archives were cut off from their organizational functions. Many records with continuing usefulness to their creators are equally useful to others. It is more accurate to think of archives as that portion of records that have continuing usefulness to later users, whether from the creating institution or elsewhere, as seen in figure 2-1.[27]

The Uses of Archives

In the research room of any archival repository, people search finding aids, identify records, request them, and read, copy, and cite them. These activities can be counted, and as we will see in chapter 9, archivists frequently compile such numbers to report the use of archives. It is more important, however, to ascertain *why* people use records. They use records to find information or evidence for a purpose. "Idle curiosity" is rarely a motive for seeking out an archival repository.

When providing reference services to individuals, reference archivists seek to understand each user's particular information need. When designing policies and programs for reference services, they seek to understand how users look for information or evidence. Understanding patterns of information seeking becomes even more important as reference services on the Internet multiply. Such services

must be designed for a variety of
groups, because the personal interaction between archivist and user
that shapes the provision of reference services is not possible on the
Internet.

Direct Uses of Archives

Direct use occurs when someone
obtains information from a record
or draws on a record as evidence of
the activity that it documents. In
these instances, users are people
"with a need or wish to know infor-

Researchers convey enthusiasm and
passion when they find documents of
importance to them and disseminate
the information far from archives in
publications and presentations.

mation found in records of enduring value."[28] Variously called
researchers, patrons, users, or clients, people initiate contact with the
repository directly, in person, or by phone, mail, or e-mail. Direct use
can be measured when someone reads a document in the repository,
obtains a copy by mail, or receives information by telephone or letter.
Loaning documents is another type of direct use. It is more difficult to
quantify the direct use of virtual documents posted on the Internet, but
it may be possible to measure the number of documents downloaded.

A direct user is also anyone "who for any reason needs the services
of an archivist or an archives."[29] For example, archivists supply administrators with information about an organization's history taken from
archival holdings or from administrative histories compiled to manage
records. Records creators also use archival services when an archivist
determines the disposition of a records series. Likewise, archivists
assist individuals wishing to preserve family papers. See figure 3-2.

Indirect Uses of Archives

Identifying *indirect use* is more difficult. Indirect users are "the potential beneficiaries of the historical information found in archives."[30]
Indirect users may never enter an archives or archival Web site, but
benefit nevertheless from archival information by using the many and

Figure 3-2 Practical Uses of Archives

Traditionally we categorize the users of records in terms of the purpose of their research, i.e., genealogical research, historical research, and the like, a custom we will hereafter refer to as definition by "occupational" categories. From a public relations view (and possibly also from the aspect of managing records), this tradition does not serve us well. First, defining use by occupational categories tells us almost nothing specific about the results of research, which may bear little relation to the occupational category itself and therefore misleads about why and even how that research is being done. Secondly, in explaining the function of an archives to the public, be aware that your listeners are seldom interested in possibilities; they are interested in results. One is reminded of the story of the successful storekeeper who was asked why his customers bought quarter inch drill bits. "They don't buy quarter inch bits," he replied. "They buy quarter inch holes." The public relations minded archivist understands that people in our market oriented culture are far less interested in knowing what an archives contains and even less what archivists do than they are in learning about the products created by research and how these products help them.

In thinking of our users as primarily historians or administrators or genealogists, rather than thinking of the products of their work, we have created categories that conceal products and therefore deny us public relations opportunities. In a section following, we will expand on this proposition. Just now, let's consider some of the general uses of archives, exclusive of the names we give to those who use them. None has ever said this as well as the staff of the New York State Archives, whose 1984 publication, *Toward a Usable Past,* was published as a report to the governor and citizens of the state. In addition to the more abstract uses of records related to the documentary heritage and the advancement of scholarly knowledge, the writers list nine practical uses of records that help expand our sense of the significance of records, the service to which they are put, and the products created from them in our society. These practical uses and the publics who benefit from these uses are worth remembering. We have paraphrased them here.

To individual citizens, organizations and institutions—Records are used to document agreements and obligations, to substantiate claims, and to back up contentions. Government records on the formulation of legislation, for example, are essential for understanding legislative intent. . . . Court records . . . are useful to attorneys and judges dealing with similar cases and to legal scholars charting

(continued)

Figure 3-2 continued

long term judicial trends. "Vital records" . . . are often crucial to establishing individual rights.

To institutions and organizations, including governments in conducting their affairs—Archives are used to study the origins of policy and program decisions . . . and to ensure the continuity of administration. Through ready access to their own past, such organizations achieve perspective on their progress and partially compensate for the rapid turnover in personnel that often leads to repeated changes in program direction and to policy discontinuities.

To the schools—Records enable students to understand their community's past, and to relate that past to the present. Use of historical records also develops reading and cognitive skills . . . [Students] analyze evidence . . . reach their own conclusions from evidence that may be inconclusive and contradictory.

Environmental issues—Engineers and investigators have used land use permits, maps, photographs and other archival records . . . to determine the location and nature of . . . toxic dumpsites.

For repairing and maintaining the physical infrastructure.

To illustrate and entertain—Businesses use historical records in advertising campaigns, newspaper writers draw on them for background for stories, and movie makers and television producers seek them out. . . . Writers of fiction draw on them for portrayals of past conditions and lifestyles.

Historic preservation—Records are used, for example, to determine the original appearance of the buildings and the location and type of their framework, electrical wiring, and plumbing.

To document land ownership—Land grants, maps, deeds, and other records are used by public authorities, corporations and individual citizens to determine property boundaries and ownership.

To improve health care—Medical researchers study patient records to understand genetic and familial diseases. . . transmitted from generation to generation, and to trace the spread of contagious diseases within geographical regions. . . .

Seen thus, these products become a rich source of public relations material, interesting to the public and essential to the well being of society, providing the specificity that no simple listing of occupational categories could achieve.

Elsie Freeman Finch and Paul Conway, "'Talking to the Angel': Beginning Your Public Relations Program," *Advocating Archives: An Introduction to Public Relations for Archivists* (Lanham, Md.: Scarecrow Press, 1994): 17–18.

varied products arising from their direct use. Though a relatively small number of researchers actually uses archives, their work has a "multiplier effect," transmitting information that affects how others think about themselves and their past.[31] Books, newspaper and periodical articles, dissertations and theses, genealogies, speeches, term papers, films, television documentaries, slide shows, exhibits, Web sites, legal briefs, environmental impact statements, and other policy documents are some of the products that convey information and evidence derived from archival holdings. Some refer to information in archives; others quote it, while others actually display documents for indirect users. See figure 3-2 and turn again to *The Information Tree* in figure 2-2, which graphically summarizes the indirect uses of archives.

Understanding Individual Needs

People come to archival repositories because they need to solve problems that require historical information or evidence found in archival holdings. Patrons generally seek solutions to their information problems, not particular objects, so in most cases they do not come to archival repositories because they want to use historical records as such. If archival repositories do not meet the information needs of users, users will not seek out archives.[32]

Although uses are practical, users often find the age, authenticity, or beauty of original documents as important as the information or evidence they contain. Authentic documents move and even awe people. The tangible, direct link to the creators of documents touches them emotionally. As an undergraduate once said, "Do you mean this letter was actually written by a Civil War soldier? Cool!" American history came alive for him in a personally meaningful way. The opportunity to touch a document as artifact also explains much of the joy of working in the archival profession.

It is also true that people who could benefit from information available in archives do not use archives. It may be because they do not know that archives have the kinds of information they seek. Others do not use archives because they think using archives is too time consuming or too daunting. Some may think that archives are not open to them.

Reference archivists need to understand who is consulting what types of information for what purposes. The needs of direct users differ depending on their research purpose, the uses they intend to make of archival information, the type of information sought, the types of questions they ask, and their experience and preparation.

Research Purpose

Research purpose is in part determined by whether the user's information problem is motivated by work requirements or by personal interest. Archives can be used for "profit" or for "fun," for love as well as money. Most people come to archives because their work, often on behalf of a business, government, association, university, class assignment, or client, requires it. This is "extrinsic motivation"; the work is performed for external rewards. Other researchers come to archives because they want to, seeking information for enjoyment, recreation, or personal growth. This is "intrinsic motivation, . . . the desire to learn for its own sake."[33]

The user's occupation or discipline has a large impact on the information requested and research methodologies employed. On a practical level, a user's occupation affects time available for research. Those whose work requires archival research find repository hours from nine to five satisfactory, as may retired individuals who have finally gained the time to devote to research. Many of those seeking information for enjoyment, recreation, or private use, however, find business hours, or abbreviated weekend and evening hours, very limiting.

Intended Use

The intended use of information—report, film, exhibit, family history, book, article, legal brief, advertisement, or environmental impact statement—affects the types of information sought and the questions asked. It is helpful to distinguish between the form or genre of information and the media on which it is stored. Reference archivists need to understand the form of evidence that researchers require for their intended use. For example, minutes of meetings or hearings may be found as paper summaries, paper transcripts, audio-recordings, video-recordings, or electronic documents.

Type of Question

Users typically bring two types of questions to archives: factual and interpretive. Some information needs are "applicational," such as the need for a specific document to provide evidence to solve a particular problem or to illustrate a point. An exploratory study of reference queries found that 56 percent of all questions about holdings sought specific items.[34] Researchers with factual questions approach archives with closed-ended questions, seeking a particular document, or seeking specific information about a particular person, place, object, or event. Their questions are precise and focused, asking, "Who, What, Where, When, How many, or How much?" Although such questions are precise, they may require considerable time and ingenuity to answer.

In contrast, other information needs are "abstract," intended to increase general understanding or competence. Researchers with interpretive questions read comprehensively through a body of material to tell a story, develop a narrative, or test a hypothesis. Posing open-ended questions, they seek to answer broad questions of motivation, causality, and change. They ask the question, "Why?"[35]

Experience and Preparation

Another variable affecting user needs is degree of experience in archival research. Many users, regardless of education, occupation, or nature of inquiry, are not well versed in archival research and need help in conceptualizing the research process. They need help from archivists to analyze the process of finding relevant documentation and devising search strategies. Once novices are launched on their research, they may need assistance deciphering handwriting, understanding dating conventions and abbreviations, or interpreting slang and references to contemporary events—in other words, helping them understand the context of the records. Many ready reference questions can be answered with such standard reference tools as the *Dictionary of American Biography*, the *Encyclopedia of American History*, local reference sources, or the Internet, and the archivist may have to teach newcomers to use these sources. Although archivists may imagine that it is particularly urgent to teach young or novice users proper care of documents and photographs, they often find that new users, more in awe of original sources than experienced users, treat materials with more respect.

It is difficult to predict how much staff time will be required to assist users. In general, the less experienced the researcher the more important the educational role of the reference archivist. In some cases, however, more experienced researchers require greater assistance from the reference archivist because they bring more complex reference requests. Since they are more efficient at using larger quantities of material, more experienced researchers may also require more time from support staff for retrieving materials and photocopying from them.

The degree of preparation for or the research stage of any particular project also affects reference requirements. Paul Conway suggests that the use of records generally moves through four stages: discovering potential sources; orienting oneself to procedures in the particular repository; searching records; and applying information found to the research problem.[36] Each of these stages requires different reference services.

Identifying Vocational User Groups: Using Archives for "Profit"

Staff of the Parent Organization

Staff members of the parent institution are an important user population. Archives, the corporate memory of the institution, are preserved so that the parent institution can understand its history and the sources of current policy and can maximize its return on its investment in information resources. Archives are used to ensure continuity, build on experience, and identify solutions for current problems. Use of archives can help prevent repetition of failed solutions for recurring problems. The entertainment industry was perhaps first to recognize the continuing usefulness of its business products as assets, to reuse or repurpose them. Other organizations do the same.[37]

Staff members use records to document the infrastructure of the organization, be it the buildings that house it, or, in the case of governmental records, the very fabric of public life, such as roads and bridges. Maintenance, repair, and public safety depend on good records. Members of the legal staff seek precedents, the terms of gifts, or evidence for current litigation.

Other employees turn to the archives to prepare for celebrations of notable events because archival records document the founding, purposes, and development of the institution. Marketing, public relations, and human relations staffs seek illustrations and other visual materials for advertisements, commercials, training films, employee information brochures, publications, exhibitions, videos, films, slide shows, and Web sites to explain the organization to employees and the public. They request apt and colorful quotations for speeches and publications. Corporate staff members use archives for customer-service research, and those in the development office of membership organizations find archival information useful for fund-raising.

Many staff questions are factual, not interpretive. Staff members often seek an illustration, quotation, or verification of a "first." Employees often request a known document in the records of a particular unit. Such seemingly simple requests may require considerable reference time if the exact date and circumstances of creation of the document are imprecise, or if the existence of the document is only remembered or only noted in brief subsequent references.

Since administrators of the parent institution are simultaneously creators and users of archives, access and reference policies may give priority to their requests. Prompt and appropriate response justifies the archives to its resource allocators. For administrative archives, especially those newly established, a successful program requires a wide range of reference services to the parent. "Through a continued effort to establish an image of usefulness through its reference services, the archives can establish its validity and role in the organization of which it is a part."[38] Manuscript repositories need similar policies for determining levels of service for donors of personal papers and for organizations that deposit or donate their records.

Archives can fulfill their roles in the parent organization only if administrators are aware of the resources of the archives and know how to use them. Archivists have many tools to educate staff. They may send brochures and copies of finding aids to new employees. Inviting department heads and administrative assistants to visit the archives and to discuss information needs can build effective relationships. Archivists can use organizational newsletters, publications, and exhibitions to inform employees of archival holdings. Celebrations such as anniversaries provide opportunities to demonstrate the resources and services of the archives. Because of their knowledge of organizational history, archivists can be key contributors to such events. In these cases the archivist often functions as a primary researcher.

An archives can become indispensable to its parent organization if it serves as a broker for information about institutional history, functions, internal operations, and activities—that is, if it truly acts as a corporate memory, not only storing such information but making it known. The archives itself uses such information to identify, organize, and describe organizational records; if promoted aggressively, this information may become the basis for making the archives the center of the organization's information system.[39] A good example is the Massachusetts Institute of Technology Archives, which uses administrative histories and biographies, developed as front matter for finding aids, as an information resource for internal or external users.[40] Elizabeth Yakel urges reference archivists to become knowledge brokers in their organizations, "the reference archivist as an equal and active participant with users in the knowledge creation process."[41]

Archivists themselves may be among the most important users of their own archives, particularly as intermediaries for other users within the parent institution. Responding to inquiries by telephone, fax, mail, and e-mail is an important reference service. Archivists interpret the inventories, catalogs, and other finding aids, and use them to look for information for records creators or other users. Archivists locate specific information or documents for factual researchers and assist interpretive researchers in finding relevant sources. Archivists disseminate information about the organization through letters, phone calls, e-mail, copies, publications, exhibitions, Web sites, and educational programs. Many organizational Web sites include historical documents and images in the pages headed "about us." As staff members themselves, archivists are the employees most likely to know an institution's history and organizational changes. They can draw attention to precedents, policies, and documents relevant to current issues and provide copies for current decision makers.

Staff Members of Other Organizations

In much the same way that staff members use archives on behalf of the parent institution, others also use archival resources in their work. Staff members of other organizations, here called "professional users" for lack of a better term, represent many professions, including but not limited to lawyers, legislators, engineers, landscape architects, preservationists, urban planners, architects, film and television producers, picture researchers, journalists, and publishers. Although they may not be trained as historians, they ask historical questions and use archival sources to answer them.[42]

These professionals are direct users linking archival sources to many indirect users. They use archival information on behalf of groups, clients, firms, governments, or professional associations. Examples of the dramatic impact of historical information on current policies abound. Environmental impact statements identify toxic waste sites threatening municipal water supplies. Civil rights suits document discrimination and gain monetary awards or reinstatement. Archaeological impact statements alter building plans. Geneticists trace the genealogical component of many diseases. Historical preservation documentation qualifies structures for tax credits and encourages the adaptive reuse of old buildings. Indian tribes win large settlements by establishing the true value of lands ceded for token payments in the nineteenth century. Mining companies use historical records to locate former mines and tailings for reworking. Historical accounts are used to locate and map the activity of earthquake faults. And in the West, vital water rights depend on historical allocations.

Films, especially television documentaries, are an important means by which historical information is disseminated to the public. Approximately seven million viewers have seen each of the historical films in the Public Broadcasting Service series *The American Experience,* and millions more see classroom rebroadcasts. Some fourteen million people watched *The Civil War* in October 1990, and the Illinois State Historical Library received thousands of requests for copies of the moving letter written by Major Sullivan Ballou to his wife Sarah. Documentaries using historical materials explore such topics as prohibition, the civil rights movement, or the internment of

Japanese-Americans during World War II. In the 1990s, cable channels such as the History Channel and the Discovery Channel dramatically extended the reach of these programs, which shape present-day conceptions by the narratives they present of the past. These programs, which tell stories in ways that people can enjoy, often simplified for dramatic effect, are sometimes called "edu-tainment" or "info-tainment." Photographs used in publications, posters, and advertisements are another important means by which historical information is transmitted to the public.[43]

Professionals using archives often expect considerable reference assistance. Most are not trained in archival research and many work under time constraints. They may be paid on an hourly basis or work for an employer with a deadline, or both. Reporters, both print and television, epitomize the deadline problem. Professional users, expecting to find ready reference collections or detailed indexes that will answer their questions quickly, may be disconcerted when told they must search through documents in many collections or records groups. For example, information needed by a historic preservation architect to preserve a building is seldom found in one folder, but must be assembled from unpublished and published sources, including city directories, maps, tax records, building permits, photograph collections, and newspapers.

By requiring scholarly credentials, many repositories once denied access to these professional users. Today, archives and manuscript repositories strive to define access as broadly as possible because professional users put information from archives to work in the real world and affect public policy and public understanding in important ways.

Scholars

Many assume that scholars are the primary constituency for archives, but in most repositories their numbers are significantly smaller than other user groups. As direct users of archives, however, scholars transmit and transfer historical information from archival sources to the indirect users of archives. Scholars from numerous disciplines—history, geography, political science, demography, sociology, literature, medicine, epidemiology, among others—use archival holdings. Scholars may not always be affiliated with academic institutions; independent scholars are found in many fields, including genealogy. Whatever their field, scholars are more likely to be interpretive rather than factual researchers, with research of broad scope. Reference archivists need to understand the nature of scholarly inquiry, research methodologies, and use of archival evidence in all disciplines using the archives.

The scholarly research process has been variously characterized. One model identifies five processes: first, identifying sources, searching, and gathering data; second, communicating with colleagues; third, interpreting and analyzing data; fourth, disseminating research findings; and finally, developing curriculum and teaching the next generation.[44] Another model suggests that historians, one group of scholars, go through three stages in the course of their research. First, a historian canvasses large bodies of material to define the scope of a research problem and the sources available. Second, after defining a topic, the historian uses particular bodies of records intensively. Finally, after writing has begun, the historian seeks to verify particular points and asks very specific questions.[45]

Research in archives calls for a partnership between archivists and researchers, but the relationship between archivists and scholars is not always as smooth as might be expected. Changes in technology are dramatically changing scholarly research and scholarly communication. Changes in research methodology and in the nature of archival sources also affect the relationship between archivists and scholars. Although archivists often expect scholars to be skilled in historical research, courses in research methodologies are no longer taught in many history departments, and other disciplines may lack specific historical knowledge and research training. Access restrictions limiting the use of recent materials also have been a source of disagreement among scholars and archivists.

Even well-prepared scholars need assistance with intellectual aspects of their research, and, as discussed in the next chapter, many users, including scholars, need mediation in provenance-based systems to translate subject requests into names of particular record groups and series. Archivists can assist scholars in evaluating archival information by sharing their knowledge of organizational activities and the technological processes that brought the documents into being.

Archivists share information about their holdings by entering descriptions of archival sources in national databases such as OCLC (Online Computer Library Center) and RLIN (Research Libraries Information Network) and by posting finding aids on the Internet on the repository Web site or through regional consortia posting finding aids. Organizing means to make these databases and finding aids readily available and teaching all potential users to use them are continuing professional tasks.

Archivists may be surprised that scholars often learn about research sources through footnotes and bibliographies in journals and through conversation in informal networks, not from archival guides and finding aids.[46] This should not be surprising because previous scholars' use of material is a clearer indication of relevance than any index or catalog. To promote the use of archives, then, archivists must go beyond publishing guides and finding aids to become part of scholarly networks, the "invisible colleges," by participating in conferences of learned societies and by writing about archival sources in journals and newsletters of scholarly associations.

In many cases, scholars are away from home and need to accomplish much research in a limited time. Consequently, they expect to handle large quantities of material and obtain copies of large numbers of documents. In fact, they may request thousands of copies and then read them later. Notwithstanding their appreciation of the importance of documents, scholars do not always handle them with care. In their haste to "get through" great quantities of documents, they may be careless in using them. Indeed, one scholar described the "prosaic problem of obtaining maximum poundage of document inspection for a given hotel bill."[47]

In addition to serving individual scholars, repositories can serve as intellectual centers for scholarship. They can organize roundtables and seminars to discuss research in progress; such forums are useful for archivists as well as scholars. Repositories may sponsor conferences for scholars and archivists to discuss research trends or common concerns about documentation. Some well-endowed repositories offer grants-in-aid to assist scholars with travel and other research costs.

Students

Not all academic research is conducted by experienced scholars. Students are a major constituency for many repositories, particularly university archives and manuscript libraries on or near college campuses. Secondary school classes have become significant users of archival material as some state curriculum standards require this component. In addition, the National History Day competition brings requests from students as young as middle school, following instructions to use primary sources in their research. Using archives can make history come alive for students, whether young or old. In the traditional model, the teacher owns information that students lack. Students see history primarily through thoroughly digested and neatly packaged textbook accounts. Providing access to archives empowers students to learn and discover on their own.[48]

Most students, like the general public, respond enthusiastically to the authenticity of original source materials. For example, the Bentley Historical Library provided a laboratory for a 225-student class in the politics and culture of the sixties. Students, in small groups, used the collections to write papers. One student wrote, "I realized that it is the first assignment I have ever had that I really enjoyed and got a lot out of."[49]

Historical documents, as artifacts, engage the physical senses: sight, touch, and in some cases hearing and smell. They also evoke emotions created by the tangible links to the creator of the document. Historical documents can be artifacts or illustration, but more importantly, can be evidence that provokes questions and stimulates hypotheses. Working with documents demonstrates the complex reality of the past. As one student said, "I'll never look at a footnote the same way again; I want to know how he knows that!" If guided through archival research, students can be stimulated to think more analytically and to look for the connections between past and present. Analyzing documents and evaluating them are important life skills for most workers and all citizens.[50]

Further, archivists have an important opportunity to help students appreciate historical documents and archival institutions. Archivists endeavor to impart an appreciation of archives and teach students to understand the research process in archives. Although most students will not become professional historians, they are citizens and potential voters. Working with students offers an important opportunity to demonstrate the value of history and the institutions that preserve it and make it accessible. It is useful to consider their parents as future archival supporters as well. See figure 3-3.

Paul Erickson leads the students of the Cross Cultural Research class as they work on an assignment using historical documents at the Billy Graham Center Archives. Courtesy Billy Graham Center Archives.

In some ways, the enthusiasm and excitement that students bring to research can make working with them very rewarding, but student questions are frequently repetitive, simplistic, or naive. Busy reference archivists may find it difficult to muster enthusiasm for yet another term paper on the frontier experience, the Gold Rush, or the Great Depression. As William Maher notes, students can be "high volume users that place heavy demands on the program but whose use generally touches only the surface of the archives and utilizes only the simplest techniques of historical research."[51]

Planning reference services for students requires understanding of the types of assistance needed. A doctoral student writing a dissertation presents different demands than a high school or elementary student. An exceptional student who independently identifies a subject calling for archival resources requires a different degree of assistance than the more usual case of a class of students sent to the archives with instructions to use primary sources for a term paper.

Even graduate students in history are not well prepared for archival research. In 1992, the Organization of American Historians sought information about the training of graduate students through a survey of history departments in 143 institutions granting Ph.Ds. It found that training focused on published bibliographic tools with little exploration of primary sources; "the historical profession no longer has a core understanding of research principles and practices that are essential for graduate students." This study suggested core research competencies:

- developing a research strategy
- understanding archival principles such as provenance and original order
- understanding archival principles as a means of locating evidence
- and understanding the nature and use of archival evidence.[52]

A decade later, most graduate students still do not have these competencies.

If the research experience is not structured, students can be overwhelmed. They frequently need help in adapting topics to available time and sources. For example, a proposed term paper on the Great Depression may need to be focused on a narrower topic such as a university's response to government work programs for students. Students often appreciate suggestions for manageable term paper topics. In many cases, the archivist also may need to recommend secondary sources for background reading. Students also need help in understanding and

Figure 3-3 Use of Historical Documents for Students

Addressing the educational needs of K-12 communities represents an unparalleled opportunity for archivists to

- expand the relevance of archival repositories in society;
- begin to grow a 'records literate' as well as 'information literate' audience that is aware of the importance, relevance, and complexities of records as bureaucratic, social, political, and cultural evidence;
- promote the role of archivists as active participants in the communication of cultural heritage;
- take advantage of the technological and financial resources that are being allocated nationally for the application of information technology in the classroom and for educational reform; and even
- promote archival education as a possible college choice.

Anne J. Gilliland-Swetland, "An Exploration of K-12 User Needs for Digital Primary Source Materials," *American Archivist* 61 (Spring 1998): 137.

evaluating the mass of information in documents and assistance with the difficult task of generalizing intelligently from details.

The educational role of the reference archivist is perhaps most obvious in work with students, which is in many ways similar to working with other unskilled researchers. Other users, however, usually define their needs more precisely than most students writing an assigned term paper because they are usually motivated by an actual information need rather than by a class assignment. Experienced archivists have learned that many students need no more assistance than other users who are not particularly skilled in archival research or who bring complex research projects requiring considerable reference time.

It is usually not the complexity of teaching students, but their numbers that pose difficulties for repositories. Most repositories can provide reference services for occasional students with well-defined questions, but most do not have resources to meet the needs of large classes with poorly defined needs. It can be a joy to work with a motivated, well-prepared student. Unprepared, reluctant students are likely to find little pleasure or value in using archival resources and will be more likely to require assistance beyond staff resources.

Providing these educational services to students depends in part on the mission of the parent institution. Teaching any unskilled user is time-consuming, and some archivists hesitate to commit scarce staff resources to it. Academic archivists generally feel obliged to teach students because of the instructional role of their parent institution, although the parent institution may not recognize the educational role of archives, even in academic settings. Participating in introductory programs offered by college and university libraries can reach many students. These programs, once called "bibliographic instruction," are now more often titled "information literacy" programs. In repositories that must limit services for students, the access policy should state that a student must have a letter of introduction from an instructor.

College and University Teachers

Ideally, archives are laboratories for research in the social sciences, and archivists and teachers work together to instruct students in historical research. Successful collaboration requires effort but can be very rewarding. Many of the problems encountered in working with students can be resolved by working directly with their teachers.

Teachers understand their curricular needs and their students. Teachers use primary sources to develop critical-thinking skills and thus support state-mandated curriculum goals. Most teachers have an idea of what they want their students to gain from archival research, but many do not know what services to expect from archives. Unfortunately, a few teachers believe in the "sink or swim" method of learning research skills, and others may not understand the contributions that archivists might make as fellow educators. Many reference archivists learn about a class assignment only after the first few students ask variations of the same question. Archivists can turn this problem into an opportunity to impress on teachers the importance of structuring the research experience and of making it an integral part of the course of study. Making this phone call, however, particularly in university settings, may require tact and diplomacy.

Archivists have a deep knowledge of research in primary sources. They also know their holdings and how their documents and collections might enrich a course of study. Teachers and archivists can collaborate to identify workable topics for student papers or to develop specific exercises for reading and understanding historical documents. By working together, teachers are better able to understand how to make best use of staff time, and archivists are better able to understand and meet the goals of the assignment. Together, archivists and teachers can develop background reading, review intermediate outlines and bibliographies, and discuss research in progress. Regular meetings with the teacher provide the archivist an opportunity to help students by discussing their experience and progress with instructors. By reviewing student papers and projects, archivists can learn what difficulties the students encountered and can assist teachers in improving the use of archives in the future.[53]

Archivists and teachers can also work together to locate suitable documents and other primary sources to enhance classroom lectures or discussion. Facsimile documents are a proven method of reaching students. Reproductions of historical documents for classroom exhibits, slide shows, videos, or teaching packets can, if well done, enhance learning and bring historical events to life. Archivists can also visit the classroom to talk with students about historical documents, using facsimiles.[54]

Public programs and publications are often effective ways to meet the needs of students, as well as other groups of unskilled users. For example, more can be accomplished in a one-hour introductory orientation class than in hours working with individual students. Structured orientation sessions are usually more successful than tours. Class sessions work best when teachers attend with their students so that they also understand the archivist's objectives and presentation. These orientation programs have been successfully translated to on-line tutorials.[55]

A well-prepared orientation session, focused on the subject area of the course and supplemented with handouts on repository procedures and research, can prepare students for productive work in the repository as well as stimulate a general understanding of and appreciation for archival research. Providing examples of research projects, having class members read vivid passages from documents, showing photographs, and illustrating the use of original sources bring the research process alive.

Demonstrating how communication patterns and changing technologies for making and keeping records combine to produce documents is critical to understanding the documents students find. Students today have probably never seen a typewriter or carbon paper, a mimeograph or ditto machine. Linking the process of records creation and use to the archival concepts of provenance and original order, as we will do in the next chapter, builds archival research competencies. Developing exercises using finding aids, proper care of materials, procedures for requesting materials and photocopies, and methods of taking notes and citing materials can save time and effort for both students and archivists. The key to the success of these sessions is often their interactive or "hands on" nature. It is important that the archivist not merely lecture to the group. Structure the session so the participants are asked to answer questions from the documents and finding aids; remind them that these documents are just earlier examples of documents they create every day.

If education is a high priority in the archival mission, as is especially likely in college and university archives, approaching faculty with a list of potential research topics or resources and offering to lead an orientation session, preferably in the archives, are means to extend the archival mission. Reviewing course catalogs and schedules can assist the archivist in identifying courses for which the resources of the archives might be beneficial. Repositories looking for potential users should not overlook neighboring community colleges, which are unlikely to have extensive archival holdings. The Organization of American Historians (OAH) notes that more than half of first-year college students receive their first collegiate experience at community colleges.[56]

K–12 Teachers

Archivists have a new opportunity to collaborate with local schools and universities to improve teachers' knowledge, understanding, and appreciation of American history through grants authorized under the Teaching American History Grant program, funded under Title II-C of the *Elementary and Secondary Education Act,* signed into law in January 2002. Under this program, local educational agencies can partner with organizations having extensive content knowledge. The projects bring together a local educational agency, an institution of higher education, and one or more of the following: a nonprofit history or humanities organization, a library, or a museum. The goal of this program is "to demonstrate how school districts and institutions with expertise in American history can collaborate over a three-year period to ensure that teachers develop the knowledge and skills necessary to teach traditional American history in an exciting and engaging way."[57]

Larger archives, or archives in institutions with education departments, have developed on-line curricula, teacher outlines, and pre-packaged and digitized documents for study. The resourceful archivist in a less well-funded institution can recommend these same Web sites to teachers to spark discussions about possible collaborations. Several examples are the National Archives and Records Administration, the American Memory site at the Library of Congress, the University of Virginia's Valley of the Shadow, and the Minnesota Historical Society.[58]

Another means for collaborating with teachers is National History Day, a year-long educational program that culminates in a national contest every June. *Our Documents Teacher Sourcebook* is a free resource created by National History Day, Inc., in cooperation with the National Archives. The sourcebook provides a hundred "milestone documents," an annotated time-line, guidelines to primary sources, lesson plans, and activities related to the classroom curriculum.[59]

Identifying Avocational User Groups: Using Archives for "Fun"

Avocational users such as genealogists, amateur historians, and hobbyists are sometimes called "recreational" or "leisure" users. Some archivists seem surprised by requests from such users. Their requests may seem less important or less justifiable in the face of pressing needs. That researchers find joy in archival research should not be surprising, however, for such intangible rewards brought many archivists to the field as a vocation.[60]

Archives can play a significant role in educating the general public, providing opportunities for lifelong learning for a public that is better educated and living longer. Many people who found classroom history boring or even alienating search eagerly for a personal, usable past. One study noted that "personal engagement with history marks a fruitful path toward self-knowledge."[61] A survey of users of British repositories found that "Archives are a key resource for life-long learning," as 83 percent of visitors came because of personal interest or a hobby.[62] Some of these users are experienced researchers, in that 31 percent had been using archives for more than five years. Most significantly, this survey found that although over two-thirds of the visitors began by getting involved in an activity such as family history, 61 percent went beyond their family history to research other subjects, and 81 percent later used other repositories.[63]

In a pluralistic, mobile society it is important for individuals, families, and groups to have a sense of time, place, and identity. As the Organization of American Historians noted, "all people have been significant actors in human events . . . history is not limited to the study of dominant political, social, and economic elites. . . . It also encompasses the individual and collective quests of ordinary people for a meaningful place for themselves in their families, in their communities, and in the larger world."[64] Memory, both personal and cultural, is critical to a sense of identity.

Genealogists

Many Americans seek meaningful connections with the past through family history. Genealogy, one of the most popular hobbies in America, appeals to all economic, racial, and ethnic groups. Genealogists have been called "historians of their own family,"[65] and they often share the results of their research with other family members.

Because the direct impact of genealogy beyond individuals is not easily measured and because of its past association with elitist societies, its value may be discounted or dismissed as idle curiosity. A few repositories do not consider genealogists qualified researchers. This is wrong. Many genealogists are expert researchers who have completed many projects using primary sources and have wide-ranging and sophisticated interests and research skills.[66] As in the case of perceived problems in dealing with students, it is usually the number of genealogists that presents problems for understaffed archives, not the nature of the research itself. The information needs of genealogists are often simpler and more predictable than those of other constituencies.

Archivists have good opportunities to serve genealogists effectively through educational programs and self-help devices. Pamphlets, brochures, and other handouts can explain the use of popular sources. Many how-to books are available. Instructional videotapes make information about using archives readily available and can be shown to groups outside the archives. Genealogists have eagerly embraced the Internet, and archivists who post detailed information about genealogical sources on their repository's Web site can ease direct reference work.[67]

Microfilming frequently requested materials and placing copies of heavily consulted sources on open shelves can expedite reference services. Today, scanning and indexing heavily used sources meet the needs of many genealogists and extend the use of repository records to other groups as well. Some repositories then provide copies at a fee and recoup costs of posting such records.[68]

Because the needs of genealogists are often routine and repetitive, well-trained para-professionals may be able to provide many of the services they require.[69] Archives can work with genealogical societies to develop educational programs. Classes that teach genealogical research skills are well attended. One British survey found that nearly half of the repositories surveyed engaged in "family history open days, courses, or fairs."[70]

Experienced genealogists often serve as volunteers to help novices. Genealogical societies can be a source of volunteers to index commonly used sources such as censuses, cemetery records, or newspapers. For example, volunteers from the Church of Jesus Christ of Latter-day Saints transcribed the arrival manifests of more than twenty-two million immigrants, passengers, and crew members who came through Ellis Island and the Port of New York from 1892 to 1924.[71]

For many repositories, genealogists are the most numerous clients, even though they may not be identified or recognized in the institutional mission statement. Their numbers help justify allocation of increased resources to reference operations. Genealogists have been a valuable constituency for archival agencies, especially government archives and historical societies, because they are numerous, knowledgeable, and vocal about the value of preserving historical records. "Without this large user group, drawn from a range of social classes, funding for record repositories might be even lower than its present levels."[72]

Historians

Prominent examples of avocational historians are local historians and hobbyists. Like genealogists, their interests reflect a modern society's need for a usable past. Community celebrations and anniversaries often stimulate interest in local history. These may focus on the community as a whole or on its many parts: churches, civic groups, businesses, schools, labor unions, ethnic groups, hospitals, or other institutions. Homeowners or business owners seek information about the history of their house or company. To show their involvement in the community, local businesses often use archival resources in marketing or public relations, in much the same way that large corporations turn to their own archives.

Few community organizations have organized their own archives, and they may recognize the value of archives only when they try to celebrate their past. This interest in archives provides the opportunity to offer advice about records management and archives. In many cases, anniversaries motivate organizations to deposit their historical materials with a suitable collecting agency, such as a county historical society or manuscripts library, and to institute a records program.

Lectures, classes, exhibitions, and publications can help local historians. A lecture series provides a forum for historians and other community members to communicate the results of archival research, presents information about the community to citizens unable to undertake their own research, and provides a showcase for repository resources and services. Exhibitions, either in the repository or in other public forums, present information about the community and encourage use. Slide shows or videotapes can be shown in classrooms or at civic meetings. A column in the local paper, well illustrated by historical photographs, can stimulate community interest and teach research skills. If a community celebration is underway, orientation classes to teach research skills lessen the need for individual orientations by reference staff members. Archivists can join local Speakers' Bureaus or make known their interest in giving talks on local history.

Hobbyists

Hobbyists find meaning in the past by focusing on selected historical objects and events, often by collecting them. For almost any common object or event one can name, there is a group devoted to its preservation and history: trains, ships, lighthouses, bottles, circuses, automobiles, carousels, prospecting, and military engagements, to name a few. Hobbyists come to archives to search for documentary evidence about the history of their interest, to ensure authentic restoration, or accurate reenactment. Because of their intense interest, hobbyists can perhaps generate greater reference pressure—or support—than any other user group. They are often collectors themselves and sometimes locate valuable historical records still in private hands. If they are impressed with a repository's care of records and service to researchers, they may recommend the repository to private owners of historical materials.

Information Seeking

We have identified some of the important constituencies using archival holdings as the reference archivist might meet them in the reading room. Now let us examine archives as they might be seen from the user's point of view. How do people seek information as they conduct their day-to-day work in organizations? How do these patterns of information seeking relate to the use of archives? Searching for information in archives is often an extension of information-seeking behavior in everyday work in organizations.[73]

For the most part, archivists and librarians focus on *information retrieval*, that is, the identification, preservation, and description of information, anticipating user queries. In contrast, focusing on *information seeking* emphasizes the needs, characteristics, and actions of the information seeker. If we focus on the actions of the information seeker, rather than on methods of information retrieval, we also break out of the institutional patterns that dictate that libraries have books, that archives have obsolete records, and that computers *are* information systems. Most information seekers do not know or care about such perceptions or distinctions.

The Information Seeker

An information seeker is a whole person, not an abstraction. Information seekers have a personal information infrastructure, which consists of interacting mental models for specific information systems, whether they are human, tangible, or electronic. Gary Marchionini defines mental models as dynamic mental representations of the real world. Mental maps are critical to navigation in any context and are also critical to organizing information and understanding it.[74]

Marcia Bates highlights the complexity of information seeking and the necessity of emphasizing it over information retrieval. In figure 3-4, she represents the classic model of information retrieval, which posits that "a user brings a single query to the information set, yielding a single answer." She argues instead that searching for information is an evolving process. The search terms change as the user proceeds; the query changes as information is acquired. In figure 3-5, Bates illustrates that the "nature

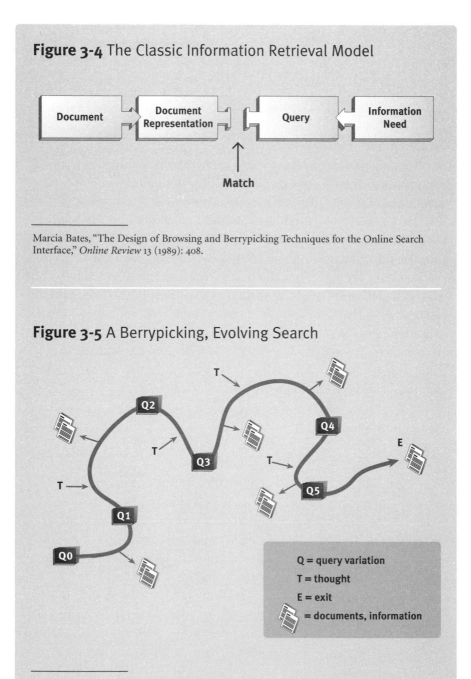

Figure 3-4 The Classic Information Retrieval Model

Document → Document Representation → Query ← Information Need

↑

Match

Marcia Bates, "The Design of Browsing and Berrypicking Techniques for the Online Search Interface," *Online Review* 13 (1989): 408.

Figure 3-5 A Berrypicking, Evolving Search

Q = query variation
T = thought
E = exit
= documents, information

Marcia Bates, "The Design of Browsing and Berrypicking Techniques for the Online Search Interface," *Online Review* 13 (1989): 410.

of the search process is such that it follows a 'berrypicking' pattern, instead of leading to a single best retrieved set." Further, "a bit-at-a-time retrieval" is like picking huckleberries, which are scattered about on bushes, not in bunches. A searcher "uses a variety of types of information sources and search techniques." Bates sums up: "typical search queries are not static, but rather evolve, searchers commonly gather information in bits and pieces instead of one grand best retrieved set, searchers use a wide variety of search techniques which extend beyond those commonly associated with bibliographical databases, and searchers use a wide variety of sources other than bibliographical databases."[75]

Today information surrounds us all. People use their mental models for events, experiences, and domains of knowledge to run scenarios for contemplated actions. In their daily work, information seekers in organizations tend to turn first to people, then to readily available print sources, and increasingly to readily available electronic resources to answer information needs.[76] Archives and libraries are seldom the first choice. See figure 3-6.

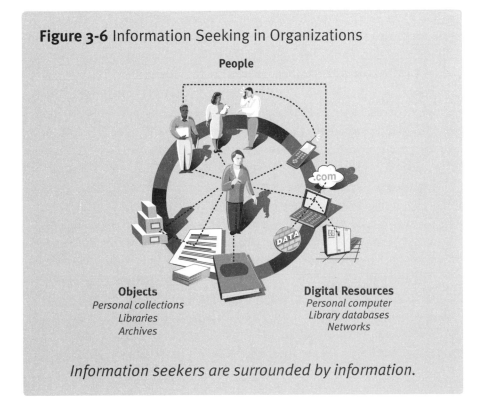

Figure 3-6 Information Seeking in Organizations

People

Objects
Personal collections
Libraries
Archives

Digital Resources
Personal computer
Library databases
Networks

Information seekers are surrounded by information.

Seeking Information from People

All human communication begins nonverbally. Our most fundamental, primary relationships are nonverbal: parent-child, husband-wife. A child first learns through touch, and touch remains a powerful means of communication through life. Parents remember their child's first smile and the communication that it established.

On a daily basis, we communicate with most people orally, regardless of all the tools we have invented to extend our powers of communication. We are programmed to learn through oral, face-to-face, human interaction. For most of human history, people learned survival skills, as well as culture, modes of thought, and religious expression, from other people. Archivists, like most educated people, have privileged literacy as the only mode of learning, and tend to under-estimate other forms, or even to denigrate them. Communication tools are additive. People did not stop talking when they learned to write, nor did they stop going to schools and universities when books were printed. People still read words on paper even as multimedia proliferates.

People learn from other people in many contexts. They learn in unstructured settings through primary, personal relationships, such as family, friends, and colleagues. They also learn from people in structured settings, such as teachers in schools and universities. Perhaps less obvious are sources deriving from functional needs, such as doctors, lawyers, bankers, or realtors. Information specialists such as librarians, archivists, records managers, systems designers, and even the staff in data centers or institutional research offices on campuses can be seen as special experts teaching in these structured settings, organized by functional needs. We also learn from other people at professional conferences such as the annual meeting of the Society of American Archivists.

Face-to-face oral communication remains a preferred means of communication because nonverbal elements carry meaning. Research shows that 50 percent or more of human communication is nonverbal. Personal interaction also provides the opportunity to clarify meaning. Seeking information from others is so ingrained in our daily behavior that we take it for granted. When we have pain, we go to a doctor rather than to a library or the Internet, even though appropriate information is likely available in all these settings. People seek information from other people because such information is filtered and, more importantly, authenticated by experience. Information givers responsible for their actions are given credence.

Seeking Information from Documents

Although there are many other information-bearing objects and locations, let us examine objects with embedded information commonly found in personal collections and libraries. Research suggests that people will use the most accessible information, regardless of whether it is the best. The "principle of least effort" is well documented:

> . . . most researchers (even "serious" scholars) will tend to choose easily available information sources, even when they are objectively of low quality, and, further, will tend to be satisfied with whatever can be found easily in preference to pursuing higher quality sources whose use would require a greater expenditure of effort.[77]

This formulation of observed behavior reflects the reality of information seeking, but blames the information seeker and not the information system. As mediators of information resources, archivists cannot simply blame users for not availing themselves of the useful sources to be found in archives. This attitude fails to recognize the limited resources and time pressures facing staff and administrators on a daily basis. More importantly, it fails to recognize the structure of information flows in organizations. Studying behavior reveals how archives can better serve staff, administrators, and indeed all researchers.

PERSONAL COLLECTIONS

As noted in the "principle of least effort," people tend to turn first to personal collections of information-bearing objects. Some tools are compiled personally such as Rolodexes, calendars, and lists. Others are familiar books close at hand, such as telephone directories, procedures manuals, professional periodicals, and reference books. Also close at hand are likely to be personal working files, which may include reports, copies of articles, research notes, and correspondence files. Most of these information sources are organized and retrieved by physical location and by form, such as size, shape, and color. People select sources close at hand, not because they are lazy, but because these sources have been authenticated by personal experience, are frequently annotated to reflect recent changes, and accommodate time constraints in the press of daily business.[78]

Libraries

Beyond their own collections, people often turn to libraries. To select a library as a source, the user must first conceive that someone might have published a book or article on the subject of interest, that is, the user must have a mental image of finding the information in a publication. Library users have an array of informal but effective search techniques beyond the catalog, and studying actual information-seeking behaviors in libraries offers insight into the assumptions and expectations of information seekers.

For example, browsing in library stacks is a common behavior. Librarians criticize this technique, knowing that the catalog is more complete. Browsing, however, provides full-text retrieval, which is very useful in evaluating the relevance of the text to the inquiry. By scanning the table of contents, bibliography, and list of illustrations, users can quickly determine the relevance of a publication. Furthermore, library classification systems mean that related materials are likely to be collocated, and this propinquity reinforces the serendipity of discovery. This preference for browsing further emphasizes the physical nature of information seeking. Archivists must realize that users accustomed to this powerful technique are likely to be frustrated by the closed stacks they encounter in archives. Shelves of gray boxes organized by provenance are alien to most users. Archivists should recognize the importance of explaining the power of provenance as a retrieval mode.

As a second example, reference archivists know that chasing footnotes is one of the most common actual behaviors of researchers. What is the power of the footnote? A footnote is information in context. The nuances of the subject reference can be very precise when the footnote barks at the heels of a sentence, in a way that Library of Congress subject headings in a catalog cannot. Further, the footnote evaluates a source in a way no catalog or finding aid can. That is, the author of a text that the reader finds useful cites further information. Thus, the source noted in a footnote is identified as a potentially useful source for the reader. Footnotes are a means of authenticating an argument, but they are equally, if not more importantly, a means for people to communicate about sources of information. In one study, almost 80 percent of legal historians relied on footnotes to find additional information.[79]

Other actual search strategies, such as citation searching, searching a straight run of a journal for related articles, or searching for works by an author whose work has been useful in the past, also demonstrate how information seekers select sources for further investigation that have been ratified or referred by other people.

Bates notes that these strategies "can be seen as a different way to identify and exploit particular regions in the total information store that are more likely than others to contain information of interest for the search at hand" and as "different ways of identifying berry patches in the forest."[80] Although we might think that users are looking for all bits of information, these search techniques indicate that they are in fact looking for authenticated, evaluated information in context.

Seeking Information from Electronic Resources

The personal reference files previously kept and annotated on paper are now more likely to be created and retained in personal computers. People maintain their address books, calendars, directories, and working files of reports, memos, directives, and the like in their personal computers.

As computers have been linked in local area networks within organizations or through the Internet to other organizations, users have come to rely on on-line tools and information resources. These tools are convenient and add powerful modes of retrieving and using information. For example, rather than maintaining a collection of maps or going to the library, users can now gain interactive access to maps of any place in the world from their computers. Further, the hypertext link exponentially expands the power of the footnote. By providing the link, the author of the Web page, whether personal or institutional, evaluates and authenticates the information source and provides full-text retrieval instantly.

Given the pressure of time, the tendency is to think that if information is not in electronic form, it does not exist. The "principle of least effort" takes on new meaning as searchers use only those information resources readily available in electronic form. In some cases, the information resources on the Internet are so chaotic that information is as good as lost. At the same time however, many records are no longer captured in a tangible form. Multimedia records are created, communicated, filed, retrieved, or lost only in electronic form.

The centrality of electronic networks for day-to-day business in a modern organization was dramatically displayed when Judge Royce C. Lambeth, U.S. District Court for the District of Columbia, ordered the Department of the Interior to disconnect all its computer systems from the Internet on 5 December 2000, until the Department could demonstrate adequate on-line security for Indian trust accounts, cutting off 71,000 employees in fourteen bureaus. Employees could no longer receive or send e-mail, produce personnel and payroll actions, pay vendors or contractors, post vacancy announcements, take on-line reservations for National Park Service campgrounds, or use planning and reporting databases. One employee reported, "We had to revert back to 1980s technology. People still remember how to use the fax machine and pick up the phone. But it was surprising; at first, you think, 'How am I going to get my job done?'" Most agencies were not back on-line until February; some not until April.[81]

Information Seeking in Organizations

Now let us apply these observations to work settings in organizations. When seeking information in organizations for their daily work, staff members typically rely first on their own memory. Second, they rely on convenient reference tools, readily accessible records that document their knowledge and actions, or known Web sites. Thus, when searching for information, a staff member is most likely to draw first on personal knowledge or on the records documenting his or her actions immediately at hand, whether actual or virtual.[82]

As noted in chapter 2, records are created in the course of practical activities. Their format reflects the recording technologies available at the time they were created, and their filing structures and locations reflect the communications patterns in the organization that created them. Documents pool in filing systems located where the information is needed. Staff members find information in current files through knowledge of an organization's activities and its filing systems. In the recent past, knowledge about the forms in which information is recorded and filed was obtained from clerical staff, in filing manuals, or through filing guides or indexes maintained by clerical staff. Today such information is sought on the organizational intranet.

For information beyond their own memory, files, and scope of activity, staff members are likely to consult other people in the organization. One survey of university administrators found that 94 percent of all respondents cited other university staff members as their primary information resource.[83] Brown and Yakel found further that "administrators rely most on human information networks resulting from years of experience and personal relationships built on trust and prior provision of reliable information."[84] It is natural for people to trust information that has been selected and authenticated by a knowledgeable and trusted expert and information given by the person responsible for the action. Robert Cross states that "people help other people to create actionable knowledge via provision of

1. solutions (both know what and know how);
2. meta-knowledge (pointers to databases or other people);
3. problem reformulation;
4. validation of plans or solutions; and
5. legitimization from contact with a respected person."[85]

Archivists use this path, too, when they consult current office staff about likely filing locations.

An employee summons knowledge of the organization and its functions to infer what person or department would collect the desired information. Such knowledge may come from personal experience or other staff members, or it may be set forth in standard practice manuals, organization charts, or staff directories. Organizational employees (and their clients or customers outside the organization) find information by asking, "Who is responsible? Who keeps that information?" Staff members ask themselves, "Who would know or need to know about this problem?" To locate the right person, they use their knowledge of organizational structure to identify the individual or office responsible for the sphere of activity, or they ask others more knowledgeable about the organization. They are likely to use the telephone in search of information.

Staff directories and organizational charts serve as guides to people with knowledge. Titles of both individuals and departments indicate responsibility for organizational functions. The information seeker relies on the responsible official to know the answer, to know their files well enough to be able to find the information, or to refer the information seeker to another person, department, or organization. In academic circles a community of scholars is known as the "invisible college." Scholars may share their personal files with colleagues as well—files that often contain photocopies, more or less well cited, from archival repositories.

In short, to find information, staff members employ a variety of techniques. They consult either their own memory or the memory of their actions embedded in their records, or they analyze the functions of the organization and then consult people or records resulting from that function. Often, however, this information-seeking behavior is so ingrained that employees do not think about these processes, and the search for information is so obvious that the process is transparent.

This pattern of information seeking is grounded in a world of personal networks. Information-seeking behavior in organizations is, however, changing rapidly as information is increasingly recorded in electronic forms, especially in networked electronic environments. For the past two decades, personal computers were primarily used to produce "fast paper," that is, people used software packages for word processing, database management, or spreadsheets to automate the production of paper documents. The flow of information continued largely through transmittal of paper documents.

Now, however, information is often transmitted only in electronic form. Internal organizational information is distributed by electronic mail or is shared via the organizational intranet. Electronic bulletin boards and discussion groups provide means to reach a wider pool of people than the telephone does, allowing for asynchronous communication. Public information and reports previously disseminated via the printing press are now available instantly through the World Wide Web.

Information once found in paper form in department files, such as benefits information, employee records, patient records, customer records, library catalogs, archival finding aids, and other departmental databases, are now accessible through local area networks that people can access from their desktops. They no longer have to call the responsible official, though Robert Cross found in his study of organizational information seeking in 2000 that "these databases at best perform a complementary role to personal networks when people are seeking answers to problems. . . . [and] make salient the point that technology itself is only one form of memory likely tapped in solving organizational problems."[86]

Information Seeking in Archives

Information seeking in institutional archives builds on patterns of information seeking in the parent institution. With the passage of time, people leave, but the organization continues. With good records management, records documenting significant actions with continuing consequences are transferred to organizational archives so that later information seekers, whether later incumbents or others seeking evidence of past actions, can find them. We will see in the next chapter how these insights inform the work of reference archivists.

Archives in the World of Information

Perhaps the most important question for the reference archivist to answer is, "How do people find archives?" As noted above, people are surrounded by information. What are the mental maps for navigating through this surfeit of information? How do users perceive archives, and how can archivists position themselves and their resources to provide what users need?

Archivists have begun to study how researchers learn about archival holdings. Initial studies indicate that researchers find their way to archival repositories through informal personal networks, that is, by word of mouth. In 1994, Paul Conway studied research use at the National Archives. He found, "Across the board, personal networks are the most important means by which people find their way to the National Archives; over half of those issued new research cards men-tion oral sources of information."[87] These findings are confirmed by recent studies at the Western History Collections at the University of Oklahoma Libraries and the University of North Carolina, which found that personal networks remain the most frequently cited source. Earlier studies also found that researchers located repositories through professional networks, that is, through footnotes and bibliographies in published sources.

Electronic networks are, however, becoming increasingly important. Kristina Southwell found in 2000 that the Web pages of the Western History Collections at the University of Oklahoma were the second largest means by which researchers found their way to the archives. This study also found that researchers who used the Web typically found the repository Web page through a general subject search using major search engines as opposed to a search for the archival institution itself.[88]

Elizabeth Yakel goes beyond the question of how researchers find archives to look at "the underlying conceptions and sensemaking involved in the archival research process and how researchers think through their search problems." She found much uncertainty about what archives are and where they are housed, making "archivists and users very dependent on others: librarians, paraprofessionals sought out in increasingly self-service microfilm reading rooms, as well as the current owners of records."[89]

Archives and the Economics of Information

Much discussion in recent years has centered on the new "information economy." As David M. Levy notes, "information seems to have become a kind of god for many of us today. Our assumption is that if we can just get the right information at the right time, good things will happen."[90] Many information seekers in the Internet age expect "instancy—or the demand for quick delivery of small bits of information." Vivid images describe this Internet phenomenon: "the one minute researcher" and the "McDonalds of information."[91]

Like many archivists today, Barbara Craig asks, "How do we understand the place of archives within an economy increasingly dependent on information products which are bought and sold, consumed, and replaced like commodities?" Archival documentation may meet ". . . immediate needs, more enduring organizational needs, or the more traditional requirements of a broad research community." Craig suggests the utility of the concept of social resources. "Some social resources are allocated to society for consumption. Others, by contrast, are protected as capital goods." Certainly the records of private organizations and individuals are often seen as "information commodities," while the records of public institutions may be regarded as "more durable social resources." Craig notes that archivists "should promote the authoritative value of archives as fundamental to social well-being. . . ." and that "there is much to recommend this view of archives in an information economy because it recognizes that archives' special nature as evidence, much of it critical, warrants protection."[92]

Conclusion

The search for information in archives about past actions is similar but more complex than searching for current information in organizations. Furthermore, new technologies are dramatically transforming these information-seeking patterns. Locating information about past actions in archives depends on interaction among three archival functions: arrangement, description, and reference services. We will discuss these archival functions in greater detail in the next two chapters.

CHAPTER 4

Providing Intellectual Access to Archives

The arrangement and description of archives in large measure inform the role of the reference archivist in providing intellectual access. The first part of this chapter discusses archival arrangement and description, including common reference tools and finding aid systems.[93] Archives and manuscripts are arranged as groups, following the principles of provenance and original order, and they are also described collectively. Researchers often need reference assistance to understand these principles and to make effective use of the available descriptive tools. The second part of this chapter discusses the role of the reference archivist in providing access to five types of information:

1. information about the repository;
2. information *about* repository holdings;
3. information *from* repository holdings;
4. information about record creators; and
5. referrals to sources outside the repository.

It is useful for reference archivists to understand the evolution of arrangement and description in archival theory and practice. As archivists face rapid change at the beginning of the twenty-first century, they must understand the descriptive tools they inherit as well as the new ones. In the first half of the twentieth century, repositories used a variety of methods to arrange and describe archives and manuscripts. In the second half of the twentieth century, methods became more standardized, but many repositories will use inherited descriptive tools for at least another decade as they bring legacy data to new descriptive standards and new formats.

Users of archives have varying degrees of skill and comfort with automated tools. Some continue to prefer earlier forms of retrieval. Furthermore, because users bring citations from published sources, it is helpful to understand descriptive practice at the time of the publication. It is also useful to understand inherited descriptive tools because archivists are researchers themselves, and the better they understand the universe of information beyond their own repository, the better they can serve their clients. As information professionals in the parent organization, reference archivists also provide information for referrals beyond it.

Arrangement

Archivists follow the principles of *provenance* and *original order* in organizing and arranging records. These principles are grounded in the contextual information that made the records usable as they were created. These principles for organizing information rest on principles we use every day.

Provenance and Original Order in Everyday Life

How do we find things in the physical world? We know intuitively that a physical object can be in only one place. All of us learned from our mothers, "A place for everything and everything in its place." We do not make finding aids, catalogs, indexes, or inventories to find objects in our daily lives. We find the objects of everyday life by their function and form. The potato peeler is in the kitchen, and the toothbrush is in the bathroom. Everyone has discovered the force of this functional arrangement when moving from one house to another, when everything is in boxes, divorced from the context of the function in which they are used. Only when household possessions are unpacked in the rooms where they will be used can we find them again.

Records from the Spaulding Boat Works can only be understood by their function and location. PHOTOGRAPH COURTESY SAN FRANCISCO MARITIME NHP 00-10-04-28.

Elizabeth Shaw states these ideas more elegantly when she says that much "metadata is implicit in the physical environment." She observes, "Place plays a significant role in our information-seeking behavior by providing visual, social and physical clues about the nature of our environment and the information provided within it." "Place imposes a set of relationships on objects," for example, in library classification schemes or office filing systems.[94]

Provenance and Original Order in Archives

After people learned to embed information in tangible objects, they needed to be able to find them. Like the tools of daily life, these information-bearing tools, the "working files of working folks," tend to pool in the offices where they are used. To return to our everyday analogy, when we asked where something was, our mothers said, "What were you doing when you had it last?" or "Where did you use it last?"

Records are given meaning and structure in records systems by the functions that use them. Remember that records systems comprise documents received, copies of documents sent, and documents used internally. Records are usually organized in records systems by form in the course of the work according to the needs of the users, whether chronologically, numerically, geographically, or alphabetically, so that they can be retrieved by date, number, place, person, or subject.

When records are transferred to archives, archivists keep them together as a group linked to the person, office, or organization that maintained them. Archivists retain the provenance and original order of the files; that is, records from each entity are kept together in the original order imposed by the department that kept them. Provenance links records to the functions that created them, reflects organizational functions, and follows the lines of communication outlined in an organizational chart.

The Power of Provenance

The most important reason for retaining provenance is to ensure that the evidence in the records is authentic. A chain of continuous custody from the action that created the document to the user ensures the authenticity of evidence. No later hand has added, subtracted, or moved the evidence from the actions that created it. In archives, unlike libraries, individual documents are not located physically according to a predetermined subject scheme. If a later person, following a library model of information retrieval, mixes documents from a number of organizations or creators, the chain of custody is broken and evidence cannot be trusted. Shaw writes, "place can have social meaning and provide a sense of authority."[95] Information seekers evaluate information on the basis of where it is found.

Second, provenance is a powerful method for locating evidence and predicting content. By following the principles of provenance and original order, archivists retain the physical organization of records as found in offices when they are transferred to the gray boxes on shelves in archives. If one knows the functions and forms of the records, one can find evidence of the actions that created them. Shaw notes that "Place provides context" and that predictable spaces make it easier to find one's way.[96] People can predict what kinds of information are found in the tax department, the school office, the water department, or the land office.

If records are kept in the same order as they were filed, the location of each item in the filing structure can usually be predicted. Since records are generated by activity, information can be found, without extensive indexing, by analyzing organizational structure and function to infer the location of files likely to hold needed information. These files can then be searched by their internal structures. For example, by knowing form and source, one can infer the probable content of the minutes of the governing board of a university or of scrapbooks of the advertising department of a bank. If the organization created inventories or indexes to use the records in the office, these indexes remain useful for later users.[97]

Thus, the organization and retrieval of information in archives rest on very simple premises. The same principles of organization and retrieval of information in the creating organization hold true for records after they move from active to archival status. Reference archivists help information seekers by asking, "What office would have been responsible for that function, and where are its files?"

For example, the records of the Alaska Packers Association and the records of San Francisco Maritime National Historical Park both contain information about actions relating to the historic vessel *Balclutha*. The records were created, however, in the course of business of two different organizations. The Alaska Packers Association employed the vessel to carry goods and men to Alaska to fish for salmon in the first third of the twentieth century. San Francisco Maritime National Historical Park is charged with preserving the vessel into the twenty-first century. Information seekers can predict the kinds of information in each of the groups of records by knowing the functions of each of the organizations.

Records resulting from the activities of large modern offices may reflect thousands of subjects. The records of a United States senator, for example, contain information about every significant issue during his or her tenure. Indexing such records by subject requires hours of staff time; yet, if a user knows that the senator was involved in tobacco liability cases, it is possible to locate information on that topic by using the internal structure of the files, even though the collection has not been indexed.

Third, the archival arrangement system based on provenance and original order is timeless; the relationship between activities and records remains constant, no matter how later users approach the records. Archival arrangement reflects its time and place. Indexes or file guides developed by creators are also useful for later researchers. In contrast, a classification scheme imposed after the fact by some later hand is arbitrary. It reflects knowledge and modes of thought at the time of the classification and may not be useful for later users.

Hierarchy of Control

Archivists gain control over records, which are often voluminous, by identifying a conceptual hierarchy. Although this hierarchy is often oversimplified, it is a useful construct for thinking about information in archives. The first three levels of the hierarchy of control described below, *document, file unit,* and *series,* are physical manifestations that relate function and form. Other levels of the hierarchy, such as *record group, subgroup,* and *collection,* are in some respects intellectual constructs that archivists use to manage larger aggregates of records. The application of this intellectual construct (this mental map, if you will) is most obvious when analyzing the form and structure of organizational records. It can also be useful for analyzing and understanding the relationship of groups of documents in collections of personal or family papers. See figure 4-1.

Figure 4-1 Hierarchy of Creation and Control

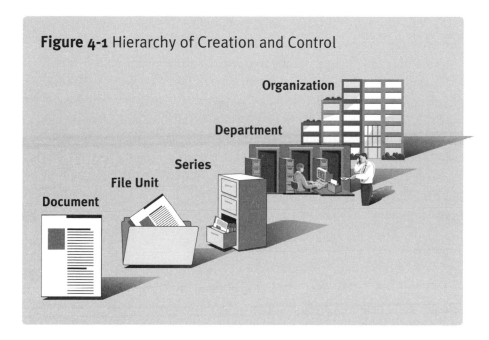

DOCUMENT

The smallest unit in this hierarchy is an individual document, which usually results from one action, for example, an incoming communication such as a letter or an e-mail; a copy of an outgoing communication such as a carbon copy of a typewritten letter or a copy of an e-mail; or an internal document such as the minutes of a meeting, a report, a form, a photograph, or an architectural drawing. Documents may be analog or digital.

FILE UNIT

Over time, most organizations devised means to bring documents together in file units that have both physical and intellectual meaning. For example, a file unit may be a volume of chronological entries such as minutes, a folder of correspondence relating to one subject, or a tube of rolled vessel plans relating to one vessel. In their personal papers, people tie together a packet of love letters, put family photographs in a shoebox, keep baby books, and make scrapbooks of memorabilia.

The word *filum* means *string*. The earliest files were related documents tied together. In the nineteenth century, documents such as letters were folded and bundled together, often tied by "red tape." Financial records were often kept in large bound volumes. The file folder and filing cabinet were inventions of the early twentieth century. The classic file unit is easily envisioned: incoming letters and copies of outgoing responses relating to a given event placed together in a file folder. Current computer operating systems extend the metaphor of the file folder by allowing users to create "folders" to bring documents together in some meaningful way, although they usually call each document a "file" and each folder a "directory."

Series

Filing units relating to one function are usually brought together into a series, organized by one filing convention, so that they can be retrieved. The file folder described above would be placed in an alphabetical sequence by subject in a file drawer. Lecture notes might be arranged first by course, then by topic, then by date. Financial records are often organized by fiscal year. In automated systems, directories can provide the same function of bringing related files together. In many offices, piles of documents are brought together relating to one project, and what should be "file management" becomes "pile management."[98]

In personal papers, series are often less distinct, but the functions of documents and filing units can usually be discerned. Manuscript repositories often collect the personal papers of authors and usually find aggregations of drafts of manuscripts organized by publication, subject files for research materials, financial records, legal documents, diaries, scrapbooks of reviews, and other functional categories useful for organizing the papers into meaningful series.

Record Group or Collection

A *record group* is an aggregation of all series and all records from one organization. There may be subgroups, which are aggregations of series or records from one department or function within the organization. A *collection* is an aggregation of personal or family records with a common provenance.

In many ways, a record group or collection is an intellectual construct. Archivists use these concepts to link records to their organizational origins. But this link is not necessarily a one-to-one relationship. The organization changes, even though the functions reflected in the records continue. The series of records may continue, regardless of the "name on the door" or the "name on the building." For example, the federal government started to build and manage lighthouses in 1789. The agency history in the *Guide to Federal Records* notes that this activity (and thus its records) has had many titles. This activity and its records were administratively part of the Secretary of the Treasury from 1789 to 1903, the Department of Commerce and Labor from 1903 to 1913, and the Department of Commerce from 1913 to 1939. In 1939, this function was transferred to United States Coast Guard, which was itself transferred to the Department of Transportation in 1967 and to the Department of Homeland Security in 2002. The records are now used by the organizations taking responsibility for lighthouses as the federal government decommissions them.

A *collection* is an aggregation of personal or family records with a common provenance in the same way that a *record group* is an aggregation of organizational records of common provenance. The term is commonly used in manuscript repositories. For example, the collection of Alexander Winchell at the University of Michigan contains letters received by him, copies of his outgoing correspondence, and his diaries and journals. The Weld-Grimké Family Papers at the Clements Library at the University of Michigan contains papers of Theodore Dwight Weld (1803–1895), Angelina Grimké Weld (1805–1879), and Sarah Moore Grimké (1792–1873), American abolitionists and reformers, including drafts of outgoing letters, letters received, essays, and diaries.

Description

As time passes, knowledge of the functions and forms of records fades from memory. No one remembers, "Oh, we did a study on that issue," or asks, "Who has the report?" Users are new staff or researchers from outside the organization who have little or no knowledge of the institution or its activities. Organizational records, especially those of organizations that no longer exist, may be transferred to collecting repositories, such as the records of the Alaska Packers Association at San Francisco Maritime National Historical Park. Manuscript repositories collect personal papers because they have interest for researchers who are not part of the family.

The farther removed users are from the activities that created the records, the more they need detailed information about the circumstances under which the records were created and the more they rely on archival description and reference assistance. Information seekers, whether archivists or researchers, need information about the functions, forms, and content of records.

Archival description is meta-information, that is, information about information that guides users to records and helps users understand them. It is also management information that allows archivists to acquire and preserve records. Description traditionally has focused on *products,* the finding aids that give access to archival holdings, partly because they were produced in forms not easily changed.

It is more useful, however, to focus on the *process* of capturing information about records through the entire life cycle, from creation through use, than on the physical form of the description. A useful definition of archival description is

> the process of capturing, collating, analyzing, and organizing any information that serves to identify, manage, locate, and interpret the holdings of archival institutions and explain the contexts and records systems from which those holding were selected.[99]

Collective Description and Progressive Refinement of Control

Archivists describe groups of records, that is, they provide information about the functions and activities of the creator, and about the formats of the records and their filing structures, content, dates, and the relationships among them. Descriptive control over a collection is progressively refined from the top down through the hierarchy of control, working from the broadest group to the appropriate level of description, whether series, file, or item.

Elements of information about records may be captured as they are created, acquired, arranged, and used. These data elements may be embodied in a number of products, such as donor records, accession lists, inventories, finding aids, catalogs, indexes, registers, card catalogs, indexes, databases, or guides, and they may be displayed on paper or on-line. An ideal descriptive system allows archivists to collect all data elements about a collection in one system and produce any number of products. If such a system is based on national standards for data structure and data values, information about collections can be shared with other repositories.

The users of archives may also enhance description of them. Reference archivists and users may add to their description information gained in using the records. "Each time a researcher interacts with a collection, something new is learned about the materials; ideally, even information gleaned during reference activities should be captured and integrated with more formal descriptive compilations."[100] As more attention is being given to use and user studies as we will see in chapter 9, archivists should seek user input as finding aids are redesigned. Most reference archivists know from experience that current finding aids are undecipherable by many users.

History of Descriptive Systems in the United States

In an ideal world, descriptive systems would be designed after assessing the needs of users. Instead, librarians, archivists, and curators inherit finding aids from previous eras in the life of the repository. These often reflect the influence of tradition, an evolving mixture of styles, and a lack of descriptive standards. They also reflect the tools available for recording information. Descriptive tools may, therefore, include

- handwritten index cards,
- typed catalog cards and lists,
- published guides,
- inventories and registers produced by word processing and database programs but used in paper form,
- stand-alone local database systems,
- national bibliographic database systems, and
- Web-based catalogs, inventories, and lists.

A thorough search for all resources in a repository may require use of all these tools.

Generally, two types of finding aid systems evolved in the United States: provenance-based descriptive systems and content-indexing descriptive systems. In provenance-based systems, descriptive information "derives only from what is known about the file—the activities of the creating person or organization and the structure or organizing principles of the file itself." Such descriptive systems developed primarily in institutional archives. In content-indexing systems, derived from librarianship, "information is gleaned by an indexer who examines the records." These systems were more likely to develop in manuscript repositories.[101] Let us look more closely at each of these types, because each has implications for the reference services offered by each type of institution.

Evolution of Provenance-Based Descriptive Systems in Archives

To cope with the masses of modern governmental and institutional records, archivists devised methods of collective description to describe groups of records identified by provenance. In the 1930s, building on European models, the National Archives developed a document it called the "inventory" as its basic descriptive tool. This became an important model for other public archives.[102] Usually prepared for each major creating agency or office, an inventory describes the activities and functions of the record creators in an administrative history and summarizes the forms and arrangement of the records in series descriptions. Most inventories include only minimal information about the content or the subjects of the records.

To provide integrated intellectual access to the inventories, repositories published compilations, usually called "guides," briefly describing the larger aggregates, whether collections or record groups. The guide indexed names, places, and subjects. In theory, users first consulted the guide to identify records of interest and then used the inventories to locate specific series of interest. In practice, however, since they were produced by using only the typewriter and the printing press, guides failed to cope with ever-changing record holdings and new inventories, and they could not provide sufficient depth of indexing to meet the need for subject access.

Thus, in most archival repositories the reference archivist was, and still is, critical to making provenance-based systems work. The archivist links subject requests with archival materials. The reference archivist draws on knowledge of records and of the functional and administrative structure of the agencies that produced them to develop a search strategy. The reference archivist helps a user link a topic with relevant sources by identifying the functions of records creators, locates the relevant finding aids, and identifies series likely to contain needed information. That is, together, the archivist and the user answer a series of questions, "What information or evidence is needed?" "Who would have needed the information initially?" "How would they have recorded it?" "Where are the files now?" "How is the information filed?"[103]

An analysis of reference work at the National Archives suggests that archivists rely heavily on a personal "institutional memory" built on their experience and knowledge of the Archives' organization, finding aids, administrative histories, and rules-of-thumb about how to search specific holdings for particular kinds of information. This interaction works best when users are staff of the creating organization or subject specialists, because they can associate names of participating organizations and individuals with events and subjects of interest.[104]

EVOLUTION OF CONTENT-INDEXING DESCRIPTIVE SYSTEMS IN MANUSCRIPT REPOSITORIES

Manuscript repositories, because they collect personal papers or institutional records from outside organizations, developed other methods to organize and describe their holdings. Many of their holdings were not complete collections. Institutional archives collected by manuscript repositories have been removed from the context of the creating organization. Personal papers often lack the structural integrity of organizational archives, and original order is often chaotic.

The earliest systems found in such institutions as the Library of Congress filed documents from many sources in a classification scheme, following a library model. Later, however, many collecting repositories began to retain the provenance of records, keeping records of one individual or organization together, but arranging documents within the collection by form, correspondent, subject, or date.[105]

Many manuscript repositories, therefore, developed descriptive systems based on direct subject indexing of content.[106] Like the Manuscripts Division of the Library of Congress, manuscript repositories typically described items by rules similar to those used to catalog books. Individual items were indexed in card catalogs by author, recipient, date, and subject. Some manuscript repositories also used calendars, or abstracts of manuscript items arranged chronologically, to describe their holdings. With such detailed control, based on examination of each item, collection-level description seemed unnecessary. Information about provenance, records creators, and a collection as a whole existed in the curator's memory.

Such catalogs and calendars may have worked reasonably well until the mid-twentieth century. Most repositories and collections were small; users could quickly learn about a collection by examining it. As collections grew larger, however, description at the item level proved too time-consuming to produce and too cumbersome to use. Some manuscript repositories published guides to provide collection-level description, but important information about collections was often difficult to find. Curators were needed to provide information about collections, just as archivists were needed in provenance-based systems to provide integrated subject access.

EVOLUTION OF INTELLECTUAL ACCESS TO AUDIOVISUAL MATERIALS

In the past, many repositories did not apply the principles of provenance and original order to nontextual materials. Photographs were often removed from their original locations and filed in self-indexing subject files, neither described nor cataloged further.

Description of audiovisual materials such as photographs and sound tapes has been less standardized than description of textual records. If available, description was idiosyncratic, consisting of item catalogs or lists. Few national tools developed for locating and describing audiovisual holdings. In most repositories, successful research in these materials still depends on assistance from knowledgeable reference archivists or photographic specialists.

Most repositories now treat nontextual materials as they treat textual materials, preserving provenance, maintaining original order if it is usable, describing them in inventories, and indexing them in integrated access tools. Photographs are more likely to be described at the item level than are other nontextual materials, but within the context of a finding aid. Audiovisual materials received as part of larger textual collections and record groups are described as part of the whole. Individual photographs may be retained with the documents to which they relate, although many repositories physically remove series of nontextual materials for housing in separate storage. If nontextual materials are removed from a series, separation sheets are left in place, and the finding aid notes both the intellectual location and the subsequent physical location.

CONVERGENCE OF FINDING AID SYSTEMS

By the late twentieth century, experience proved it dangerous to rely too heavily on the archivist's knowledge of subject or the curator's knowledge of provenance to provide intellectual access. The quality of reference service can vary from day to day as staff members are absent from work, and from year to year as archivists change jobs, retire, or simply forget. Archivists and curators developed descriptive systems to free users from dependence on archivists and curators and to free themselves from dependence on memory. Descriptive systems merged elements from both the public archives and historical manuscript traditions. Most manuscript repositories described collections in a "register," similar to the archival inventory, to provide information about each collection of records.[107]

Both types of repositories also maintained "bridging" tools to provide access to all inventories or registers through index terms for the record groups or collections. Index terms included subjects, personal names, corporate names, and place names. The index terms for all record groups were cumulated in a master index so that users who do not know the functions or forms of records can be pointed to the records likely to be of interest to them. Card catalogs, cumulative indexes, or published guides provided integrated, collection-level access.[108]

Although much interest focuses on improving subject access to provenance-based systems, archivists also recognize the "power of provenance." They use terms for organizational functions, such as monitoring or reporting, and for forms of records, such as minutes, logbooks, architectural drawings, photographs, or videotapes, as index terms in addition to subject headings.[109]

Most archives and manuscript repositories use a two-stage system to provide intellectual access. From the user's point of view, a catalog, index, guide, database, or Web site is the primary finding aid. Researchers bring names or subject queries to the primary finding aid to identify collections or other sets of records of probable interest. This primary tool then refers users to inventories or registers, which provide more detailed information about the creators of the records and their structure and content. These frequently include lists of box or folder titles, which users scan to select particular boxes or folders of interest.

Continuing Evolution of Descriptive Systems

Modern computing systems and telecommunication networks make both repository systems and national systems for access to information about archival and manuscript holdings accessible to users around the world. Today, all these descriptive tools are called "finding aids." Automation has made it possible for one document in electronic form to serve many functions, including the functions of both the inventory/register to describe records and of the indexes to provide pointers to records, at any level of the hierarchy. Increasingly, a database or Web-based description is the primary finding aid, the first point of entry into the descriptive system. What had been a two-step process in a paper-based system often is seen as one step in an automated system. Or the steps in the process become links in an on-line environment. See figure 4-2.

Shared descriptive systems depend on standard formats for exchanging information, rules for describing archives and manuscripts, and authority control of indexing terms.[110] Archivists have created standards for structuring descriptive information so that it can be shared now and migrated through time for preservation. Most repositories, however, still hold many descriptive tools that have not been converted to national standards and remain only in the repository. National standards and shared systems provide a pathway for

Figure 4-2 Integrating Access Points Across Finding Aids

Indexes	Catalogs
Point to location	*Provide pointers and*
handwritten	*description*
typed	card catalogs
printed dBase index terms	databases
published index terms	published guides
Internet search engines	Internet search engines

retrospective conversion of such inherited tools as well as a vision of a seamless integrated system of finding aids available to all users regardless of location.[111]

The first national standard for structuring information about books was MAchine-Readable Cataloging, or MARC. In the 1980s, archivists and manuscript curators adapted this format for archival and manuscript collections and called it MARC AMC or Archival and Manuscript Control. This data structure allowed archivists and curators to participate in Online Public Access Catalogs (OPACs) and in national bibliographical databases. These catalogs analyze collections, parts of collections, and single items by personal name, organization, subject, and format.

In the 1990s, archivists developed another standard for structuring information from the full array of finding aids, and for presenting information in hierarchical displays reflecting the organization of the records. This standard is the Encoded Archival Description (EAD) in the Standard Generalized Markup Language (SGML). The standard is maintained by the Library of Congress, which provides useful links to other sites of on-line finding aids.[112] It provides a tool for navigating and searching the full text of finding aids in an on-line environment. It also provides a structure for viewing digital representations of documents in the context of hierarchaical descriptive information. The Encoded Archival Description codifies the "finding aid" structures agreed upon by archives and manuscript repositories in the 1980s.

Whether this is the best format for delivering information in an on-line environment is yet to be determined.[113]

Electronic Access Systems

Electronic access systems extend searching capability because they allow postcoordinate searching not possible in traditional indexes or catalogs. That is, researchers can search for any word or combination of words, rather than depending on only the terms provided by the cataloger. Digital systems also can accommodate the power of provenance by providing means of searching interactive hierarchical displays rather than only the sequential linear text displays of finding aids on paper. They also enable scanning or browsing large amounts of information quickly. Electronic access systems provide remote access to information about repositories, about holdings, and to documents themselves, and they also better accommodate the nonlinear nature of research and discovery. Hyperlinks enhance the power of footnotes exponentially by linking directly to the source.

Automating descriptive systems and linking them via the Internet means that users and other staff need not rely so heavily on the knowledge of reference archivists. It also means, however, that users do not have the advantage of interacting with a knowledgeable reference archivist, nor can archivists answer questions that arise as users move through automated finding aids.

No finding aid can address all future uses of the records, and novice users will need instruction and assistance no matter how complete the finding aids. It may be that the more sophisticated the finding aids become, the more some users will require assistance to use them. Although knowledgeable reference archivists always will be needed, finding aids should capture their knowledge so that users can be as self-sufficient as possible.

Providing Information about Repositories

To use records, users must know that they exist and how to find them. If users know the scope of the collection of a repository, they can often predict whether its holdings will have information or evidence for them. Researchers often search for the archives of institutions by going directly to them, so they want to learn about all the repositories in a geographical area to plan their research trips. Information about repositories includes practical information about mission, location, telephone numbers, Web sites, public hours, services, and access policies.

Directories

In the past, researchers found such information through national, regional, or thematic directories, and such tools are still useful because some information has not been posted to the Internet. Other traditional publications, such as brochures, signs, and guides, remain helpful because they can be easily carried about. Public programs, such as lectures or workshops, provide information as well. Increasingly, researchers find information about repositories and their holdings through the Internet. Many tools once published in print form are now published in electronic form and are available through subscriptions to electronic publications.

Terry Abraham at the University of Idaho maintains a useful on-line directory of archival Web sites called "Repositories of Primary Sources."[114] Leon Miller at Tulane University maintains "Ready, 'Net, Go! Archival Internet Resources." This site includes lists of archival Web sites as well as links to tools for archivists, archival search engines, and professional sources.[115] The National Association of Government Archivists and Records Administrators provides links to the Web sites of all state archives, and the UNESCO Archives Portal provides links to international organizations.[116]

For some time, an important directory of archival repositories was the *Directory of Archives and Manuscript Repositories in the United States,* compiled by the National Historical Publications and Records Commission and frequently referred to as the NHPRC *Directory,* or DAMRUS.[117] Today a similar directory is maintained on-line by the publishing firm Chadwyck-Healey as part of a subscription to *ArchivesUSA.* Currently, the directory provides information for over 5,480 repositories. It is useful for finding repositories in a particular location or for identifying the records of institutions that maintain their own archives.[118]

Donald L. DeWitt has published both a *Guide to Archives and Manuscript Collections in the United States* (Greenwood, 1994) and *Articles Describing Archives and Manuscript Collections in the United State: An Annotated Bibliography* (Greenwood, 1997). Society of American Archivists roundtables and sections, such as the Lesbian and Gay Archivists Roundtable, maintain lists of special subject repositories and collections. They can be accessed via the SAA Web site.

Other directories also list archival and manuscript repositories. The American Association for State and Local History publishes the *Directory of Historical Organizations in the United States and Canada,* now in its fifteenth edition. It contains listings of local historical societies and museums, genealogical societies, oral history centers, folklore societies, and living history groups, as well as archives and manuscript repositories.[119] The 2001 edition lists some 13,000 historical agencies. The brief entries give location and a general description of repository holdings.

Library directories include some archival and manuscript repositories. The *American Library Directory* is a two-volume set currently published by Information Today, Inc. Volume 1 lists public, academic, and special libraries in the United States, arranged alphabetically by state, thereunder alphabetically by city. Each entry includes staff and contact information, with the library's address, phone number, fax number, Web site URL, and e-mail address, if applicable, as well as information about the library's finances, population served, and holdings. It is available on CD-ROM and on-line for a fee through The Dialog Corporation.[120] LibWeb lists library servers available through the World Wide Web; at this writing it lists 6,600 Web pages in 115 countries.[121]

Although increasingly superseded by Internet resources, a number of specialized directories describe and locate repositories. *Subject Collections: A Guide to Special Book Collections and Subject Emphases as Reported by University, College, Public, and Special Libraries and Museums in the United States and Canada* provides access by subject to special collections as noted in the title. The last edition, now out of print, contains 65,818 entries for collections held by 5,882 institutions, classified under 15,875 subject headings based on the Library of Congress subject headings list. For each collection, the directory gives the name of the institution; telephone, fax, and e-mail address; and a general description of holdings.[122]

Organized alphabetically, the *Directory of Special Libraries and Information Centers* contains directory information for some 34,000 special libraries and information centers maintained by various government agencies, businesses, publishers, educational and nonprofit organizations, and associations around the world. Subject areas include science and engineering, medicine, law, art, religion, the social sciences and humanities. It is updated annually by the *Subject Directory of Special Libraries and Information Centers,* which is arranged by subject matter.[123]

Information about visual materials can be found in the *Picture Researcher's Handbook: An International Guide to Picture Sources and How to Use Them.*[124] Another directory of repositories holding photographs is the *Index to American Photographic Collections: Compiled at the International Museum of Photography at George Eastman House.*[125] Film sources are described in *Footage 91: North American Film and Video Sources,* which is updated and expanded in *The Worldwide Moving Image Sourcebook,* edited by Rick Gell. *Footage.net: the Stock, Archival and News Footage Network* provides access to stock footage sources.[126]

Repository Publications

Repositories publish brochures, pamphlets, and other handouts both through their Web sites and in paper form to convey general information about themselves. Such publications save reference staff time by answering frequently asked questions about access, holdings, and services. In analog form, such publications can be provided in response to requests for information, distributed at meetings, and placed in libraries and other locations accessible to potential users. They also can help educate administrators in the parent institution as well as actual and potential donors.

A general repository brochure should include both administrative and descriptive information. Practical matters such as location, hours of operation, access policy, information about public transportation to the repository, parking, and handicapped access, should be explained. The availability of specialized reference and copying services should be mentioned, a telephone number given for additional information, and, if appropriate, a fax number or e-mail address. A repository brochure also should describe generally the holdings and types of uses that they can support. A summary of the collecting policy is helpful to potential donors and users, as is a list of subjects. For large repositories, a map of the reading room may help orient users to the range of resources available and ease navigation for those who prefer to explore finding aids by themselves.

Reference staff members should help prepare repository brochures. Depending on the nature of the holdings and user interest, they also can prepare supplemental brochures describing particular bodies of records or areas of inquiry, such as sources and services for genealogical or pictorial research.

Repository Web Pages

Both electronic access systems and traditional access systems must be consistent with program mission and goals. They must be sustainable using available resources. The home page is analogous to the introductory sections of a repository guide, containing repository-level information.[127] Some of the elements of information found on the Web site are similar to the elements found in a good repository brochure, such as name, address, phone numbers, e-mail address, public hours, scope of collections, and services available. But each of these elements can be expanded on a Web site, and links can be provided to more detailed information: maps and detailed directions to the facility, expanded descriptions of services, e-mail links for reference inquiries, summary descriptions of collections, detailed descriptions of holdings, digital surrogates of heavily used or representative documents and photographs, frequently asked questions (FAQs), profiles of selected staff members, press releases, and virtual exhibits.[128] See figure 4-3 for examples.

Repository Web sites should be organized logically, with graphics used to assist navigation rather than for decoration or special effects. To the extent possible, the site should be written for the general public, and archival language explained simply and clearly. The site should be maintained and updated frequently, displaying the date of the last update. Ideally, the repository should be a top-level link on the institutional home page. Reference services should be a top-level link on the repository page.[129] It is important to register the institutional pages with search engines; ". . . registering a page is the best way to

Figure 4-3 Repository Web Sites

Manuscripts Division, Library of Congress
    http://www.loc.gov
National Archives and Records Administration
    http://www.archives.gov
Bentley Historical Library, University of Michigan
    http://www.umich.edu/~bhl/
Rare Book, Manuscript, and Special Collections Library, Duke University
    http://scriptorium.lib.duke.edu/
Manuscripts and Archives, Yale University
    http://www.library.yale.edu/mssa/

facilitate its appearance in a web search."[130] Metatags are provided so that search engines can locate the site.

Public Programs

Many other activities can be used to disseminate information about a repository. Reference staff members can help to identify constituencies of current and potential users and develop programs to reach them. Such outreach activities as speeches, exhibitions, publications, audiovisual presentations, videotapes, tours, and festivals inform potential users about archival resources and how to use them.

Providing Information *about* Holdings

The distinction between descriptive tools found only in the repository and those descriptions published to disseminate information about holdings beyond the repository has been dramatically blurred since the last edition of this manual. Until the last decade, most finding aids, such as card catalogs, registers, and inventories, were found only in the repository in unique formats either handwritten or typed. As a general rule, only repository guides were published and available for use beyond the repository. Today, as finding aids are increasingly produced in electronic form, they can be shared immediately with the world through the Internet.

Repository Guide

In the past, many repositories published guides that summarized information about groups of records, and some still do, both in print and electronically. For example, the *Guide to Federal Records in the National Archives of the United States* (1995) includes useful agency histories that identify the functions of the federal government from its founding, its organizational entities and their reporting relationships, as well as descriptions of the forms and contents of records. It is extensively indexed. The Web version of this guide incorporates the information in the published guide, but augments it with descriptive information about federal records acquired or described by the National Archives since 1995. It is regularly updated.[131]

Also on the National Archives Web site is an on-line catalog, the Archival Research Catalog (ARC). It incorporates the information previously found in the guide and includes information about holdings in Washington, D.C., the regional archives, and the presidential libraries. It provides hierarchical displays of archival descriptions and links to agency histories. It provides navigation up and down the archival hierarchy, as well as keyword searching; Boolean searching; date searching; filtered searching for digital images, locations, and records types; and browsing of and filtering by selected authority files for organizations, people, and topical subjects. The National Archives also maintains "Reference at Your Desk," by the National Archives Library and Information Center (ALIC), which includes links to laws, copyright regulations, and legal, biographical, and geographical resources.

Similarly, manuscript repositories published guides to their holdings, such as the *Guide to Manuscripts in the Bentley Historical Library*. This volume replaced the previous *Guide to Manuscripts in the Michigan Historical Collections of the University of Michigan*. Both gave brief collection-level descriptions, with extensive indexing of significant correspondents and of some general subject terms. This information now appears on-line in several venues, including RLIN and the repository Web site.[132]

Subject Surveys

Published by scholars or national research organizations, subject surveys also disseminate information about holdings. Such guides typically describe holdings at the collection or record-group level. Well-known examples include Richard C. Davis, *North American Forest History: A Guide to Archives and Manuscripts in the United States and Canada* and the massive *Women's History Sources* edited by Andrea Hinding, et al. Manuscripts of notable literary figures are itemized in *American Literary Manuscripts: A Checklist of Holdings in Academic, Historical, Public Libraries, Museums, and Authors' Homes in the United States.*[133]

National Union Catalog of Manuscript Collections

The first reference tool to publish descriptions of manuscript collections in repositories throughout the United States was the *National Union Catalog of Manuscript Collections,* NUCMC, affectionately known as "nuck muck." From 1959 to 1993, the Library of Congress published descriptions of approximately 72,300 collections located in 1,406 different repositories in twenty-nine annual printed volumes. The final printed volume was published in 1994. Perhaps even more significantly, it provided the first integrated indexes that allowed researchers to search across repositories. NUCMC included approximately 1,085,000 index terms. The *Index to Personal Names in the National Union Catalog of Manuscript Collections 1959–1984* by Harriet Ostroff simplified access to over 200,000 personal and family names in the separate indexes.

NUCMC provided the first evidence that repositories could share information about collections. The success of NUCMC was, however, uneven. It relied on voluntary reporting by manuscript repositories, and many repositories did not participate. More important, its scope is limited to manuscript collections, that is, it includes only collections held by collecting repositories. It does not include archives maintained by the creating institution, and thus it omits vast quantities of archival materials by excluding institutional, organizational, and governmental archives. Indexes cumulated at uneven intervals were cumbersome to use.

As NUCMC grew, the multiplicity of volumes, the need to search several indexes, and the difficulty of revising descriptions to accommodate changes in collection content or access made it increasingly frustrating to use. However, it proved that manuscript collections could be described in a common data structure and shared with other repositories, and it set the stage for more ambitious programs as automation advanced.

NUCMC continues today as a free-of-charge cooperative cataloging program operated by the Library of Congress. All ongoing cataloging is available on-line, as is the information published from 1986 to 1993. The information in the printed volumes (1960–1985) has not been put on-line. Eligible repositories contribute data, and NUCMC catalogers create MARC (MAchine-Readable Cataloging) collection-level records in the RLG (Research Libraries Group) database, describe collections held by participants, and supply name and subject headings. To be eligible, repositories must be located in the United States, be open to researchers, and lack the capability of entering their own manuscript cataloging into either national bibliographic database. See figure 4-4.

To provide access to its on-line cataloging, NUCMC provides free access through a z39.50 gateway to the Archival and Mixed Collections (AMC) file in the Research Libraries Information Network (RLIN AMC) and to the Mixed Materials file in the Online Computer Library Center (OCLC) database. Access is not provided to other databases in either utility; that is, access is not provided through this gateway to books, maps, computer files, or visual material. These are available by subscription only.

The NUCMC site also provides links to other Library of Congress resources, archival associations, archival education, electronic discussion groups and periodicals, bibliographical utilities, preservation, and the Encoded Archival Description (EAD) standard and its use by the archival profession.[134]

The NUCMC printed volumes are currently out of print. Microfilm copies of these volumes may be available from the Library of Congress.

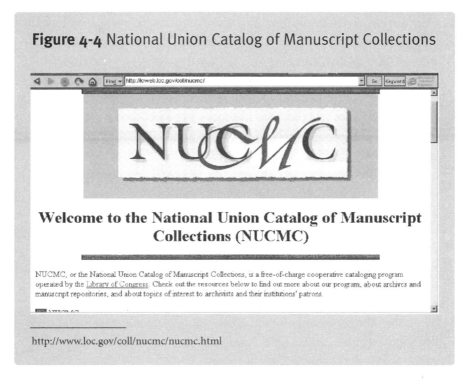

Figure 4-4 National Union Catalog of Manuscript Collections

http://www.loc.gov/coll/nucmc/nucmc.html

Access is also available through subscription to *ArchivesUSA*, as will be discussed below.

Bibliographic Databases

National bibliographical utilities, most notably the Online Computer Library Center (OCLC) and the Research Libraries Information Network (RLIN), developed means to share collection-level descriptions of archival holdings. Information in these utilities is structured in the MARC format. Both organizations began as utilities to provide the benefits of shared cataloging for published materials. Both soon found that the databases are also useful for reference staff and patrons searching for information. Both charge for searches. As mentioned above, however, the Library of Congress provides on-line access without charge to the archival components of these utilities through the NUCMC Web site.

The Research Libraries Group (RLG) developed to serve large university research libraries. It is a nonprofit membership corporation of over 160 universities, national libraries, archives, historical societies, and other institutions. Its database, called the Research Libraries Information Network, (RLIN), is a cultural resources database. Its Archival and Mixed Collections (AMC) file contains descriptions of literary and historical documents, public records, and other primary source materials. Because its mission is to support research institutions, it has developed a more robust interface for archival materials. Catalog records in RLIN provide the URL to link to on-line finding aids.[135]

The Online Computer Library Center (OCLC) developed to serve college and public libraries. A nonprofit membership organization, it serves 41,000 libraries in eighty-two countries and territories around the world. Its Mixed Materials file contains descriptions of literary and historical documents, public records, and other primary source materials. About 300,000 catalog records are available in the OCLC bibliographic database that describe archival and manuscript collections in public, college and university, and special libraries.[136]

Many library on-line public access catalogs (OPACs) or integrated library systems (ILSs) include descriptions of archival holdings, and many are available through the Internet.

National Inventory of Documentary Sources

Before the development of the Web, publisher Chadwyck-Healey began to provide access to finding aids. The company microfilmed inventories and registers in repositories and published them in a microfiche publication, *National Inventory of Documentary Sources (NIDS)*. The microfiche publication contains finding aids for some 54,000 collections in three parts. The first part has finding aids for federal records repositories, including the National Archives, the Smithsonian Institution Archives, and the presidential libraries. The second includes finding aids for the Manuscript Division of the Library of Congress. The third comprises finding aids from state archives, state libraries, state historical societies, academic libraries, and other repositories. The UMI division of ProQuest Company now publishes *NIDS;* only very large research libraries purchase this extensive microfiche product.[137]

ArchivesUSA

In 1997, Chadwyck-Healey combined several products into *ArchivesUSA: Integrated Collection and Repository Information,* available on CD-ROM or on the Web for subscribers.[138] It incorporates three tools. First is the *Directory of Archives and Manuscripts Repositories in the United States* (DAMRUS), which lists over 5,480 repositories. Second are the indexes to its *National Inventory of Documentary Sources* (NIDS), which provide access to names and subjects. Third it provides access to the entire *National Union Catalog of Manuscript Collections* from 1959 to the present, and it makes NUCMC fully searchable in electronic form.

Placing Finding Aids On-line

An increasing number of archival finding aids are now available on-line either as simple HTML documents or fully marked up EAD documents. Several studies suggest that researchers find these very useful.[139] A catalog record in MARC can link to a full finding aid.

Consortia of digital services are developing.[140] A useful example is the Online Archive of California, part of the California Digital Library maintained by the University of California.[141] It provides links to catalogs and indexes, including finding aids, as well as links to text and image collections in California. It also provides information for digital library developers, reports on research and development, software tools, and learning tools. It is important that reference archivists not assume that researchers, even scholarly ones, know any of the preceding information. Be ready with demonstrations and handouts on these various resources, linking them, if possible, to your Web site.

Providing Information *from* Holdings

In most repositories, providing information *about* holdings has been the primary focus of reference service. Most repositories, however, do provide some information *from* holdings in response to reference inquiries. Here we will consider providing information for individual requests. Providing copies and loans will be covered at greater length in chapter 8.

In addition, many repositories publish documents as a way of providing information from holdings and consider it a fundamental part of their mission. Increasingly, digital publication provides new opportunities and means to do so. This will also be considered in chapter 8.

Providing information *from* holdings will remain an important part of reference service because most holdings will not be available in digital form in the foreseeable future. When providing information *about* holdings, the archivist helps users identify likely sources, and users do their own research, identifying, evaluating, and synthesizing relevant information from documents. When providing information *from* holdings, archivists supply information from their own knowledge, from finding aids, from reference tools, or in some cases, they conduct research in their holdings to answer questions.

Requests for information *from* holdings rather than *about* them raise the delicate matter of distinguishing between reference service and research, a distinction usually clearer in theory than in practice. As discussed in chapter 3, some users request factual information; others request interpretation or evaluation of information. Many factual requests are quite simple: supplying a date, locating a photograph, finding a name. In many cases, a straightforward factual question can be answered by relatively simple research requiring little evaluation or interpretation by the archivist. In a college or university archives, for example, supplying the date that a fraternity was established is probably a simple task. In contrast, a request to identify and copy letters, diaries, and other documents recording attitudes toward fraternities in the 1890s demands research—evaluation and interpretation that are usually the responsibility of the researcher.

The appropriate response to requests for information from holdings depends on institutional mission and staff resources. Many repositories respond to requests for straightforward factual information, but will not undertake extensive or substantive research. A state archives, for example, may locate and copy a Civil War service record if the researcher supplies a soldier's name and unit, but decline to fill in the blanks in a family genealogy. Archives of academic institutions may take a more active role in orientation and instruction, but decline to conduct the research that is the responsibility of the student researcher.

Providing substantive research services for the parent institution may, however, be a significant responsibility of reference service in institutional archives. As employees of the parent institution, archivists provide research services for it. A corporate archivist notes, "The staff does the research and provides the answer—it may be one word, two hundred pages of photocopies of original documents, or a six-page synopsis of our research."[142]

Changing Researcher Expectations

Providing extracted information, rather than direction to relevant records, is likely to become more important for archives, especially as more materials are available on-line. Charles Dollar notes, "researchers will expect customized electronic services for specific information. In this environment, a critical issue for archives reference service is how to shift to a demand-driven reference service that accommodates researchers' expectations and need for information, not records per se." If they are to survive in an increasingly competitive information environment, archives, particularly those in organizational settings, must become service agencies providing information services their primary constituencies need.[143] Indeed many archivists are finding that access to online finding aids prompts many researchers, before unsure of topics covered in various collections, to request the contents of entire folders they see listed on-line.

Supplying detailed, comprehensive management information for administrative queries makes the corporate memory a living, vital part of the entity and integrates the archives into current organizational decision making. Such an activist role runs counter to the traditional notion of the archivist as the impartial servant of future scholarship, but is more likely to garner the resources for the identification and retention of records of enduring value. Angelika Menne-Haritz notes that "Archives that see their main task in preserving the past for the future become invisible in the present, when support for creating an own memory is needed." And further, "Archives do not store memory. They offer the possibility to create memory."[144]

Developing Policies

Repositories need policy statements to guide staff members responding to requests for information from records. Such statements should indicate the amount of time that can be given to one query and define how precisely the query must be stated. A repository that must limit research services may state, for example, that ten minutes will be spent searching an index for a name, and a maximum of one hour on a more general query. Written procedures and search protocols will help ensure equity of treatment and search accuracy. If requests are numerous, the use of forms or standard responses may speed response time and ensure that all users receive equal treatment. Staff members should always indicate the sources of the information supplied and the extent of the search undertaken. If additional searching might be useful, the user should be informed of the probable duration and result. Some repositories charge fees for research services. These must be precisely defined in the access policy, which will be considered at greater length in chapter 6.

Repositories, especially those with large outside constituencies, also might maintain lists of local individuals who undertake research for others. One source is graduate students at a local university; universities often maintain a job placement service for part-time student workers. Other sources are local genealogical societies, which often can provide lists of volunteers or researchers available for contract work. National organizations such as the Board for Certification of Genealogists also maintain lists of researchers.[145] When furnishing the names of such individuals, the repository should stipulate that these researchers are independent contractors and that the repository cannot guarantee their work.

Providing Information about Records Creators

On closer analysis, many requests for information, especially those received by organizational archives, are actually inquiries about records creators, not requests for information about or from holdings. Information about creating organizations or individuals is useful to agencies and departments inside and outside the creating institution and to individual researchers.

In the course of locating records, analyzing the creator's functions and organizational changes over time, and arranging and describing its records, archivists compile rich historical information about records creators and organizational functions, activities, events, and precedents. This is generally an unappreciated and untapped information resource. Archivists need to link their information about records creators with the information needs of other departments in the creating organization, individual researchers, and other information professionals.[146] Here, too, repeated queries may prompt digitization of certain categories of information so that they can be mounted on the Web site.

Some of this information is incorporated in administrative histories and biographical notes in inventories, but it is often helpful to build reference files in addition to the inventory. Compiling information about records creators, especially in institutional archives, makes it possible to respond quickly to questions. Frequently useful are

- agency or departmental histories,
- lists of officers or department heads with their dates of tenure,
- chronologies of organizational name changes,
- organization charts,
- genealogies,
- lists of publications,
- histories of buildings,
- biographies of leaders, and
- chronologies of important dates.

Lists of significant "firsts" in organizational history are useful, but in some cases it is wise to have such lists cleared by the legal department, especially if they are to be used in advertising. Such information can be produced in handouts, filed in loose-leaf binders for photocopying, or mounted on a Web site. Archivists also are beginning to capture information about records creators in automated systems or in authority files, such as agency histories in the RLIN database.[147] Administrative histories are found in the EAD structure, and there is a movement to create a standard format for them.

Reference staff members frequently maintain a vertical file of clippings, pamphlets, and brochures about people, departments, events, buildings, and subjects. The results of searches to answer complex questions can also be filed in such reference files or in electronic directories for future use. They may compile copies of frequently requested photographs arranged by topic, both in binders in the reading room and in databases on the Web site. If space in the research room permits, a reference set of frequently consulted published documents, such as minutes of the governing authority, yearbooks, annual reports, newsletters, or journals, can expedite providing information about the institution and other records creators. Indexing such publications of record saves much reference time and contributes to use of the archives. Also useful are monographs based on the holdings or relevant to collection strengths.

While such reference tools are useful for quick responses to factual questions, archivists must guard against developing a parallel finding aid system at the reference desk. If reference archivists discover that they are beginning to develop extensive sets of lists and indexes, then analysis of the descriptive program is warranted.

Providing Referrals

If their repositories do not hold needed information or records of interest to researchers, archivists may be able to provide referrals to people, institutions, libraries, or repositories that do. Most reference archivists develop a Rolodex or electronic directory of names, phone numbers, and addresses of people and institutions to which frequent referrals are made. The directories, guides to other repositories, subject surveys, and other published finding aids described above are also useful in providing referrals. Providing referrals may also include doing straightforward Internet searches, informed by knowledge of searching protocols or of the particular topic.

Through their knowledge of creating organizations or their records management programs, archivists often know which office maintains information in records not yet transferred to the archives. Because archives are the organizational memory of an institution, archivists play an integrative role in linking information sources throughout the organization. This often includes educating current office staff about the existence and availability of their own office's past files in the archives—frequent turnover makes this information "lost" more often than we would like to think.

Manuscript repositories may play a similar role for documentation created in their collecting area, even if records are not actually held by the repository. Curators often direct researchers to other archives and manuscript repositories with appropriate related materials or to libraries with related published sources.

Conclusion

In recent decades, it has become easier to search across repositories. Manuscript repositories began this trend with the publication of NUCMC in 1959, but searches were cumbersome and limited to repositories that housed the volumes. The advent of the national bibliographic databases in the 1980s furthered integration of information and fostered the ability to search across repositories, but only library staff had access to these databases. In most cases, librarians mediated such searches. The advent of the World Wide Web in the 1990s meant that almost everyone with access to the Internet is able to search across repositories.

Providing intellectual access traditionally has meant providing information about repositories and their holdings. In many settings, and increasingly in an information economy, archivists also provide information from records, information about records creators, and referrals to outside information sources. Archivists, as the guardians of memory, can play increasingly important roles in helping users find the information they need.

Archivists use a variety of finding aids, which continue to evolve as new technologies become available, to provide intellectual access to archives and manuscripts. Reference archivists provide a critical link between these finding aids and users seeking information. They educate users about the process of doing research in archives, and they help users identify and locate the finding aids, records, and information needed for their research. Because assistance from reference archivists is so often vital to the success of users in archives and manuscript repositories, chapter 5 will examine the reference process.

The Reference Process

This chapter focuses on the human dimension of providing reference services in archives, whether in person, or by phone, mail, or electronic communication systems. Because reference archivists frequently mediate among users, finding aids, and records, understanding the interaction among them is critical to providing intellectual access to archives. Beyond assisting individual users, reference archivists also provide services to groups of users and potential users through public programs and Web-based programs.

As more finding aids and records become available on-line, it may seem that there will be less need for reference services. In fact, "As more people gain access to online information services, even more guides will be needed to help."[148] As information resources proliferate, people need assistance to locate and evaluate information sources. A reference archivist is a guide not only to finding aids and records, but to the structures and forms of the information landscape of their repositories and beyond. Providing reference services is a value-added process. To paraphrase Bonnie A. Nardi and Vicki L. O' Day, the reference archivist is a keystone species in the information ecology of organizational archives, the key to making the system work. Archival reference services provide the "oil" to keep organizational information systems running well. Ideally, the reference archivist is not a barrier, nor a gatekeeper, but rather a partner, a facilitator, and a guide.

Reference Interaction in the Repository

The extent of reference interaction varies from simple to complex, depending on the nature of the repository, the kinds of finding aids available, the research problem, and users' research skills. Not all users require, or even desire, all elements of the reference process, nor do all repositories have sufficient staff to carry them out.

The reference interaction has both intellectual and administrative elements and is powerfully affected by interpersonal dynamics between user and archivist. The quality of reference service depends on acknowledging and successfully resolving the complicated dynamics of reference transactions. An effective reference interaction enables a user to exploit archival resources fully, while meeting the administrative requirements of the repository.

Intellectual Dimensions of the Reference Interaction

As an intellectual exchange, reference interaction, also called "question negotiation," consists of three activities: *query abstraction, resolution,* and *refinement.*[149] These activities usually, but not always, follow each other sequentially through time. Typically, the reference interaction proceeds through three phases—initial interview, continuing assistance, and follow-up activities. Query abstraction and query resolution usually take place during the initial interview. Since query refinement takes place during research, interaction between user and archivist may be needed throughout the research project. Interaction may be extended by phone or mail follow-up activity after the researcher leaves. See figure 5-1 and 5-2.

Figure 5-1 Intellectual Dimensions of Reference Services

Initial interview
    Query abstraction
    Query resolution
    Search strategy
Continuing interaction
    Query refinement
Exit interview

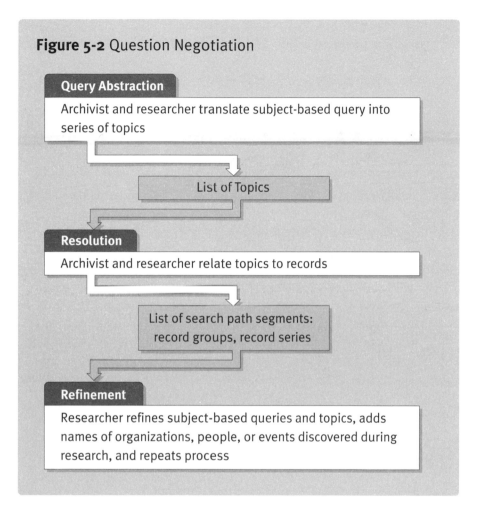

Figure 5-2 Question Negotiation

Query Abstraction

Archivist and researcher translate subject-based query into series of topics

List of Topics

Resolution

Archivist and researcher relate topics to records

List of search path segments: record groups, record series

Refinement

Researcher refines subject-based queries and topics, adds names of organizations, people, or events discovered during research, and repeats process

INITIAL INTERVIEW

The initial interview is an intellectual interchange between archivist and user. It is the archivist's opportunity to elicit information about the research project and to guide the user to the necessary sources. The archivist ascertains what information the user needs to answer a particular question, and the amount, variety, level, and complexity of the source materials needed to resolve it. The initial interview begins with question abstraction, in which the seeker and the archivist identify the topic, delimited by time, place, and the seeker's intended use.

Figure 5-3 Reference Process: Black Box

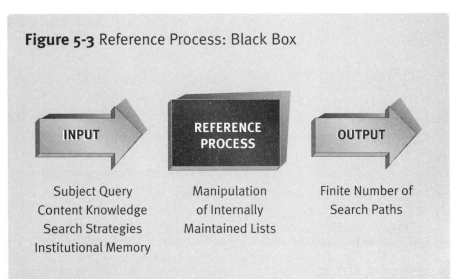

INPUT	REFERENCE PROCESS	OUTPUT
Subject Query	Manipulation	Finite Number of
Content Knowledge	of Internally	Search Paths
Search Strategies	Maintained Lists	
Institutional Memory		

This exhibit shows the modular software model developed for the expert system prototype. The modular software model shows the reference process used by the archivist as a "black box" that accepts input to create an output. The input is the query and the output is a list of records which will provide an answer to the query.

American Management Systems, 1986

Query Abstraction

Archivist and user strive to clarify questions and to state the full scope of the research problem. In some cases it is necessary to narrow the user's initial question, in others to broaden it. By asking good questions, the archivist helps the researcher raise all relevant issues. In this stage, the archivist tries to glean enough information to translate the user's natural language into the retrieval language of the finding aid system. Eliciting names of specific persons, organizations, places, and events is important, because research subjects must be linked with the collections and record groups created by specific individuals and organizations.

During query abstraction, it is frequently helpful to learn about the intended uses of the information, because the nature of the intended product may indicate which types of sources will be most useful. Is the researcher writing a dissertation or a term paper, producing a documentary film or videotape, preparing a report for a public policy agency, seeking legal precedent, or satisfying curiosity?

It is also useful to find out whether the user is asking on behalf of someone else, as is frequently the case in institutional archives. Because negotiating a question through an intermediary is difficult, it is best, whenever possible, for the archivist to talk directly to the person with the question. Ascertaining the amount of time that the researcher has available for the research project also helps determine the nature and depth of suitable resources.

Question abstraction is important whether the user or the archivist will conduct the research. In fact, precision in defining user needs may be more important if the archivist is to locate the information, since the archivist, not the user, must evaluate the relevance of sources and information.

QUERY RESOLUTION

In the second, or resolution, stage, the archivist and the user analyze the problem in terms of the sources available and form a search strategy, a plan for resolving the question in light of the sources. The archivist assesses available sources, identifies records, and suggests an order in which the researcher might use them. Based in part on an assessment of the probability of finding useful information, the archivist helps the user identify some sources as highly relevant, others as possibly useful, and others as of marginal interest. The archivist may answer some factual questions from personal knowledge or ready reference sources. For other questions, a published history will be sufficient, and for yet others multiple sources will be needed, including archives, manuscripts, photographs, motion pictures, sound recordings, and electronic data archives.

The arrangement of a series may dictate research strategy. For example, to use a series arranged by name, the researcher must have the names of individuals; similarly, to use a geographically arranged series effectively, the researcher must know the area of interest. Sometimes, one group of records must be used first to learn information necessary to use another.

Figure 5-4
Inside the Black Box

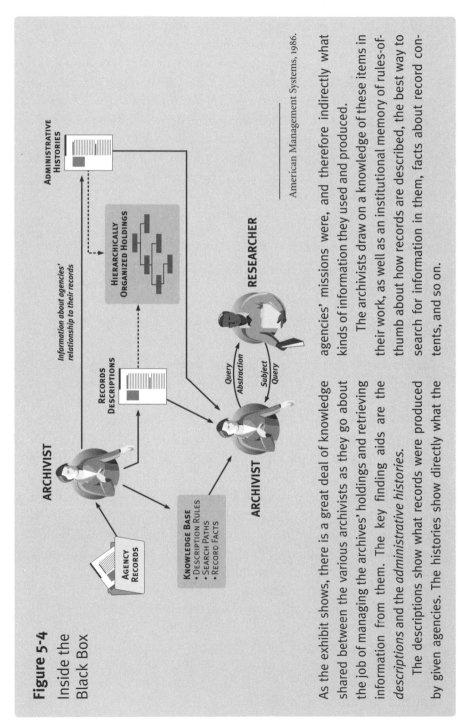

ARCHIVIST

Information about agencies' relationship to their records

ADMINISTRATIVE HISTORIES

RECORDS DESCRIPTIONS

HIERARCHICALLY ORGANIZED HOLDINGS

AGENCY RECORDS

KNOWLEDGE BASE
• DESCRIPTION RULES
• SEARCH PATHS
• RECORD FACTS

ARCHIVIST

Query
Abstraction

Subject Query

RESEARCHER

American Management Systems, 1986.

As the exhibit shows, there is a great deal of knowledge shared between the various archivists as they go about the job of managing the archives' holdings and retrieving information from them. The key finding aids are the *descriptions* and the *administrative histories*.

The descriptions show what records were produced by given agencies. The histories show directly what the agencies' missions were, and therefore indirectly what kinds of information they used and produced.

The archivists draw on a knowledge of these items in their work, as well as an institutional memory of rules-of-thumb about how records are described, the best way to search for information in them, facts about record contents, and so on.

The archivist's response to the user's query depends in large measure on the level of description and the types of finding aids available. In some cases, the archivist identifies terms for searching catalogs and databases. In others, the archivist identifies likely record groups and series. In still other cases, the archivist locates and explains the use of finding aids likely to guide the user to relevant sources.

Increasingly users have identified holdings of possible interest through national or local databases, but they still rely on archivists to explain archival arrangement and the use of inventories and other finding aids. To refer users to relevant information sources outside the repository, archivists may also use national reference sources and their knowledge of holdings of other repositories or of sources retained by creating departments within the parent organization. Figure 5-4 suggests the complicated relationships among archivists, finding aids, records, and users in resolving questions.

The resolution stage of question negotiation is particularly important in institutional archives. The archivist translates a question about a subject into a question about the related organizational functions. Knowledge of institutional history is necessary to ascertain which agencies were responsible for those functions in the period under investigation and thus likely to have recorded the needed information. The archivist also uses knowledge of the forms in which information was recorded to infer which series might bear on the subject, to suggest, for example, that annual reports will be more fruitful than minutes.

A question about a department may lead beyond its own records to an analysis of information flows within the parent organization to locate all relevant information, including that transmitted to other departments. For example, a thorough study of a university English department may require use of the records of the governing dean, academic vice president, president, faculty senate, and governing board. Further resolution may lead to a printed bibliography of faculty publications and to the database that succeeded it.

In manuscript repositories, a similar process takes place. The reference archivist uses knowledge of the activities of the people and organizations whose papers the repository has collected, knowledge of the kinds of information found in such generic types of records as diaries or field notes, and knowledge of the repository's finding aids to identify relevant collections. Since manuscript collections do not reflect functions embodied in organizations and recorded in particular record forms to the extent that archives do, the process is necessarily less distinct.

Although the query abstraction and resolution stages of the reference interaction are distinct, they often occur concurrently. For example, a researcher's interest in a particular organization, such as the Grand Rapids Kindergarten Training School, may lead directly to its finding aid to locate appropriate series, boxes, or folders. In contrast, a broad subject request, such as a request for sources for a history of early childhood education, requires more extensive abstraction and resolution. It will lead to a longer discussion, first, of the terminology used to identify this concept over time and, second, of the individuals and organizations likely to have participated in its development. This negotiation may lead not only to the records of the Grand Rapids Kindergarten Training School, but to the papers of its founder Clara Wheeler and to the records of the Woman's Christian Temperance Union, which promoted legislation to establish public kindergartens.

Locating information in archives is often inferential, based on what is known about the records, their creators, and the circumstances of their creation. In many cases, reference archivists link the records and the functions that created them, extending the user's information seeking in the creating organization into the past. Archivists play a vital role in this process because of their understanding of the universe of documentation and how a user's questions fit within that universe.

This intuitive process of inference sometimes gives archivists an "illusion of omniscience" to users unfamiliar with archival research. For example, a user inquired whether a noted Victorian author had ever visited Ann Arbor, Michigan. The archivist suspected that the author would have written to University of Michigan president James B. Angell and knew that Angell's correspondence was indexed by name. With this knowledge it was relatively simple to find a letter from the author discussing the date of his visit. Knowledge of the date gave access to local newspapers, university publications, and diaries for descriptions of the visit.

By explaining their reasoning to users, archivists can help researchers build their own research skills. It is important to help users understand record creation, finding aids, and the process leading to a particular search strategy. Archivists strive to make users as independent as possible by helping them to think archivally—that is, functionally and hierarchically. As teachers, archivists help users to think, "Who would have been likely to record the information I am seeking, how would it have been recorded and filed, and where are the records now?"

Continuing Interaction

In the third, or query refinement, stage, interaction between archivist and user continues to refine the problem and search strategy. Research in archives is iterative. As users work through archival materials, they discover new aspects of their topic, including the names of other organizations and individuals whose activities bear on the subject of research. These names must be linked with other record groups or collections. Often the introductory information in the finding aid of one collection provides additional names, places, and events for further query refinement. Additional discussions, similar to the initial interview, are needed to clarify and resolve these new questions.

Researchers also discover questions about the records as they work through them. These problems of external evidence are very much the archivist's concern. Provenance-related questions about the source, creation, or custody of records can help the user judge the authenticity of documents, understand bias or interpretation, or explain gaps in the records. Users also may need technical assistance—deciphering handwriting, identifying archaic words or references, resolving problems with dating, or using difficult file structures. Archivists also may help users understand how best to use formats new to them, such as architectural drawings, photographs, maps, or electronic records.

Other questions that arise during research concern repository policies and procedures. Nonprofessional support staff members may often answer simple questions about retrieving or photocopying materials. Substantive or complicated administrative questions—for example, regarding copyright or publication—cannot be delegated. Matters of intellectual substance must engage the attention of professional staff. Support staff members must be trained to recognize which questions to refer.

Exit Interview

Ideally, reference interaction is closed by an exit interview as long and thorough as the initial interview, but this is seldom realized. Because users do not always announce their departure, it is wise to request and, if possible, schedule an exit interview during the initial interview. Although continuing interaction during research helps to ensure that researchers have seen all pertinent materials, an exit interview provides an opportunity to review the sources used and to discover if additional materials warrant another visit. Reference archivists can clarify policies for publication, citation, and the use of copies, and request a copy, or at least a citation, of publications or other products based on repository resources.

The exit interview is an opportunity to capture the knowledge and expertise of researchers and use it to enhance collection descriptions. In many cases, the researcher who uses a collection will discover information about the collection or its creator. Reference archivists can collect information discovered in the course of research to add to repository finding aids. An exit interview also is an opportunity for users to evaluate repository services. Users can assess finding aids, report on arrangement and preservation, suggest leads for acquisition, and evaluate reference services. An exit interview is not the only way to obtain such information; other follow-up activities will be discussed in chapter 9.

Interpersonal Dynamics: The Human Dimension of the Reference Interaction

All phases of reference interaction—initial interview, continuing assistance, and exit interview—are affected by interpersonal dynamics between user and archivist. Nardi and O'Day define the reference interview as "a modest name for an impressive deployment of tact, diplomacy, and persistence, as well as a skillful interviewing technique."[150]

Most information about the dynamics of reference interaction in archives is anecdotal. Librarians have studied reference encounters extensively, and archivists can learn from this research, albeit recognizing significant differences between the two. The most significant difference is that reference encounters in libraries are usually short and voluntary, each devoted to a single question. In contrast, reference transactions in archives are more likely to be substantive, obligatory, and continuing.[151]

Nonverbal Signs and Symbols

Nonverbal signs and symbols are significant components of interpersonal communication.[152] These subtle messages can either reinforce or subvert the overt messages sent or received verbally. Often people are not fully aware of sending and receiving these covert messages. Nonverbal language is culturally determined and culturally bound. Research indicates that more than half of the information exchanged between two people is expressed nonverbally by gestures, tone, and attitude.[153] Verbal and nonverbal communications must be congruent.

Positive body language makes users feel more comfortable approaching a staff member with a question. Making eye contact, nodding, smiling, the so-called eyebrow flash, and immediate verbal acknowledgment of the user's approach are feedback signals that tell a user that questions are welcomed. Furthermore, a user will approach a standing person more readily than a seated person, so standing when a user nears sends a powerful welcoming message. Correspondingly, negative body language discourages users. Such negative behavior includes lack of acknowledgment, no change in body position, frowning, pursing the lips, grimacing, sitting with hand over brow, or writing. A person facing a terminal, sitting with his or her back to users, sends the most negative message.[154]

Physical distance between people is a significant nonverbal symbol and defines the context of the interaction. Eighteen inches is the recommended distance in our society between client and professional. Maintaining eye contact conveys confidence and openness. Staff dress also affects public perceptions. Wearing a name tag with name and function is one of the simplest and most effective ways of communicating a professional and welcoming message.[155]

Nonverbal interaction goes both ways; archivists get impressions of users, too. Nonverbal messages may influence professional roles and actions, and awareness of interpersonal factors can help archivists treat all researchers fairly. Occasionally, an archivist may dislike a user, find a user extremely difficult to assist, or provide greater attention to another researcher with a more attractive personality. Archivists must guard against making assumptions about the value of research or the level of intelligence and skill based on a user's mannerisms.

The First Question, the Initial Inquiry

Beginnings are delicate, and the initial interview sets the tone for much that follows. A survey of British archival users found that about a quarter were first time users and underscored the importance of the initial interview; "first impressions and effective induction are likely to have a critical impact both on their relationship with the archive and on long-term satisfaction ratings."[156] Because clear communication between user and archivist is essential to make best use of holdings, the initial interview often is crucial to a user's experience in an archives.

Reference archivists quickly learn that the first question that researchers ask is usually not the real question, or that the first statement of need is not a full statement of need. Some researchers do an excellent job of articulating what they need. Other users need help to articulate their needs. A few appear to conceal their needs, or even describe their needs in a misleading way. Experienced reference archivists continue to marvel at the gap between what researchers say and what they need. It is fruitless to blame researchers for this gap. Understanding why this gap exists leads to better reference service.

People often feel vulnerable when asking questions, at a psychological disadvantage because they expose need or ignorance to a stranger whose response is unknown. In this vulnerable position, users may adopt a defensive strategy. They may ask a simple directional question to see what kind of response is forthcoming. Or, afraid of appearing inept or uninformed, they may try to bluff to give the impression that they know more than they do. If users anticipate a particular response, they may frame their question in accordance with expectation. Users who anticipate rejection may ask questions defensively. Such defensiveness may be exacerbated by repository security procedures. Users who feel that they are being treated as thieves may find it difficult to discuss their needs fully with someone they think distrusts them. Some users may take a bullying approach to conceal vulnerability.

Researcher and archivist discuss on-line finding aids. PHOTOGRAPH COURTESY
MANUSCRIPTS AND ARCHIVES, YALE UNIVERSITY LIBRARY.

Some users may not ask questions at all, thinking that the staff is too busy, or that their questions are too unimportant. Users new to archives do not expect a lengthy interchange. Some users expect archives to be like libraries and look for a catalog and shelves that they can browse. Many researchers feel that they should know how to find information for themselves and are embarrassed to ask questions that might reveal that they do not. Others feel superior to archivists or lack confidence in them. Scholars are particularly prone to these behaviors. A scholar may well know more about a subject than the archivist does, but very likely does not know the holdings of the archives or how best to exploit them. One social scientist views the reference interview as a "mandatory interaction ritual" and instructs his reader on how best to overcome this obstacle, get past the archivist, and find records.[157] Many students are told that they should do research themselves and may feel that getting help from an archivist is somehow cheating.

Researchers who are not familiar with archives or the extraordinary range of materials in them are unable to ask for what they cannot conceive. Conversely, researchers may ask for a type of document that they think will answer their question, rather than stating the question in such a way as to identify a range of sources. Researchers also vary in their research styles. Some researchers prefer to work with people, some with printed sources, and others with electronic sources. Age, gender, and position in the organizational hierarchy may also affect research preferences. Figure 5-5 shows how one repository explains user choices in this matter.

These behaviors, though understandable, serve to conceal the real question. And in a complex research project, the first statement cannot possibly explore the full ramifications of the research problem. Thus, initial inquiries are especially complicated by interpersonal dynamics. Most users need to be encouraged to state their problem fully, and, in nearly all cases, the first question, whatever it may be, must be expanded. If the archivist fails to probe more thoroughly, the real problem may not be discovered, and the user may not find needed information. Or, if the first question is taken at face value and answered, time may wasted, because the user then says, "Yes, but what I really need is . . . ." It is often useful to respond to a broad query with "Is there some specific information you're looking for?"

Archivists are also at risk of setting up barriers to communication. They may prejudge the value of certain kinds of research or dismiss some users. Like users, they may suffer from tender egos and uncertain status. They may fear exposing their own limited knowledge and or think that they must be authority figures, instant experts in all fields, able to dazzle and astound all comers with their omniscience. Inexperienced archivists in particular, afraid to appear ignorant, too often hasten to answer the ostensible question instead of asking additional questions to get a better sense of the real problem. Listening is as important as talking, if not more so. Not only do most users enjoy talking about their research, but silences can also be employed effectively to give users time to think of relevant terms or concepts.

Library research indicates that "there may often be considerable variance between what users want out of the interview and what the reference staff considers appropriate."[158] For example, archivists may believe that users should find their own answers, or that some types of users such as genealogists deserve less help than others. Archivists

Figure 5-5 Reference Interview: Handout for Researchers

The purpose of the reference interview is to help you identify appropriate sources, refine your subject, and develop a more successful archival research strategy. Your job during the interview is to explain the topic, show your preliminary search, and explain your project scope, including its length and deadlines. The archivist's job is to match your interest with collections or parts of collections.

The reference interview is not a requirement. You can just fill in the mandatory registration form and request specific material already identified from your preliminary search. However, our policy is to give high level reference assistance and the interview can provide you important information. The archivist may be able to help you narrow or broaden your subject, identify material that you have missed, point out areas of research that have been neglected and collections that have not been used, or even refer you to other archives that may have relevant materials. It is also an opportunity to ask questions you may have about using archival records.

Auburn University Archives Tutorial
http://www.lib.auburn.edu/archive/user/resinterview.html

may have some unstated sense of the appropriate time to be given for certain kinds of questions.

Catherine Sheldrick Ross and Patricia Dewdney discuss the practical need of busy reference staff "to deal with the stream of questions in such a way that users are processed expeditiously and sent out of the system." With two or three people sometimes handling more than a hundred questions an hour in a busy academic or public library, reference "became a sort of tennis game; the idea was to whack the ball back into the client's court and hope that it stayed there." Ross and Dewdney analyzed patterns of reference transactions in which "the staff member concentrated on moves that would achieve an ending to the reference transaction; the user employed countermoves to keep the reference transaction going." They identified a number of strategies that librarians employ to discourage users from continuing the reference transaction before finding the answer.[159]

For archivists, the dynamics of the interaction may be somewhat different, because the result of the interaction is more likely to be a search strategy, rather than an answer. Archivists should, however, be aware of negative closures found in archives. For example, an archivist might refer the user to another library or another repository immediately, state that the information is not in the archives, or that the information does not exist at all. These statements may be true, but if they are presented before the archivist has conducted a full initial interview, they send a potential user away prematurely. Reference archivists have also been known to end the initial interview prematurely by stating that the user should have done research in secondary sources before coming to the archives. This may also be true, but all too often the user feels unwelcome and does not return after reading the secondary sources.

It is also easy to give the user information easily found in secondary sources, instead of the information actually needed, which will be more difficult to locate. Archivists know that research in archives is often complicated, so it is tempting to send a user away prematurely by indicating that the topic is too hard, obscure, large, elusive, or otherwise unpromising. Finally when a researcher asks defensively, "You don't have any genealogies do you?" it is tempting to take the statement at face value and agree, rather than discussing whether tax records, land records, or church records may have needed information.

Responding to the First Question

How can the reference archivist understand the full ramifications of a question or research project? Active listening is more important than talking. Taking time to draw out the full question and determining the level to which it needs to be answered are important for both seeker and archivist. Reflective listening is often useful in expanding the inquiry. That is, the archivist first repeats or rephrases the question to confirm shared understanding and clarify meaning.

Reference staff and researchers need to ask further questions to determine which archival and manuscript collections will be most useful. Asking such questions can also educate researchers about the process of finding information in archives. Such questions include:

- *who* would have needed this information or evidence? This question elicits names of agencies or people whose records might contain the necessary information.
- *why* would someone have needed this information or evidence? This question identifies functions that would have required this information or evidence and helps determine whose records might contain the information.
- *when* in the past would this information or evidence have been produced or gathered? This question identifies the time period important to the project.
- *how* might the information been recorded? This question identifies the forms of records likely to have this information.
- *where* would those records be now? This question identifies archival descriptions available to locate likely sources.
- *what product* will result from the research project? Almost every research project has a product as its end, such as an exhibit, video, term paper, dissertation, article, report, television or radio report, documentary film, law brief, speech, genealogy, plan, or specifications for a contract. Determining the end result will assist in identifying the range of sources needed and will also alert the archivist to potential legal ramifications of the use. For example, if the researcher plans to publish materials, he or she must be informed of the need to obtain copyright permissions for protected materials.

Asking this question may also elicit that the researcher is doing the research on behalf of someone else. It is not uncommon for an administrator to ask an assistant to find information, or for a scholar to employ a research assistant. As the question or the information need passes through others, it is altered. It can be difficult to negotiate a question if the assistant does not know why the information is needed or does not know the full ramifications of the question. If possible, try to discuss the question with the person ultimately responsible. Explain to the intermediary that you can give much better service directly. In addition to providing better service, in organizational archives, speaking to the actual user, who is often higher in the organizational chart, is an important means of advocating for the archives.

- *how much time* is available for this research? The nature of research for a speech to be given tomorrow will be very different from the research for a dissertation or book.

CUES FOR RESEARCHERS

Researchers need clear cues to identify the reference archivist. Layout and signage can facilitate the interpersonal exchange by making it clear that the reference archivist is to be approached and marking clear pathways to the reference workstation. The reference archivist should wear a name tag with title, as should support staff or volunteers. Other barriers to good relationships can be mitigated by careful building design and furniture layout. Good signage directs patrons to registration, finding aids, lockers, reference, and the restroom. Publications and good signage can be used to explain procedures.

The location of the initial interview is important. Does it take place either at a reference desk in the research room or at the researcher's table in sight and sound of other users? Finding it difficult to admit need, expose ignorance, or seek help in public settings, or not wanting to bother other users, many users respond better in a private setting, such as a separate office. Although in many small repositories all user activities must take place in one room, larger repositories should consider having an office for reference interviews. Regardless of the location of the interview, ready access to finding aids is helpful because they not only provide needed information for the intellectual components of the interview, but can ease awkward interpersonal relations since user and archivist can focus on shared inanimate objects.

INTERPERSONAL DYNAMICS OF CONTINUING INTERACTION

If a good relationship is forged during the initial interview, interpersonal communications are less likely to be a problem in continuing interaction and the exit interview. Since the direction of research can-

Good signage signals where to go for assistance. PHOTOGRAPH COURTESY NANCY CARROLL, CLARKE COLLEGE, DUBUQUE, IOWA.

not be foreseen, the archivist must maintain contact to maximize assistance to the user. Librarians have found that reference failure often results from the "unmonitored referral," when the reference librarian "refers the patron to a source within the library but makes no effort to check that the source is ever found or, when found, actually answers the question."[160] It is easy to see how this finding can be extrapolated in an archival setting. For example, the reference archivist might wave in the direction of the finding aids, or even identify a series of records but fail to ask whether it is what the user needs.

Research in library settings indicates the importance of the follow-up question. Examples of such questions are "Does this answer your question?" Or, "If this collection isn't it, come back to me and we can try something else." One study concluded that the follow-up question "may be the single most important behavior because it has the potential for allowing one to remedy lapses in other desirable behaviors."[161] Requesting an exit interview during the initial interview is another means of informing users that the reference archivist welcomes continuing interaction and wants to know the outcome of the research experience.

Ascertaining the appropriate degree of continuing contact is sometimes difficult. Some users do not want to be interrupted by staff. Others appreciate a timely question asking whether they are finding what they need, because it indicates that the archivist expects continuing interaction. The appropriate moment to intervene can be better chosen if the archivist observes the user at work.

Staff members cannot control the behavior of users, but they do have control over their responses to users.

Some researchers burden the staff by requesting continuing assistance beyond staff resources, in effect asking staff members to do their research for them. Dealing with such people is not easy. Appropriate body language can help create necessary distance, but sometimes the most dependent researchers are oblivious to subtle cues. The access policy, discussed in the next chapter, should clearly indicate how much assistance staff can be expected to give. Polite but firm explanation of the policy may be necessary as may be a referral to a list of researchers for hire. In many of these instances, good negotiation skills are key to a successful interaction. Creative problem solving and a willingness to entertain new ideas and solutions can turn a tense situation into a mutually satisfying one.

Staff members cannot control the behavior of users, but they do have control over their responses to users. They must strive to be pleasant and courteous to all users, regardless of their demeanor. If staff members cannot provide requested information or services, they must explain such limitations fully and politely.

INTERPERSONAL DYNAMICS OF THE EXIT INTERVIEW

Very little has been written about the exit interview. The unstated assumption is that the reference transaction ends by mutual agreement between the reference staff and the user when the research need has been adequately met. In these days of easy electronic communication, follow-up questions and interactions may continue for some time after the researcher has left the archives.

Administrative Dimensions of the Reference Interaction

"Administrivia" and the Initial Interview

Another impediment to successful initial interviews may be repository administrative needs. In most repositories, numerous practical matters must be settled before researchers even get to the "first question." As will be discussed in chapter 7, researchers usually register, identify themselves, and check their belongings before they begin their research. They are given handouts explaining the procedures for requesting materials and photocopies. They are required to read the rules for proper care of archival materials and are given information about copyright and citations. These administrative details can consume considerable time and are likely to be distracting.

These practical requirements, though necessary, can hamper a substantive discussion of user needs and repository resources. In some ways they are counterproductive to the primary goal of the interview—eliciting information about users' needs and devising strategies for meeting them. In many repositories, without some care, such administrative details easily prevail over more important intellectual and interpersonal aspects of reference service.[162]

Balancing the intellectual and administrative aspects of reference interaction is difficult but important. Both staff member and user will feel frustrated if they have attended to extensive administrative details only to discover that the repository has no materials of interest. Elaborate registration procedures overwhelm a ready reference question that can be answered quickly from staff knowledge or convenient reference tools.

Administrative concerns can also complicate the interpersonal dynamics of the initial interview. Without some forethought, security procedures can make the first message to potential users, "We think that you are a thief." If the archivist must enforce security rules, it may be difficult to gain the trust necessary to develop a full dialogue about the research topic. The archivist can mitigate this conflict in part by explanation and positive body language, but this takes away energy and time from substantive matters. It is also helpful to clarify that the interview is a form of orientation; the purpose is to help the researcher learn how to make the most effective use of his or her time at the repository.

Administrative matters also frequently dominate both continuing interaction and the exit interview. Requesting and retrieving materials, returning and checking them, handling photocopy orders, assuring security, and reshelving are likely to take everyone's attention. These interactions can, however, provide opportunities to check in with users, to ask whether the users found what they were looking for.

Staff

Responding sensitively and creatively to user queries takes time and effort. When faced with a difficult user or under pressure of other work, the archivist may be tempted to answer a direct question, despite suspecting that it is not the real question. Sometimes coping with indirect questions seems to require too great an effort or too much time. Reference staff members are probably more subject to burnout than other staff members. They may feel as though they are chained to the reference desk if they are not relieved for breaks. In larger repositories, delegating administrative procedures and paperwork to a receptionist leaves archivists to concentrate on the substantive intellectual work of the reference interaction.

The quality of reference service can only reflect the resources allocated to it. Unfortunately, all too often, archivists are too busy to engage in a meaningful dialogue. Meaningful interaction depends on the accessibility and continuity of reference staff and thus on staff allocations by repository administrators.

Reference Interaction with Remote Users

Off-site users direct inquiries to the archives through letters, telephone calls, electronic mail, and fax. For some users, such inquiries initiate or continue research conducted in person, but for many users they are the sole means of interacting with the repository. Archivists encourage users, especially those from afar, to write or call before visiting. This permits archivists to conduct preliminary searches to identify relevant materials, especially new holdings not widely known. Prior communication helps users decide whether a trip is warranted and helps them better plan their visits. It prevents users from coming unannounced only to find that needed materials are unavailable because they are being processed or microfilmed, in off-site storage or at the conservation laboratory. Access to other records may be restricted or have to be arranged in advance of use.

Some remote users request information about records, but many request information from holdings or about records creators. The repository needs policies to define the amount of staff time to devote to such research and the types of research to be undertaken by staff. A repository also needs policies for responding to requests for copies from off-site users. Most repositories provide copies, for a fee, of a limited number of clearly identified items, but do not provide staff time for broad subject searches or for making judgments about the relevance of particular documents. Archivists frequently must balance the needs of researchers in the research room against requests from afar. The user who has expended time and effort to visit in person is usually given priority. Phone calls may be returned after researchers in the research room have been served. Callers with complex questions may be asked to put the request in writing. Such a policy, however, may be modified by institutional mission. For example, in an institutional archives, administrators calling on the telephone may take precedence over other types of users in the reading room.

Telephone

In phone interactions, archivists may engage in the same process as in person, but the nonverbal elements of the exchange are necessarily more limited. Tone of voice and pauses in the discussion may be significant, but body language cannot be read. Nonetheless, the archivist and caller can engage in dialogue to clarify the question and discuss possible alternatives.

A British survey of visitors found in 1998 that almost half who sought information in advance of their visit used the telephone, rather than mail or e-mail. This result underscores the importance of effective telephone communication and "a professional approach to information provision over the telephone." The survey also found that many of the negative satisfaction ratings flowed from the "Failure to provide good advance information—to be proactive, not just reactive—and to manage expectations, particularly of first-timers . . . ."[163]

Mail and E-mail

In the last decade, e-mail has become the preferred method for the written inquiry, and the number of remote written requests has increased substantially, even exponentially. One reference archivist suggests that, compared to the written questions received by letter, more e-mail questions come from casual users searching for personal purposes and that e-mail requests seem to be more informal and less revealing, providing an abbreviated introduction to the researcher and the topic under study. E-mail requests may be less likely to indicate the uses to which the information will be put.[164] A public reference librarian found that initial inquiries via e-mail were less defensive or querulous than those of patrons in person. She also notes that the electronic patron wants electronic sources, and adds that "Yes, they will take easier over better."[165]

A certain number of users have always asked very general questions. For example, archivists are accustomed to letters saying, "Send me everything you have on the Civil War" or "Please send me everything you have about my family," but the number of these questions is increasing through e-mail. Other remote researchers use the Internet to explore repository holdings and services to refine their questions before writing to the repository. For example, a repository with on-line indexes to its land grant records received a large number of requests for photocopies of them.[166]

Both the mail transaction and the e-mail transaction include some elements of the reference dialogue, but the archivist has limited flexibility in negotiation. For written inquiries, whether by post or by e-mail, the reference transaction must often be extended to refine the question. In many cases, the archivist may need to request additional information to determine the researcher's real needs. An experienced reference librarian, noting that researchers may resent requests for more information, reports that she prefaces her requests for more information with statements such as, "In order to find the best answer for you ..." or "So I can correctly answer your question ...."[167] If the e-mail exchange reaches five transactions, a telephone call may be more satisfactory or the researcher may need to come to the repository.[168]

Three elements are found in effective written responses, whether by post or by e-mail. First, an opening paragraph welcomes the patron and restates the question. As in the personal interaction, it is best to rephrase the question as a guarantee of shared understanding. Second, the response states the information found, how it was found, its sources, and referrals if appropriate. Note material attached or sent under separate cover. If necessary, explain why it is not possible to provide an answer. For example, the repository may hold no materials relevant to the query, or records may be too extensive for the archivist to search. The archivist should clearly indicate sources of all information, and as time permits, identify other possible resources. Copies of portions of finding aids can be mailed or faxed, or the researcher referred to on-line finding aids. Reference copies can be scanned and attached to e-mail. Third, the closing paragraph encourages follow-up and provides the name of the archivist, title, institution, and contact information (address, phone, fax, and e-mail). The closing paragraph can be saved as a template and tailored to each response as necessary.

E-mail offers advantages over the post because of the ease of response and the virtual conversation that can develop.[169] In e-mail transactions, the dialogue may be captured in a string of e-mails, so that the negotiation can be viewed by both as it proceeds. Unlike either in-person reference or telephone reference, staff need not juggle queries; e-mail and letters can be answered in the order in which they are received, when the pace of reference allows.

Because of the ease and speed of electronic mail, however, many people expect instant answers to their questions. A standard electronic response may be developed that is automatically returned to the sender. This response acknowledges receipt of the e-mail and indicates how long it will take for a full response, especially if that time is two or three weeks. The response also presents an opportunity to educate the public about research in archives, explaining how archives differ from libraries or from stock photograph agencies. The response might also indicate that if the patron needs information immediately, he or she might hire a researcher or come to the repository to do research in person.[170]

Letters and e-mail inquiries often do not provide sufficient information to make a suitable response. Some large repositories develop forms to respond to frequent questions, such as genealogical requests for military service records or death certificates. The forms require users to supply the information needed to use the particular records in a structured format. Now, reference request forms can be placed on the repository Web site to prompt users to supply information needed to respond to their inquiry. Such forms may be tailored for specific series of records or designed for more general use. The form may prompt for a clear statement of need, the purpose for which the information is needed, and sources already consulted. The form should request a postal address so that photocopies can be mailed if necessary. Links to the e-mail address may be maintained for users whose browsers do not process forms. The form might also ask for background information about the user and provide a space for information about how the user found the repository. As we will see in chapter 9, this information is also helpful for understanding patterns of use.

Large repositories monitor correspondence, e-mail, and phone requests to assure that they are answered promptly by the most appropriate staff member. Reference staff members screen letters and e-mail and, if necessary, route them to other appropriate staff. A telephone request form, as shown in figure 5-6, collects both information necessary for a reply and information for evaluating repository use.

Automation can be used to facilitate correspondence with remote users, whether by e-mail or by post. Mary Margaret Bell describes the use of stored responses to answer common inquiries and the use of macros by which boilerplate text can be inserted into e-mail responses.[171] The use of word processing programs increases efficiency in answering written inquiries. Responses can be drafted by paraprofessionals and reviewed by archivists; responses drafted or approved by archivists can be formatted and sent by clerical staff. Using standard paragraphs to convey frequently requested information is helpful. As

Figure 5-6 Telephone Request Form

Date of Call _____   Time of Call _____

Name of caller _____

Name of institution/unit caller represents

_____

Phone number of caller _____

        Best time to call _____

Address for any correspondence_____

_____

Account number for any fees_____

Summary of request:

Services requested:

Date needed_____Date completed_____

Staff member_____

Notes:

noted in chapter 4, requests for information about the repository and its procedures are usually answered by brochures, handouts, and the repository Web site. If the archivist can identify frequently asked questions, designing appropriate handouts and publishing them in both paper and on the repository Web site can save considerable staff time.

Substantive responses, whether composed as an e-mail response or as a text file in a word processing program, can be captured in a shared directory, a staff network, or a database to build knowledge through time and facilitate future reference work. Some information learned in the course of responding to reference inquiries can be added to finding aids or to reference files.

Remote inquiries, whether by phone, mail, e-mail, or fax, can consume a significant part of a repository's reference resources. If the volume of letters and phone calls begins to exceed the capacity of staff members to respond in a timely manner, solutions must be sought. Ideally, additional employees are hired or assigned to reference service. If this is not possible, it may be necessary to send form letters explaining that remote reference requests cannot be answered.

Inquiries from remote users underscore the major constraint in expanding the use of archival holdings. The physical distance between potential users and records has been called the "death of distance." As Charles Lee, former archivist of South Carolina, remarked decades ago, "to use my archives that graduate student is still going to have to get on that Greyhound bus and find a cheap motel." As noted in the discussion of the principle of least effort, people tend to use information readily available, even if they know it is not the best information. In recent decades, remote users requested copies to diminish the physical distance between themselves and archival holdings. Digital technologies offer new opportunities to meet the needs of remote users, even as these tools raise users' expectations.

Reference Services on the Web

Many elements of reference services are moving to the Internet and the World Wide Web, which expand both archival services and researcher expectations.[172] To provide the kinds of expanded access that researchers increasingly expect, repositories must assess groups of users and their needs in the context of the repository mission. User needs differ for collecting repositories and institutional archives.

For collecting repositories, information about researcher needs may require assessment of researcher patterns in the repository, of scholarly networks, and of kindergarten through twelfth grade curriculum standards. Collecting repositories can export collection-level descriptions to national bibliographical networks such as OCLC and RLIN that provide a link to the Web-based finding aid in the MARC record. Analysis of e-mail reference questions can also assist in designing electronic information systems.[173]

Networked electronic information systems offer archivists in institutional archives the opportunity to integrate archival information

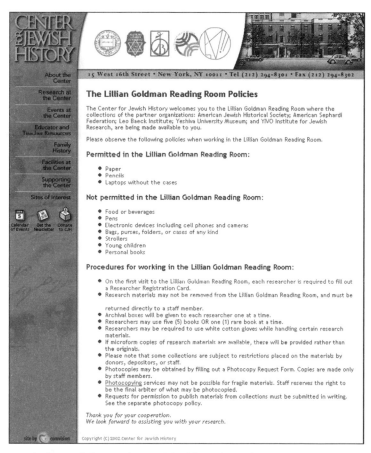

By placing policies on the World Wide Web, as demonstrated in this screenshot of the Lillian Goldman Reading Room Policies on the Center for Jewish History Web site, many questions regarding access can be answered off-site. IMAGE COURTESY CENTER FOR JEWISH HISTORY (http://www.cjh.org/archives/ ReadingRoom/reading_room_policies.html).

resources into the information ecosystem surrounding all information seekers anywhere in the institution. Representations of primary full-text information resources, whether electronic records or digital representations of documents, can be mounted on the Web and placed in context through the on-line finding aid, so that the information seeker can navigate, retrieve, extract, and understand information.

All archival information services should be accessible to users including those with disabilities. Section 508 of the *Rehabilitation Act* requires federal repositories to adopt electronic and information technology accessibility standards. Electronic information is considered accessible if it can be used in a variety of ways and is not dependent on one sense for use.[174]

Repository Web Site

The Web provides an unparalleled opportunity for archivists to serve users. The repository Web site never closes and is accessible regardless of geography. The Internet has increased the variety of users contacting archives, especially casual users who find the repository through search engines. The Web offers the opportunity for users anywhere on the planet to find the repository and its services through search engines.

Web sites draw many "accidental users," and "electronic service may unleash the power of archives as many faceted social memory by directly reaching thousands, perhaps even millions, in web-based exhibits. . . ."[175] As a British archivist notes, "The market potential for use of archival material through the medium of the web is vast." He goes on to note, "What we effectively did with the internet was to 'grow the market.'"[176]

When structuring on-line interfaces so that users will find information they need, it is important to understand the strategies that users actually use and to give them a familiar base from which to start. One interface will not likely meet the needs of all researchers. Patrons can range from students and occasional users to staff, scholars, and information professionals. Some will be searching for a particular item or fact for a specific purpose, others will be looking for an overview of what is available and how to use it. Remote researchers using the Web lack the personal assistance available in the reading room. The Library of Congress designed its digital architecture on a "modular framework that allows different interfaces to take advantage of the same catalog records and the same digital content."[177] The repository can post specialized information for different constituencies, such as genealogists. For example, the Bentley Historical Library has placed a guide to its genealogical sources on-line. As importantly, this site indicates what materials it does not hold and provides links to Web sites of other repositories holding series of records frequently requested by genealogists.[178]

A number of criteria affect the quality of a Web site. The first is browser compatibility so that a site can be available to the largest number of users possible. Stability is also important. The host server must be consistently available and able to handle the traffic generated by users. Loading time should be kept manageable. Web pages are read on a screen, so readability is crucial. It is easier to see dark text against a white or light background color than against a picture. Text should be in an easily read font such as Times New Roman, Arial, or Helvetica. Navigation is critical since hyperlinks allow people to move quickly around a site, seldom proceeding in the linear fashion of traditional text. Aids to navigation should be consistent and placed in a predictable place on every page. Short paragraphs, bullets, and lists simplify navigation. If other applications such as plug-ins or multimedia tools are required, the site should provide a means to download them.[179]

Archivists want users to understand what they find on the Web. Elizabeth Yakel points out that the on-line interface must provide *accessibility* as well as *access* for users in an on-line environment; an interface often "leaves users with websites that they can access physically, but which users cannot utilize to the fullest because cognitive accessibility is low."[180] Archivists also want users to locate finding aids on the Web when they post them. Helen Tibbo points out, "Many factors, however, including search engine features, searcher skill, and the sheer size of the World Wide Web, influence the ease with which users may retrieve a given finding aid from the World Wide Web."[181] Further, this searching environment changes rapidly. For example, Tibbo found in 2000 that the newer search engines such as Google had a much higher retrieval rate than earlier search engines studied by Kathleen Feeney in 1998.[182]

On the Web, a repository can provide—and frequently update— summary descriptions of its holdings that it might have published in a guide in the past. Search engines integrate access points in much the same way that an index does to the published guide. Full text of finding aids can be made available either on the repository Web site or through regional consortiums. Finding aids can be posted simply in HTML, but it is better to use a structure, such as the EAD format, so they may be intelligently navigated or searched. Finally, because the Web is a graphical medium, it provides an unparalleled opportunity for users to see actual images of documents, and thus reach the core of the archival mission. Combining powerful search technologies with scanned images provides a level of access impossible to imagine a decade ago.

The Web site provides an ideal location to post responses to frequently asked questions (FAQs), and it should indicate what information the reference archivist needs from the researcher to provide reference services. The Web site also provides a place to publish the annual report of the repository, along with a list of the products of use such as books and films to show how the holdings have been used, and to give a sense of the range of research possible in the repository. On-line exhibits offer another means to educate and delight the public. They also make it possible to multiply the number of exhibits available at any one time by providing access to earlier exhibits as well as current ones. Some institutions have created on-line stores where people can purchase copies of publications, reproductions of images, or merchandise such as notecards.[183]

Virtual Reference Services

Digital reference services in libraries are growing at an exponential rate and may provide archivists an opportunity to add value to repository Web sites by providing human mediation and navigation. Bernie Sloan defines on-line, virtual, or digital reference service, as "the provision of reference services, involving collaboration between library user and librarian, in a computer-based medium. These services can utilize various media, including e-mail, Web forms, chat, video, Web customer call center software, Voice over Internet Protocol (VOIP), etc." In a matter of years, electronic reference services have produced an extensive bibliography, conferences, a Web site, and draft guidelines. They are adding to the list of reference services available in some archival repositories, especially those in major research libraries.[184]

Commercial software products that support these services are developing and changing rapidly. For example, libraries have begun to experiment with Web-based customer service software developed for large on-line retailers that allows both parties to view Web pages together. The Library of Congress and OCLC are cooperating on QuestionPoint, a collaborative reference service. Most software products provide an opportunity for real-time interaction with remote users through the use of on-line chat services. In some ways an extension of telephone service, these services extend the reference interaction into new environments, such as videoconferencing, mail lists, and chat rooms.[185]

As when providing other reference services, the repository should determine the constituencies that it wants to serve electronically. Location is no longer a major defining characteristic. Is the goal to improve service to existing constituencies or to expand to new groups? What are the limitations on service? How will staff be trained and supported in this new role? How will such service be integrated into the existing work, and how will it be evaluated?

Institutional Intranets

Through an intranet—an institution's internal Internet—an institutional archives has an important opportunity to become a clearing-house for all organizational information, not just for information about the records it holds. The archives can integrate information about organizational functions, activities, and forms of records, whether paper, visual, audio, or digital, and regardless of whether records are in offices, records center, or archives. The organization chart could be used as an information interface. Better yet, using the business processes or functions of the organization provides a more useful map of the organization. The provenance method of information retrieval can be made explicit and can empower the information seeker.

Outreach

Reference archivists are integral to outreach programs in their repository. The daily activities of providing reference services profoundly affect public relations. For better or worse, the reference archivist contributes daily to the public perception of the repository and the profession. Finch and Conway state, "Good public relations begins simply with a focus on the user's interests, requirements, comforts, and intended products."[186] Tamar G. Chute notes, "Outreach can be as simple as removing the dust from a box before the archivist gives it to a researcher or as complex as removing old stereotypes about archives."[187] John Grabowski states, "Only when a large number of users join the small number of keepers and their historical allies in saying that archives, history, and heritage are important, will the funders respond in a manner that befits the work we do."[188]

Developing Personal Networks in the Parent Organization

For institutional archivists, developing networks of people and constituencies is as important as developing electronic networks. Archivists can recognize and build on the ways staff in organizations find information through other people. Developing networks within the parent institution has two important benefits. First, staff members may think to call when they have information needs. Information seeking often depends on human connections. Second, building such networks reinforces the usefulness of archives; staff will know why the repository is important to the organization.

Activities to build such networks include

- making appointments to visit with records creators in their offices to discuss their records and their information needs;
- giving tours of facilities. People are captivated by the authenticity of archival holdings;
- working with public relations and marketing staff who use archival holdings to represent the organizational image and to promote the organization;
- volunteering information from the archival holdings for current organizational projects and initiatives;
- inviting staff to parties to announce the opening of important collections, exhibits, or other public programs. Providing food increases the likelihood that people will come to any event;
- rehearsing a two-minute explanation of what the archives does and how it is important to the organization for use for chance encounters in elevators, corridors, or meetings;
- being ready to take advantage of a variety of unplanned opportunities—joining a committee, speaking at a meeting or training session, or simply advocating the use of archives in casual conversation.

Developing Networks Outside the Parent Institution

Building outside networks is another important aspect of outreach. Archivists should

- participate in conferences of scholarly associations in relevant subject areas;
- visit with records creators, donors, and collectors;
- call and get to know university instructors; and
- prepare public programs describing the repository's records and how they could assist current work.

The finding aid might itself serve as a locus for discussion among staff members and users. Light and Hyry suggest that the "annotated finding aids could become a meeting space for a textual community to share experience, form arguments, and exchange and review each others' citations." Further ". . . researchers could build a web of relationships based on their discoveries among collections and repositories."[189]

Public Programs

Some users' needs can be met more effectively through public programs for groups of users than through personal reference interaction. Planning for public programs involves

- establishing goals and objectives,
- identifying constituencies and their needs,
- developing programs to meet those needs, and
- evaluating the programs' success in meeting them.

Establishing goals and objectives for educational programs is part of the planning process of the repository as a whole. Public programs are not frills, but an integral part of institutional mission. To use resources effectively, public programs must relate to the goals of the repository and the parent institution. Goals and objectives must be realistic. Typical goals include, for example, informing potential users of holdings, encouraging potential users to visit the repository, or

The authenticity of documents captivates people. Actor Martin Sheen examines an exhibit of documents from the Dorothy Day-Catholic Worker Collection at the dedication of the John P. Raynor, S. J., Library at Marquette University with archivists Nicholas C. Burckel and Philip Runkel. DAN JOHNSON, PHOTOGRAPHER; MARQUETTE UNIVERSITY ARCHIVES.

teaching current researchers to use the repository and its resources more efficiently.

Learning about a historical event or issue may stimulate potential patrons who have not thought of using archival sources because they are unaware of them or have not related their question to archival sources. Promoting appreciation and use of records often involves locating, synthesizing, and disseminating archival information through exhibitions, publications, speeches, and other educational programs. Archivists use holdings to write books and articles, develop exhibits, produce slide shows, and create film documentaries. In these products they select and analyze historical information, tell a story, and inform a wider public of the content of records. In short, archivists are users themselves and present their products as other users do, with the goal of informing, educating, or entertaining the public. "Public programs publicize the products of research and the availability of the information in records, encouraging a variety of users who are not reached through traditional means."[190] Archives Week is an annual, week-long observance of the importance of archival and historical records to our lives. Archivists hold special events and activities during the week of the Columbus Day holiday each year to increase public awareness of the relevance of archives to modern life.

An effective schedule of public programs can also expand the acquisition and preservation of archival holdings by informing people in the community about the identification of records that should be saved and educating the public about the importance of keeping them. Public programs are also necessary to elevate awareness of the archival mission, especially to those who provide funding for archival institutions.[191] Unless archivists develop varied and vocal constituencies today, archival repositories will not likely have the resources necessary to identify, preserve, and make available the cultural resources needed in the future. As Chauncey Bell states, "your story must show how *you take care of things that matter to people.*"[192]

CHAPTER 6

Determining Access Policies

Access policies protect records from harm and some information from premature disclosure, while making as much information available to researchers as possible. An access policy mediates among the competing demands of privacy, confidentiality, public right to know, and equality of access. Some of these concepts are embodied in law, others in deeds of gift, and still others in ethical norms. Access policies also allocate repository resources for reference services as equitably as possible. Providing reference services and determining access to records are separate issues, yet they are linked in access policies.

Defining Access and its Relationship to Reference Services

The meaning of the word *access* depends on its context. In the broad sense, as we have seen, it refers to the process of locating needed information, that is, "the means of finding, using, or approaching documents or information."[193] In a narrower, more traditional sense, access is "the authority to obtain information from or to perform research in archival records," or "the availability of, or the permission to consult records, archives, or manuscripts."[194] When discussing access, therefore, we must always determine whether we are talking about access broadly defined or in this more limited, legal sense. Determining access policies in this narrow sense is not solely, or even primarily, a reference function, although it is customary to discuss reference services and access together.

Because reference and access issues have been linked, often inappropriately, they are often confused. Reference services and access are associated because reference assistance is critical to obtaining access in the broad intellectual sense. Reference and access also are linked for administrative reasons. In most repositories, reference archivists administer physical access to records in the research room and supervise researchers actually using documents. Usually, they are responsible for administering and explaining to users any restrictions on access to records.

> **Access is, in short, "Who gets to see what and when."**

Most importantly, perhaps, reference and access are linked by tradition. In the past, access to manuscript repositories was granted only to "serious" researchers or scholars. Access to the archives of private organizations was often, and sometimes still is, restricted to members. In these settings, access was seen a privilege, not a right. Determining access meant determining *who* was allowed to use records. The reference archivist decided who was allowed to enter and use records by examining the credentials of potential researchers.

In contrast, repositories of records created by local, state, and federal governments are open to all citizens. Specific information protected by law is closed for limited periods, but, in general, governmental archives and most of their holdings are open to all. In this context, access is defined as determining *when* users are allowed to use *what* information.

Access is, in short, "*Who* gets to see *what* and *when*." The repository must face this issue before users request to use records. Access policies must be determined in consultation with all interested parties, applying relevant laws, in the context of the mission and resources of the repository. When interested users approach the repository, archivists strive to treat them equally. Archival responsibilities regarding access are summarized in figure 6-1.

Equality of access is now the governing principle for use of records in most repositories. Information to be protected is identified and segregated during acquisition and processing. Access policies are therefore administered, but not determined, at the reference desk. Reference archivists must, nevertheless, understand access issues in this narrow legal sense as well as access in the broad intellectual sense so they can administer restrictions and explain them to users.

Access Concepts

Archivists have a dual responsibility to the creators and subjects of the records on one hand and to scholarship and the public good on the other. Archivists seek to make as much information as possible available to users as soon as possible, but recognize that some information must be withheld to protect legitimate interests of privacy and confi-

Figure 6-1 Archival Responsibilities Regarding Access

- understand laws and regulations relevant to information found in records in the repository, especially federal and state laws governing privacy, confidentiality, and freedom of information, and regulations relating to security classification,
- advise donors and creators about access issues,
- negotiate clear and responsible agreements with private donors and originating agencies,
- know where sensitive information is likely to be found in the types of records acquired,
- identify information that cannot be released immediately for public use,
- develop appropriate restrictions for sensitive information,
- administer restrictions fairly,
- inform users about restricted materials,
- strive to open as much material as possible,
- define policy codifying access decisions,
- promote equality of access wherever possible, and
- if necessary, advocate legislation or institutional policy that clarifies archival issues in the creation, preservation, accessibility, and use of records.

dentiality. Archivists maintain a delicate balance between encouraging use and protecting the rights of creators and third parties. Without some restrictions on access to recent and sensitive materials, individuals may be harmed. Furthermore, without such protection, creators may destroy records rather than transfer them to archives, or they may not record certain kinds of information at all.

Understanding the concepts underlying the laws, regulations, and policies governing access to archival materials is important when designing repository access policies. Four concepts are particularly relevant:

- privacy,
- confidentiality,
- right to know, and
- equality of access.

These guiding concepts are expressed in various forms. The first three are expressed in privacy and freedom of information laws affecting records generated or accumulated by institutions such as federal, state, and local governments, colleges and universities, businesses, and other corporate bodies. Archivists responsible for such records must educate themselves about these laws. All laws affecting records in the institution must be identified, and archivists also must monitor current legislation and modify access policies as needed. Other guidelines regarding privacy and confidentiality are embodied in deeds of gift or transmittal documents and in ethical norms. The following discussion only introduces the concepts and guidelines influencing access to information. Because of the complexities of legal access, consultation with competent legal advisors is often wise.[195]

Privacy and Confidentiality

The concept of privacy defines the right of living individuals to be left alone, to keep information about themselves to themselves, and to specify what information they wish to have known. Privacy protects not only good reputation, but also any personal information that individuals want to keep from being known. Some people do not care if their age is known; others feel considerable interest in keeping such information to themselves, perhaps with good reason because they have witnessed or experienced age discrimination. The dead have no privacy rights, a fact important to archivists, since as records age, protecting privacy becomes less a concern.

The concept of privacy also includes control of the use of one's name or likeness. Individuals, including public figures, have the right to control the commercial use of their name, likeness, voice, features, or other identifying characteristic for financial gain. This right, unlike other rights associated with privacy, can survive death.

The concept of confidentiality has two meanings. It refers first to private communications. Confidential communication between two people is restricted to them alone, and unauthorized inquiry into the content of the communication is forbidden. Confidentiality is vital to nourishing the trust that enables relationships to function—for example, doctor-patient, lawyer-client, husband-wife, and priest-penitent. These communications are *privileged,* that is, they may be protected by law; neither party can be compelled to testify against the other. Communications resulting from other relationships, such as friendship, may not be protected by law, but archivists may need to recognize and protect the confidentiality implied in them.[196]

Second, the concept of confidentiality also protects private information collected for one purpose from being used for any other purpose during a person's lifetime. Individuals may communicate private information to a person or agency because the law requires it of all citizens or demands it as a prerequisite to participation in social programs. In exchange for revealing private information, people are promised that it will be protected from all other uses. People who have entrusted personal information to government agencies, employers, social agencies, or private corporations must feel confident, not only that the information will not be used against them, but also that it will not be seen by anyone without legal authority. Records created or accumulated under promise of confidentiality include personnel records, social service case files, disciplinary board files, and investigative files.

Right to Know

Another concept relevant to archivists is the public's right to know. During the French Revolution, the Assembly recognized that citizens must have access to government records to protect themselves and to monitor the actions of public officials. In the twentieth century, however, governments have become more involved in the day-to-day lives of citizens; hence, the question arises, what information does the public have a right to know?

In a democracy, the public has a right to information about the actions of its government, but people do not have the right to know private information about each other. Thus, the public's right to know must be balanced against privacy and confidentiality. Political scientists, historians, demographers, epidemiologists, geneticists, sociologists, genealogists, biographers, and other researchers request information about individuals or groups to carry out studies that may have profound social implications. Archival access policies and decisions allow for such research while protecting individual rights.

Equality of Access

Equality of access to archival materials is another fundamental concept affecting archival access policies. It is an ethical norm of the archival profession embodied in the access statement of the Society of American Archivists. Promoting the broadest possible access for all users on an equal basis, it states that it is the responsibility of a repository "to make available research materials in its possession to researchers on equal terms of access."[197]

Equality of access is not always easy to practice. Although archival ethics call for all archives to open as many of their holdings as possible, most archivists serve two constituencies, their employers and the general public. As David Bearman states, institutional archives on the one hand are "clearly a housekeeping function of the organization of which they are a part, and are beholden to that organization for efficient management of an information resource," and on the other hand, serve "a broader cultural master, one who rarely pays the bills and is stingy in its praise."[198]

For archivists in institutional archives this dilemma is particularly obvious; institutions often attempt to protect themselves by limiting access by outsiders.[199] Archivists in institutional archives frequently find themselves advocating to the parent institution (and its lawyers) the broader cultural values of archives. Archivists in manuscript repositories founded on a research rationale are today less likely to face pressure for unequal access policies, although the heritage of the great manuscript repositories often favors the academic scholar over other user groups.

Laws Affecting Access to Information

Privacy

The federal government and most states have enacted privacy legislation to protect private and confidential information in governmental records and in other select classes of records such as medical and adoption records. Privacy acts generally state that the government must tell individuals why personal information is collected and what will happen to it, and they must declare that personal information will be used only for the stated purpose. Privacy acts generally give individuals the right to see what information has been collected about them, to correct it if necessary, and in some cases to expunge it. These laws also give individuals the right to sue.

In general, people may sue for invasion of privacy on four grounds, although the exact standing varies from state to state. The first is "intrusion into seclusion," in which someone must intrude or pry, in a way that is offensive to a reasonable person, to obtain something that is private. To be photographed in public does not provide grounds for a suit. The second group is "public disclosure of private facts." Public figures generally have fewer privacy rights. Third, the ground of "false light" means that the public disclosure of private facts places the offended individual in a false light with the public. Fourth, "(mis)appropriation" refers to the misuse of the person's likeness for "fraudulent exploitation." This latter is very similar to the right of publicity, by which people control the unauthorized commercial use of their name, likeness, or other attribute.[200]

Records with personal information usually may be made accessible for research after the death of the individual or after the passage of seventy-five years. The United States Census, which serves as a model for handling personal information, is opened for research seventy-two years after the date of creation. Archival repositories also are interested in maintaining the privacy rights of their researchers. Many states have explicit laws protecting the privacy of public library patrons, that would, in most cases, extend to public archival repositories as well. Archivists should know the laws in their state.[201]

Freedom of Information

Freedom of information acts (FOIA) are intended to ensure that records of governmental activities are open to all. The federal statute states that any person has the right to know anything about the operation of the federal government, with nine specifically defined exceptions, including personal privacy and confidentiality. The person requesting information does not have to give a reason for asking for it; but if the agency denies the request, it must show why the information should not be made available. The federal law also specifies time limits to respond to requests. Nearly all states now have freedom of information laws in some form.[202] The procedures for handling a *Freedom of Information Act* request are usefully summarized for federal agencies in the National Park Service Museum Handbook.[203] It is worth mentioning that many users are confused about the applicability of FOIA laws. Some assume that the federal statute covers state and local records—or indeed all records, even those created by non-governmental bodies. The archivist may need to educate users about the nature of these laws and their rights under them.

Classification

In some cases, the need of the federal government to keep information about some of its actions secure limits the public's right to know. Such information has been *classified* to prevent disclosure of military or diplomatic information deemed vital to the national security of the United States. The right of the federal government to restrict information about sensitive military and diplomatic activities is recognized, though often controversial and challenged.[204]

Security classification rests on a series of executive orders, and its terms may vary from one presidential administration to the next. Federal officials with responsibility for security-classified documents must not remove them from federal custody, so that records with security-classified information should be found only in federal archives. Manuscript repositories collecting papers of public officials or archives holding records of federal contractors, however, sometimes find security-classified documents. Such materials must be withdrawn from use and secured. The repository must apply to have them declassified, and unless declassified, they cannot be made available to users. The National Archives and Records Administration can help archivists who find security-classified information in their holdings to follow proper procedures to protect the records and to secure declassification if possible.[205]

The Family Educational Rights and Privacy Act of 1974

The *Family Educational Rights and Privacy Act* of 1974, known as FERPA or the Buckley Amendment, pertains to records of students in educational institutions. The law gives the student or the parent of a minor student the right to examine or challenge educational records and prohibits the release of personal information without permission of the student or parent. The law appears to deny all access to educational records with personal information and has been applied retroactively to student records created before its passage. It prompted many colleges to destroy student records rather than transfer them to archives. Many archives have not accessioned student records because of potential access problems, and most have closed student records to research. A few archivists, arguing that scholarly research is allowed under the ten narrow exceptions to the law, have made student records available to users who sign a waiver agreeing not to use or publish personal information; others have deleted names or otherwise screened records. It appears that student records may be opened after seventy-five years.[206]

Institutional Policy

Issues of privacy and confidentiality also arise in collections of personal papers and in the records of private organizations. Personal collections may contain correspondence from writers who do not know that their letters have been given to a public repository, or personal information about family members including medical, legal, and psychiatric information of a highly sensitive nature. The commingling of personal and professional lives raises issues of privacy and confidentiality as the distinction between home and workplace frequently breaks down. Personal papers may contain letters of recommendation, grant application review files, peer review files, and other records about third parties.

Private organizations, particularly businesses, seek to protect internal information regarding proprietary processes, business strategies, or information about clients. In addition, the organization may expect archivists to protect intellectual property, corporate trade secrets, and research and development data. In many organizations, records management is used to protect the organization. Records are destroyed, rather than transferred to archives, as soon as the immediate need has passed, on a systematic and regularly scheduled basis.[207] Case files from social service organizations also contain confidential information. Archivists in private organizations and businesses are most familiar with these issues, but collecting repositories may also inherit them when they accession records from such organizations.[208]

Donor Restrictions

The terms of access to personal papers and organizational records transferred to manuscript repositories are usually spelled out in deeds of gift. The terms of access to institutional records transferred to an archives are usually defined in transmittal documents. A sample deed of gift and transmittal document and instructions for completing them should be drawn up and reviewed by legal counsel. They should indicate the categories of information to be restricted and identify the length of restrictions.

For example, the Social History Welfare Archives at the University of Minnesota tries to negotiate a three-stage access policy for case records. For the first period, usually up to fifty years, access requires permission from the agency. After that, typically from year fifty-one to year seventy-five, the archives may grant access to researchers with the agreement that they will not reveal personal names. After seventy-five years, access is open.

Ethical Norms

Archivists work to open all materials for research eventually. The SAA policy states, "Repositories are committed to preserving manuscript and archival materials and to making them available for research as soon as possible." Although it may be necessary to close certain bodies of information for reasonable periods to all but the creator, all records will be opened to all researchers at some time. Joseph L. Sax argues that the archival profession should adopt standard guidelines for donor-imposed restrictions so that repositories might deter inappropriate restrictions.[209]

Insofar as possible, records open to one user are open to all users.

In general, repositories grant access to all users to all materials, with the exception of those covered by law or other restrictions. Insofar as possible, records open to one user are open to all users. Deeds of gift and other transmittal documents should state that materials will be available for research on equal terms of access.

In addition to advocating equal access for all users, archivists strive to give equal service to all users. Archivists in both archives and manuscript repositories are unlikely, however, to have sufficient resources to be able to serve all users equally and must therefore devise policies to administer reference services fairly.

An ethical question arises when archivists learn new information about their own holdings from discoveries of researchers, such as the identification of authorship of an important work or the discovery of hitherto unknown writings of an important writer. To what extent does sharing such information expropriate the intellectual property of the researcher? There are no easy answers to this question, but it should be remembered that both archivists and scholars are engaged in furthering scholarship and are committed to equal access to materials. In general, such information should be incorporated into finding aids.

While research in records generally enhances archivists' knowledge of holdings and enables them to serve users better or to publicize holdings, in some situations archivists conducting research in their own holdings face a conflict of interest in their ability to assist other users. For example, they may be tempted to withhold information from users to protect their own publication plans. The SAA Code of Ethics recommends handling this potential conflict of interest by clarifying and publicizing the role of archivist as researcher. That archivists are engaged in such research should be made known to other researchers. Archivists should clearly understand their access and publication rights and not overstep these rights.

Restrictions

In general, there are two ways to apply restrictions to specific bodies of records: screening users or screening records.

Screening Users

The earlier method of protecting information—screening users and admitting to the repository only those persons deemed capable of using information properly—is now discouraged. In the past, repositories often granted access to "serious" users, such as scholars holding a doctorate, but denied it to others deemed less responsible, such as journalists or students. Such restrictions are flawed because there is no guarantee that even the most qualified scholar will not find information that invades privacy or breaches confidentiality.

Requiring the donor's permission, another method of screening users, is also flawed. The donor may not be qualified to judge credentials, may not grant access fairly, or may come to resent requests. Donors may be difficult to locate. They age, become ill or senile, and die, often leaving the access question unresolved. Most important, a user who gains a donor's approval may still find information that should be protected. Such donor restrictions should be discouraged, although many repositories find that they must still administer them for older acquisitions.

Some repositories review researchers' notes to be certain they do not contain sensitive information. This is an unacceptable solution because users can remember sensitive information even though they do not note it. Some repositories require that users allow archivists to review manuscripts before submitting them for publication. Such restrictions place the archivist in the role of censor and should be discouraged. In short, screening users is frail protection for sensitive information.

Screening Information

Screening records and closing sensitive portions as long as is necessary to protect legitimate needs is far better than relying on the ability of reference archivists or donors to screen users. Screening records before they are made available for research better protects creators and third parties mentioned in the records, and it is fairer to users. Access restrictions specified in donor or transfer agreements should describe the precise materials to be closed and the reason for their closure. Restrictions should specify the length of time the records are to be closed and a date when they will open.[210]

When restricted material is withdrawn from an otherwise open body of records, a withdrawal form left in its place should describe it, the reasons for its removal, and the length of time it will be closed. Withdrawn items should be placed in a separate secure place and clearly identified so that staff members do not mistakenly retrieve them for users. A system for identifying withdrawn records is needed so that they are opened at the expiration of the restriction. Reference archivists can advocate for physical separation of restricted materials, where possible, though processing archivists often prefer to keep temporarily restricted materials within open series and boxes.

Removing or masking names or other personally identifiable characteristics is another form of screening records. This process is called *redaction*. It is particularly useful for case files because they can be made available for aggregate studies without revealing personal information. This method is relatively simple for electronic records, but regardless of format, such information should be removed only from copies of records so that information is not lost.

For the Stanley Milgram Papers at Yale University, the donor stipulated in the deed of gift that all records of a confidential nature be sealed for seventy-five years. The donor, however, left the decision of specifying which records were to be sealed to the archival staff. Unlike archivists who screen records covered by privacy statutes, no guidelines were available to archivists screening these personal papers. In the collection were data files from experiments in social psychology, many with identifiable subjects. Today, university committees review proposals for studies that use human subjects to ensure the well-being of the subjects and the confidentiality of data. The Manuscripts and Archives Department found that the guidelines used by such committees were helpful in guiding access decisions. The Department provides redacted copies for researchers upon request and has established procedures by which researchers pay for the costs of redaction as well as copying. The sanitized copies are kept and are available to future users.[211]

Reference archivists maintain a list of closed materials and publicize newly opened materials. It is important not to conceal the existence of material, even though it may be restricted or closed. Archivists are obligated to review restricted collections periodically and to open them when possible.

Elements of a Repository Access Policy

A well-considered written access policy that reconciles equality of access, the right of inquiry, and the rights of privacy and confidentiality is a basic requirement for sound archival management. It should be written as one of the repository's founding documents, adopted by its governing authority, and reviewed regularly. Its provisions must be known to all—staff, donors, and users. Acquisitions staff members should consult this policy when negotiating with records creators and donors; processing staff members when identifying and segregating sensitive materials; and reference staff members when administering legal access. In developing this and other reference policies, it is often useful to consult with other, similar, repositories. These days, one can simply access their Web sites and compare listed policies to one's own.

Figure 6-2 Elements of an Access Policy

1. **User Communities.** Identify the communities of users to be served by the repository.
2. **Resources and Restrictions.** State generally the types of records held by the repository. State the types of information that may need to be restricted. Identify applicable laws and institutional information policies that apply to information in the repository, and append them to the policy. Indicate how restrictions will be applied.
3. **Intellectual Access and Reference Services.** Describe the finding aids, levels of reference services, and the relationship between the two. If necessary, specify distinctions in service levels. Describe searching services, copying services, and services for remote users, whether by phone, e-mail, fax or mail.
4. **Fees.** Indicate fees for services.
5. **Physical Access and Conditions of Use.** Describe how records will be made available for research. Include rules for using materials and policy statements for researchers.
6. **Use of Information.** Establish policies to respond to requests for permission to publish from holdings. Indicate forms for citations. Determine terms for staff use of holdings.
7. **Loan of Materials.** Specify conditions under which materials will be loaned.

The access policy, whose elements are outlined in figure 6-2, also guides priorities for the reference services necessary to provide intellectual and physical access, and it outlines policies for the use of information taken from the repository.[212] Finally, Finch and Conway remind us that "Access is a matter of general program planning and daily implementation; that it is largely cost-free; and that it is intimately related to good public relations."[213]

Identifying User Communities

The access policy states *who* is admitted to use materials in the context of the repository mission; that is, it identifies the communities of users the repository serves. Governing legislation defines the users of most repositories; for example, the National Archives is open to all. Access to some institutional archives is limited to employees of the parent institution. The institutional mission of other repositories identifies categories of primary users, such as administrators of the parent institution or students of the parent university. The policy should define user constituencies as broadly as possible.

The access policy should state the principle of equality of access and give access to research materials to all. To the extent possible, repositories should admit users who do not belong to identified primary constituencies, even though services for these users may, in some circumstances, be limited.

No exclusive use of materials should be allowed. In the past, some manuscript repositories granted exclusive rights to use particular collections. In some archives, staff members of the parent institution have been granted similar rights. Such exclusionary policies should be discouraged. As the SAA access policy states, "A repository should not deny access to materials to any person or persons, nor grant privileged or exclusive use of materials to any person or persons, nor conceal the existence of any body of material from any researcher unless required to do so by law, donor, or purchase stipulations." If materials are temporarily withdrawn, such as for microfilming or loan, other users must be informed of these special conditions. Archivists also should discourage donors from granting exclusive use to their papers, although the custom of granting access only to authorized biographers is difficult to end. Deeds of gift should not be used to institutionalize unequal access.

Any exceptions to the fundamental principle of equality of access to archival holdings should be spelled out, as appropriate, in the access policy. There are six categories of exceptions.

First, the recipient of documents, who is usually the donor, and the creator of documents stand in a special relationship to the material. Repositories may allow access by the person or the staff of the agency that created, received, or assembled the records, while restricting access by others for a reasonable period. For example, staff members from a department of social welfare, in the course of current departmental work, may be granted access to case files closed to outside researchers.

Second, the policy may deny access to anyone who has a claim against the institution. Explicit rules of discovery under the law cover such instances, and archival records may be subpoenaed for use in litigation. The access policy should describe procedures for responding to a request from someone with a claim, to a request for discovery, and to a subpoena. In general, the institution has a period of time to respond to a subpoena. If served, the reference archivist must contact the institution's legal department as soon as possible. The archivist is not obliged to deliver the subpoenaed records upon demand before obtaining legal advice.[214]

Third, minimum age limits are acceptable; it is common to require that students under the age of sixteen be accompanied by an adult, as well as a certain number of responsible adults per underage group.

Fourth, the access policy should deny further access to researchers whose demonstrated carelessness or irresponsibility threatens the integrity of holdings.

Fifth, the policy should deny physical access to the repository to those not using archival materials. For example, in universities, students frequently seek a quiet place to study; they should be referred elsewhere.

Last, the use of original documents may be restricted if facsimiles are available.

Research Resources and Restrictions

An access policy should include a general statement of the types of records available for research and describe the kinds of information that may be restricted by law or donor agreement. Federal and state laws and regulations or information policies of the parent institution applicable to the types of records acquired by the repository should be cited, and the texts appended to the access policy. Likewise, a sample gift agreement or transmittal document and instructions for completing it should be part of the access policy. The policy should spell out in some detail procedures for administering applicable laws and donor agreements. In particular, it should indicate how restricted materials are identified, and their length and review. The access policy should specify an appeal process for users who believe they have been unfairly denied access to materials.

Occasionally, a user will discover materials that should have been restricted. Because information about taxes, investigative methods, clients, disciplinary actions, proprietary business, or other confidential subjects can appear in unanticipated places, reference archivists should be alert for sensitive information that may not have been adequately screened. Although it may seem unfair to the user, such material must be withdrawn from use. It has happened that the first time the reference archivist sees such documents is when copying them. The access policy should outline the procedures for the reference archivist to follow if such circumstances occur. Staff at all levels should be aware of this possibility and how the repository will handle it, including how the researcher is to be informed and what recourse they have for petitioning to see the material again.

The access policy also should state clear procedures regarding the use of unprocessed collections. Many repositories limit their use, while others allow access to unprocessed materials if their order and condition allow it. Some records arrive with well-organized file order and detailed lists or indexes. Such materials might be used without staff intervention or with minimal processing. Others arrive in such disarray that they cannot be used before at least preliminary processing. If the archivist could reasonably expect from the activities of the creating office or individual that records might include sensitive materials, they should not be made available without processing, regardless of their organization when received. Reference archivists should have input into what information about these collections appears in collection-level descriptions.

Intellectual Access and Reference Services

Availability of Finding Aids

The access policy should spell out in some detail access in the larger intellectual sense: the relationship of finding aids and the role of reference assistance in locating information. To the extent possible, the repository should strive to make all materials equally accessible to all users through arrangement and description, while realizing that this ideal will not always be met.

LEVELS OF REFERENCE SERVICES

Archival resources are limited, and it is a rare repository that has sufficient resources to provide all services requested by all users. Although striving to treat all users equally, archivists recognize that equal access does not necessarily mean equal service. That is, equal access in the narrow sense (authority to use materials) does not necessarily mean equal access in the larger sense (assistance in locating or using information). Some repositories, because of their mission, find it necessary to provide greater levels of service to their primary constituencies. In other cases, limited resources may limit services.

The access policy must acknowledge necessary limitations and priorities. The definition of services available to each constituency will depend on the repository's institutional mission, the nature and size of its holdings, and the available resources of staff, space, and equipment. The type of staff assistance available should be spelled out, by category of user if appropriate. Distinctions in service levels should be articulated.

The level of reference services that can be provided to remote users by telephone, mail, and e-mail should also be identified. If resources are scarce, specific time limits may be prescribed. The repository should determine the number of pages and types of documents that can be copied, mailed, faxed, or scanned for off-site users. The policy also should set forth the kinds of copying services available, fees charged, and time required to process orders.[215]

LEVELS OF RESEARCH SERVICES

Similarly, if the repository staff provides research services, the access policy must identify the extent of research that the staff can provide and identify necessary limitations for each constituency. In general, archivists assist users in locating relevant records, but in some circumstances, archivists also conduct research for them. For example, some research services may be provided for organizational staff in an institutional archives but not for external users.

Physical Access and Conditions of Use

The access policy should specify the physical conditions under which research materials may be used. Archivists have an important responsibility to protect the integrity of their holdings. Rules governing the use of materials must be written, distributed to all users, and equitably enforced. They will be discussed in greater detail in chapter 7. Permissible methods of note taking and procedures for requesting copying also should be specified.

If a repository's resources for providing physical access are inadequate to meet the demands of its potential users, it faces difficult decisions. For example, what is done if all seats in the research room are taken and another user arrives? How can the repository balance its responsibility to make materials available while also protecting the integrity of the materials? Materials needing less security such as microfilm or publications may be used in an auxiliary reading room, but what should be done after all satisfactory compromises have been exhausted? If a repository is likely to face such circumstances, its access policy should indicate the circumstances in which the archivist is justified in turning users away and establish priorities for determining who will be denied access. Will access to the reading room be on a first-come, first-served basis, or will some users, such as staff of the parent institution, take precedence? Will time limits be placed on use of microfilm readers or other equipment? Will all users be required to make appointments? While such decisions may need to be made in emergency situations, such constraints on research should not be allowed to continue indefinitely. The repository must seek resources of space and staff to meet demands for physical access.

Fees

The access policy should explain all fees related to the use of materials. Since making materials available for research is a fundamental archival responsibility, charging fees for access to the repository or for using research materials in the repository is discouraged. Fees for services such as photocopying or extended searches are customary.[216] Publicly supported repositories should not charge fees for access or for providing information about holdings; some state archives, however, charge fees for out-of-state requests for information from holdings. Some private historical societies require that researchers become members of the society, usually at a nominal level.

Occasionally, when copyrights held by a repository have significant monetary or symbolic value, the repository must decide whether it will charge publication fees for commercial use of its materials. Many repositories charge publication fees for commercial use of photographs, but few charge for publication of other documents.[217]

Use of Information

The use of information taken from the holdings also should be explained in the access policy. As will be discussed in chapter 8, provisions of copyright law that apply to the repository and its holdings must be identified and policies for copying and publishing from the holdings specified.

CITATION

Users need guidelines for adequate citations, and the access policy should specify them. Clear and accurate citations are required for good scholarship. They also facilitate administration of reference services because users frequently use footnotes in others' publications to guide their own research work. In the access policy and in procedural statements for users, the repository should indicate the elements necessary to identify items in its holdings; illustrative examples are helpful. In general, citations should identify

- the item (including, as appropriate, author, recipient, title, date, page number),
- all filing levels necessary to find it (file, series, subgroup, record group, or collection),
- and the repository. See figure 6-3.

Archivists often must educate users to provide full citations for photographs and other nontextual records as well as for written sources. Few scholars cite photographs, for example, with the same detail as they use for textual materials, perhaps because they regard photographs as decoration or illustration rather than as source material. For some publications, such as a newspaper story, a credit line giving the repository name may be all that can be obtained. A full citation— including, as appropriate, collection, series, folder, and image or negative number—is preferable, however, especially because publication of a photograph frequently results in additional requests for it. By fully citing photographs in repository publications, archivists set a good example for other users.

Figure 6-3 Suggestions for Citing Records in the National Archives of the United States

The National Archives and Records Administration is frequently asked to provide recommendations regarding information to be included in footnotes or other references to records among its holdings. The following suggestions should serve this purpose and their use will also enable our staff more readily to locate records that have been cited.

Sequence of Elements in Citation

The most convenient citation for archives is one similar to that used for personal papers and other historical manuscripts. Full identification of most unpublished material usually requires giving the title and date of the item, series title (if applicable), name of the collection, and the name of the repository. Except for placing the cited item first, there is no general agreement on the sequence of the remaining elements in the citation. Publishers, professional journals, and graduate faculties all prescribe their own style. Whatever sequence is adopted, however, should be used consistently throughout the same work.

(continued)

Figure 6-3 continued

Full Identification of Archival Material

Because of the greater complexity and more formal structure of archival material, additional elements may be needed in citations not only to fully identify an item, but also to indicate its relative location within a given record group. The record group is a unit of control for records based upon their administrative origin, and, for citation purpose, is comparable to a collection or an organized body of personal papers. The elements that may be necessary for full identification of archival material, depending upon its complexity, include:

(Item)
Charles G. Hewett to Aubrey Williams, December 28, 1936,

(File Unit)
File "Adm. Reports, October through December 30," Maine,

(Series Title)
Administrative Reports Received from N.Y.A. State Officers, 1935-38,

(Subgroups)
Records of the Deputy Executive Director and Deputy Administrator, Office of the Administrator,

(Record Group Title and Number)
Records of the National Youth Administration, Record Group 19,

(Repository)
National Archives Building.

In this example, all of the elements before record group title and number indicate how the agency received or created the document and where it filed the record.

Guide to the National Archives of the United States (Washington, D.C.: National Archives, 1974), 761.

Publication

Responding to requests for permission to publish is often a reference function and will be discussed in chapter 8. It is the responsibility of the reference archivist to clarify the nature of copyright—that it belongs to creators and their heirs—in most cases, to neither the donor nor the repository. Repositories need procedures for answering requests to publish from those holdings for which they hold copyright and procedures that they themselves must follow when contemplating publication.

Use by Repository Staff

The access policy should discuss access and use by archival staff. In the course of their work, archivists may discover private or confidential information or have access to restricted materials. Staff members must not use or reveal such privileged information. Archivists may not give anyone special access to such information, including themselves, other staff members, or researchers. In the course of their work, archivists also learn about users' research plans. This information is confidential. Archivists should not disclose users' research strategies nor the sources they consulted.

Both the SAA statement on access and the SAA Code of Ethics suggest, however, that archivists endeavor to inform users of parallel research in the same materials. If the individuals agree, archivists may arrange introductions. As will be discussed in chapter 7, the simplest way to do this is to request on the registration form a researcher's permission to share such information.

Loan of Materials

In general, archival materials do not leave the repository. Occasionally, circumstances allow exceptions to this rule. The conditions under which materials will be loaned, which are discussed at greater length in chapter 7, also should be specified in the access policy.

Conclusion

Access policies are necessary to sound administration of reference services. Policies for access in its larger intellectual sense and its narrower legal sense must be in place before users actually examine records and obtain information from them. Archivists strive to provide equality of access to repository holdings, although they find they often must educate both records creators and records users about appropriate access to sensitive information. Access policies rest in part on laws relating to privacy, confidentiality, and freedom of information and on contracts found in deeds of gift and transmittal documents. Sensitive information should be identified and segregated during acquisition and processing so that the reference archivist does not have to judge the motives or wisdom of researchers.

Archivists also try to provide equal services to all researchers, but in some settings limitations on services must be acknowledged. Policies and procedures help the archivist to balance user needs against the staff resources available to meet them while also protecting archival holdings from harm.

CHAPTER 7

Providing Physical Access to Archives

After identifying records of potential interest, users usually want to examine them. Chapter 3 discussed the many ways that people look for information. To find information in records, someone must consult documents, whether in analog or digital form. This chapter examines the elements of providing access to documents in the repository. Often, however, because it is not easy for people to come to the archives, remote users request archivists to locate documents, search them, and provide information from them. Chapter 8 addresses ways of providing information and documents for remote users.

Most information in archives remains in tangible forms in unique aggregations, although information is increasingly "born digital," created and maintained in electronic form. Records must be protected from tampering and from accidental or careless damage. The evidential value of archives depends on preserving their integrity, proven through an unbroken line of responsible custody. Information in archival documents is often unique, and the aggregations of records in one record group are unique. If the document or the order of documents is lost, it cannot be recovered. Records need physical protection from all types of hazards. Repositories protect records from environmental threats such as fires, floods, and other natural catastrophes, and extend the life of records by creating a stable environment.

Archivists protect records while making them available to users. Policies aim for a balance between protecting the materials from irresponsible use and providing the best service for users. The repository must determine policies and procedures for using materials before researchers are given access to the records. These policies and procedures should be codified in the access policy and explained in a procedures manual so that reference staff members treat all users fairly and equitably.

Archival services should be accessible to all. Access for people with disabilities is a matter of public law. Title II of the *Americans with Disabilities Act* covers libraries, museums, and archives of federal, state, and local governments. Title III covers institutions owned by private organizations if they are public accommodations. Most states and some cities also have laws and statutes relating to accessibility for all. For new construction, these provisions are usually specified in building codes, or in the Uniform Federal Accessibility Standards. Universal design aids all and makes a space feel more welcoming: wide doors that are easy to open, uncluttered lobbies and corridors, elevators, and ramps. In older buildings, public archives must remove architectural and communications obstacles and barriers and provide auxiliary services to those who need them. Adaptive technologies, software, and human assistance may be needed to use archival services.[218]

Reference Facilities

The research room is variously called the *reading room* or the *search room*. Security and preservation are two central concerns in planning reference facilities, but the convenience and comfort of users and staff are equally important. Finch and Conway remind us that "the built environment and the way it is maintained is rich in sensory clues that tell visitors about the nature of the place they are in." To the extent possible, archivists strive to make the reference facility accessible, comfortable, and current.[219]

The research space should be easily accessible from the outside. The entry to the public space is best located in relation to other institutional spaces in a way that informs the user that it is important to the institution and accessible to the public. Unfortunately, archives are all too often housed in the basement or the attic, reinforcing stereotypes about their value. Directional signs are important in all facilities but doubly so when pointing to an archives in a poor location. Good

The reference desk is prominently placed within the Ohio University Archives and is visible through the windows of the welcoming entrance. On the left are lockers, which are available to researchers for safely storing their personal items, and also provide added security for the archives. PHOTOGRAPH COURTESY OHIO UNIVERSITY ARCHIVES.

directional signs leading to the archives are as important as the signs within it. Master location maps or directories in large complexes should indicate the location of the archives. Within the archives' public space, signs should clearly locate restrooms, exits, reference assistance, and reference tools.

A well-designed research room is quiet, comfortable, and well lighted. Ultraviolet filters on all fluorescent lights help protect documents. A northern exposure, which allows natural light but no direct sunlight, is ideal. If the room has other exposures, shades, ultraviolet filters, or curtains are needed to control sunlight.[220] Furnishings and equipment are required to facilitate the use of the variety of materials held by the repository. Table space for each researcher should provide sufficient room to open a folder of records and to take notes next to it, either by hand or by laptop. Generally forty to fifty square feet are recommended per user. This will allow for table space, a chair, and space

The reading room of the Library of Congress Manuscript Division provides comfortable space for using collections. Photograph courtesy Library of Congress.

to maneuver around the table.[221] The chairs must be comfortable; some people will use them for days. Since people have a variety of ergonomic needs, it is wise to have some fully adjustable chairs, especially for long-term users taking notes on laptops.

Providing access to large-format materials, such as maps, blueprints, and drawings, requires additional space to avoid folding or draping the records over the side of the table. More space is needed if researchers wish to compare two documents. The ICA Architectural Records Section recommends 85 to 110 square feet for each user. Tables with wheels can be moved together as needed to accommodate large-format materials.[222]

Space should be configured for circulation of people and materials on book trucks or carts. It is convenient to plan enough space to place a cart next to each researcher to hold boxes and volumes. Space must also accommodate the oversize flat carts used to transport large-format materials. Materials being held for use or awaiting return to the storage area also need space.

Reference staff members need a desk or table equipped with a telephone and a computer workstation. The reference station should be located close to the reading room, if not in it, so that users have ready access to knowledgeable and helpful staff. Staff members need easy access to a photocopier, scanner, and a fax machine and access to finding aids and databases describing archival materials. Ideally, to reduce noise in the reading room, an adjacent room should be made available for interviews, database searches, consultations, and telephone reference calls. Such an office should allow visual surveillance of the reading room and easy communication with users.

Users should have the freest possible access to finding aids in or near the reading room without staff intervention, since the purpose of finding aids is to make the user as independent of the archivist as possible. Although the SAA statement on access urges that finding aids be made available to users, not all repositories comply. The need to ensure security of finding aids does not justify denying researchers access to them; security copies of finding aids stored off-site provide adequate protection against fire, flood, theft, or abuse. As more catalogs, finding aids, and research tools are created and stored digitally, it is important to have an adequate number of computer terminals for researcher use. Unique indexes compiled by records creators may be treated as part of the record group, and users should be required to sign for them.

A selection of general reference tools appropriate to the subject matter of the holdings also should be available to users in the research room. Tools such as dictionaries, directories, biographies, bibliographies, gazetteers, almanacs, handbooks, manuals, and a perpetual calendar readily at hand will save time for researcher and archivist alike. Institutional archives also might have available reference copies of minutes, annual reports, yearbooks, directories, organization charts, and other reference sources discussed in chapter 4.

Many record forms require special equipment for use: for example, microfilm, microfiche, motion picture film, sound recordings, and electronic records.[223] Equipment of professional quality is more likely to protect records and be more reliable. Though it is tempting to house such equipment separately, it is important to remember that audiovisual materials must also be used under direct supervision. Earphones can enable the use of most media equipment in regular reading rooms. Regular inspection, cleaning, and maintenance according to manufacturers' instructions will keep equipment working and reduce the possibility of damage to materials. Every piece of equipment needs a regular schedule for inspection and maintenance, and a checklist to document its care. Equipment replacement should be budgeted on a regular schedule.

Instructions for use of each type of equipment should be posted neatly and prominently on or near each machine, but trained staff members should always be available to manage audiovisual equipment and to load and unload original materials. The record button on tape players should be disabled so that sound tapes cannot be accidentally erased. Using flat-bed viewers for motion picture film reduces wear and tear caused by projectors.

If the repository does not own the necessary equipment, it should locate reliable and well-maintained machines elsewhere and make arrangements for researchers to use materials under supervision there. If equipment to use early document forms, such as turntables for glass radio recordings, is unavailable, it is best to copy such holdings onto currently usable formats to use for reference, especially given the fragility and temperamental nature of sound recordings and motion picture films.

Security

Because repositories must protect records, security is a basic function for all staff members, not just those in reference.[224] Three components interact to provide security for documents: secure storage, description of holdings, and protection of materials while in use. Secure storage space should be inaccessible from outside the facility and also from users within it. Spaces used to process and store archival materials should be segregated from the research space. If it is not possible to have two separate rooms, the reference workstation can provide a barrier between the public and staff areas of the archives.

Because archivists seldom describe individual documents, archival descriptive systems compound security problems and make proving loss difficult or impossible. In some repositories, manuscript curators once counted documents before and after use, or numbered individual items, but the size of modern collections generally precludes such precautions.

The third component of security is protection while in use. Records are most at risk when they are in active use, and reference archivists are generally responsible for ensuring that they are protected during use. All portions of the reading room must be under staff supervision at all times. It is best if at least two staff members are on duty so that one remains in the reading room while the other retrieves requested materials. Ideally, a third person should be stationed where users enter and leave the room. In small repositories, the archivist may have to work in the same area as users during public hours to provide such supervision.[225]

Tables offer better visual surveillance than desks, and researchers should all face the front of the room. A few repositories use closed-circuit television to monitor users. Others mark volumes with "tattle-tapes" that sound an alarm when removed from a designated area without being desensitized, but such measures are not, of course, practical for loose pages.

Understanding the motives of thieves and vandals helps archivists to protect documents. Monetary profit is the most obvious motive for theft. Similar but less obvious is the desire to own an important document. Some collectors simply seek the joy of possession. Some items in archival custody carry important symbolic value, and even items with little monetary value may arouse personal interest. Some users, particularly those working under tight deadlines, may rationalize theft as a convenient, short-term loan. Surprised to find restrictions on loans or copying, they may fully intend to return the item later. Some recent thieves have also been motivated by a need to "protect" records they see as ill-cared for or not fully appreciated by archives. Thus, any document may be a potential candidate for theft, and it is not enough to protect only those of monetary value.

Deliberate destruction and altering of evidence are perhaps greater threats, from which there is less chance of recovering than from theft. People disturbed by an institution's actions may react by damaging its archival holdings because they are an accessible, value-laden part of the institution. Employees may attack their institution in insidious ways by destroying or defacing documents, particularly those of monetary or symbolic value. Similarly, participants in an event or advocates of a cause may wish to purge or alter evidence in contemporary records, to leave the "correct" view of events, to change perceived errors, or to damage someone's credibility.

The integrity of records also may be threatened by careless use, especially if items are left out of order. Provenance and original order are critical both to locating documents and to evaluating their contents. If order is disturbed, either by accident or design, documents may be "lost" or evidence distorted. It is important to establish procedures to protect records from misuse by both users and staff. Archival staff members, who have greater access to documents than other users, may pose the greatest risk. All staff must receive training and ongoing review in archival security.

Figure 7-1 Repository Security Checklist

❏ Is there a repository security officer?
❏ Is there a procedure to check all applicants' backgrounds before hiring?
❏ Is the repository insured against theft by employees?
❏ Is access to stack and storage areas on a need-to-go basis?
❏ How many employees have master keys and combinations to vaults and other restricted areas?
❏ Is an employee assigned to the reading room at all times?
❏ Do employees recognize the seriousness of the theft problem and the need for vigilance in the reading room?
❏ Have employees been instructed in the techniques of observation?
❏ Have employees been told what to do if they witness a theft?
❏ Has contact been made with the crime prevention unit of the appropriate law enforcement agency?
❏ What type of personal identification is required of patrons?
❏ Are patrons interviewed and oriented to collections prior to use of collections?
❏ Has there been an effort to appraise patrons of the need for better security?
❏ What are patrons allowed to bring into the reading room?
❏ Is a secure place provided for those items not allowed in the reading room?
❏ Do call slips include the signature of patrons? What other information is included? How long are call slips retained?
❏ How much material are patrons allowed to have at any one time?
❏ Are archival materials stacked on trucks near the patrons' seats or kept near the reference desk?
❏ Has the reading room been arranged so that all patrons can be seen from the reference desk?
❏ Do patrons have access to stack areas?
❏ Are patrons allowed to use unprocessed collections?
❏ Are patrons' belongings searched when they leave the reading room?
❏ Do accession records provide sufficient detail to identify missing materials?

(continued)

Figure 7-1 continued

❑ Are archival materials monetarily appraised as part of routine processing?

❑ Are particularly valuable items placed in individual folders?

❑ Are manuscripts marked as part of routine processing?

❑ Do finding aids provide sufficient detail to identify missing materials?

❑ Does the insurance policy cover the loss of individual manuscript items?

❑ Does the insurance policy reflect the current market value of the collections?

❑ What is the procedure for the return of archival materials to the shelves? Are folders and boxes checked before they are replaced?

❑ Are document exhibit cases wired to the alarm system?

❑ Are all exterior doors absolutely necessary? Are there grills or screens on ground floor windows?

❑ Are doors and windows wired to a security alarm? If located in a library or building with easy access, does the repository have special locks and alarms to prevent illegal entry?

❑ Is a security guard needed to patrol the repository after closing?

❑ Are fire and alarm switch boxes always locked? Are security alarms always secured, tamper-proof, and away from the mainstream of traffic?

❑ Does the repository have a vault or very secure storage area?

❑ Is a master key system necessary?

❑ Does the repository have special key signs to prevent addition, removal, or duplication of keys? Is after-hours security lighting necessary? Does the repository have a sprinkler system or other suitable fire suppression system?

❑ Does the repository have adequate fire extinguishers in accessible locations?

❑ Does the repository have a low temperature alarm in event of heat failure to prevent frozen pipes? Are manuscripts and records stored in areas near water pipes or subject to flooding?

❑ Does the repository have written procedures for fire alarms, drills, and evacuation?

Timothy Walch, *Archives and Manuscripts: Security* (Chicago: Society of American Archivists, 1977), 30.

Repositories must also protect people, both staff and the public, from dangers in the workplace, including the reading room. A good safety program is proactive and makes safety the first priority of the management line. It cannot be left to a safety officer. Management must conduct safety hazard analyses and integrate regular inspections into daily work to ensure that safe practice is followed. Perhaps the most common hazards in the reading room are related to retrieving, lifting, and carrying heavy boxes and to repetitive stress related to use of the computer. Ergonomic evaluations are critical for staff members who spend four or more hours a day at a computer keyboard. The reading room should have a variety of adjustable desks and chairs for patrons who spend long hours at their laptops.

Organizations also need a plan for responding to emergencies, whether natural disasters or human threat. Employees must practice responses to a variety of threats regularly. All fire extinguishers must be checked every month, and every employee must be trained in their use.[226]

In the reading room, staff members must know what to do if they suspect a theft or if they are threatened by a member of the public. Every repository needs a plan for responding to suspected theft or abuse and for apprehending suspects without endangering staff, other users, or documents. Archivists often work with local law enforcement personnel when devising procedures for apprehending suspected thieves or vandals. If a suspect is caught, archivists should prosecute in the courts. Some repositories shrink from prosecuting or publicizing thefts because they fear negative publicity. Failure to prosecute simply rewards and encourages thieves, trivializes serious abuse, and abdicates responsibility. Archivists must work to have thefts, abuse, or destruction of archives taken seriously and to have meaningful penalties assessed. They should also work to diminish the stigma of admitting that theft has occurred. This means they must be ready to pursue "insider theft" as rigorously as thefts by non-archivists.

Repositories have different security needs, and each must evaluate its needs in light of its holdings, descriptive systems, physical facilities, staff, and use policies. Archivists must plan procedures that allow users to read and study documents and devise sensible plans that provide an acceptable and prudent level of care. Use policies and procedures

should be developed in the course of repository planning and documented in policy statements and procedures manuals. See figure 7-1.

All but a few users value and respect archival materials. In emphasizing security, archivists can easily lose sight of the needs of users in a
thicket of rules and suspicion. It is vital that archivists' concern for the
protection of materials not make users feel like thieves and vandals. A
welcome smile and cordial greeting must accompany instructions
about security provisions. Most users respond sympathetically to
security regulations when they understand the reasons for them. And
sadly, after 11 September 2001, all Americans are becoming familiar
with increased security measures in every part of daily life. The measures that archives impose to protect documents now seem less intrusive than they once did.

Preservation

Records also need protection to minimize the wear and tear inherent
in handling, copying, loaning, and exhibiting them. Ultraviolet light
from sunlight and fluorescent lights weakens and embrittles paper.
Light also causes fading, and light from photocopy machines is particularly intense. Acid, sweat, and dirt from hands attack the cellulose
fibers of paper and photographic emulsions. Physical stress also
threatens records. Forcing bindings open, pulling volumes from
shelves by the headbands, unfurling tightly rolled maps, or even opening a heavy scrapbook may cause paper to break or glue to separate.
Removing items from envelopes and folders may scratch or abrade
them if care is not exercised.

Educating users and staff about such problems is vital. Any
devices or supplies that can alleviate or prevent such problems should
be readily available in the research room. Heavy volumes may need
the support of book cradles or reading stands. Tables with tilt tops or
cradles may be needed for large bound volumes such as newspapers,
tax rolls, censuses, and financial records. Sand-filled cloth snakes gen-
tly hold pages of tightly bound volumes open without breaking their
spines. It is also helpful to provide a supply of pencils, a pencil sharp-
ener, and a magnifying glass.

Anyone using photographs should wear lintless gloves to protect images from fingerprints. Making use copies of fragile or heavily used materials can help preserve them and promote use of the information in them. Staff members should model for users the handling of archival materials, remembering that in the press of daily work, they may be the most careless users of all.[227]

Preservation and access are further integrated when the reference staff assess the physical status of documents as they are used. Staff members should remove dust from boxes and volumes, using proper techniques, before delivering them to users. This prevents dirt and grit from becoming embedded in papers and bindings. It also helps to dispel the image of archives as dusty and musty! See figure 7-2.

A point-of-use preservation survey may be a reasonable alternative to a systematic survey of all holdings, because the most heavily used materials are likely the most valuable and most vulnerable holdings. That is, frequency of use indicates a probable high informational or evidential value, and repeated use threatens the physical integrity of documents. Analyzing records of use can identify frequently

Figure 7-2 Preservation Actions During Reference

These actions can be done before giving records to researchers.

- Dusting exteriors of boxes and bound volumes
- Placing fragile items in polyester sleeves
- Photocopying damaged documents
- Placing photographs in polyester sleeves
- Adding spacer boards to underfilled boxes
- Replacing damaged folders/adding folders as required
- Removing and replacing damaging fasteners
- Noting presence of oversize materials and ensuring their safe access
- Counting items in folders containing valuable or sensitive materials
- Withholding records that will be damaged by use

Mary Lynn Ritzenthaler, *Preserving Archives and Manuscripts* (Chicago: Society of American Archivists, 1993), 113.

requested materials. Examining materials as they are used provides a basis for planning conservation treatments, especially preservation copying. Disaster planning should consider materials in use in the research room as well as material in storage.

Public Hours

Every repository should have a regular schedule of hours when it is open to the public. This schedule should be posted prominently and published in brochures, handouts, and on the Web page. It is common to open a repository to researchers one-half hour after the staff arrives and to close one-half hour before the staff leaves. This time can be used for staff meetings, often difficult when reading rooms must be supervised, and used to review circulation records (call slips) to assure the security of collections.

Repositories committed to serving a full range of users maintain evening and weekend hours. Some repositories staff such hours only with paraprofessionals, while others limit reference or retrieval services during the extended hours and require users to arrange in advance so that needed materials can be made available. Another solution is to offer Saturday hours, but close to the public one weekday, often Monday.

Opening only by appointment may be necessary but is difficult for both archivist and users. In a one-person archives, where other duties must be accommodated, regular hours of operation, albeit limited, allow both archivist and users to plan the best use of time.

Directions

Maps and information about parking and public transportation posted on the Web site and printed for distribution help users find the parent institution and the repository within it. Information about accommodations is helpful for out-of-town users. Information about restaurants is useful for researchers spending the day.

A well-publicized phone number, signs, and other directional devices also enhance ease of access. Well-designed and attractive signs

Figure 7-3 Policy Statements and Forms for Researchers

- Location and Hours
- Access
- Accommodations
- Directions (by car, public transportation)
- Parking
- Registration and Security
- Finding Aids
- Requesting Materials
- Use of Materials

- Copyright
- Ordering Copies (policies, instructions, prices, and forms for each)
  - Electrostatic Copies
  - Photographic Copies
  - Microfilm Copies
  - Audiovisual Copies
  - Digital Copies

and brochures make users feel welcome and save staff time. All staff members should be able to give clear instructions to users who call for directions, whatever their means of transportation. A telephone answering machine offers small repositories the ability to provide information about hours and services and to take messages when no one can answer the phone.

Policy and Procedure Statements for Users

Staff members usually give statements about the practical procedures of conducting research in the repository to new users as part of the registration process. Users will also need other information, such as procedures for using finding aids and catalogs, requesting documents, requesting copies, and citing documents. An attractive set of policy statements conveys such information, clarifies expectations, saves staff time, and ensures that all users receive the same procedural information.

It is unrealistic, however, to expect most users to read and digest a large document before they begin work. To what extent does a large amount of information overwhelm users and hinder good communication, and to what extent does it codify and simplify communication?

The balance depends on the researcher, the institutional mission, and the resources available.

Statements for users may be issued in a single document, or in individual handouts focusing on specific topics to be distributed as needed. The basic document should include

- hours of operation,
- access policy,
- registration procedures,
- materials allowed in the reading room, and
- rules for using materials.

To assist users in locating and requesting records, another handout can

- describe the finding aids and reference services available,
- give instructions for filling out request forms,
- state limits on amounts of material that can be requested at one time, and
- explain procedures for holding materials for future use.

A third handout might

- discuss procedures for requesting copies,
- explain copyright law,
- explain procedures for requesting permission to publish, and
- suggest forms of citation.

These materials may also be posted on the Web site. Figure 7-4 shows how the Special Collections and Archives, University of Idaho explains its policies to users. It recognizes that archives frequently present a negative image and directly confronts it.

Registration and Identification

Registration and identification of users are customary means to enhance security of documents and to help ensure that all users have

Figure 7-4 The "No" in Special Collections

To aid your research, forestall misunderstandings, and acquaint you with current practices in other similar repositories you might visit, we offer these explanations of some of the "No's" relating to Special Collections.

"No, the shelves are not open for browsing." Special Collections is a closed-stack facility consisting of over 50,000 titles in nine different collections, over 5,500 linear feet of manuscripts and archives, over 100,000 photographic images, and a great deal of uncataloged ephemera. Materials are retrieved by the staff for use in the reading room. It is essential to completely identify the items desired, so that we may efficiently serve you. Please note that "Day-NW," "Idaho," "Oversize," and any dates are all important parts of the call number.

"No, you can't check out books or take them out of this room." The materials in Special Collections are non-circulating, as they are all, either individually or in the aggregate, rare, unique, or hard-to-replace. All materials must be used in our reading room, under our watchful eye. Although some may be new books, they are frequently more difficult to replace than older books that were once printed in the thousands. Some may duplicate books in the general collection, but those support different curricular requirements and, unlike the books in Special Collections, may be checked out and unavailable just when you need them most.

"No, we are not open evenings and weekends." Maintaining a secure area while providing access to the books, manuscripts, archives, historic photographs, and early maps stretches our small staff to the limit. Additional hours are just not possible at current funding levels.

"No, you cannot use a pen in Special Collections." Pencils, or keyboards, are required note-taking tools. We've all seen the results of a single careless slip, where indelible ink transforms a pristine page into one forever scarred.

(continued)

Figure 7-4 continued

"No, not all materials can be photocopied." The photocopier is a boon to researchers but a guillotine for books. Careless use of the copier breaks their backs requiring expensive (and at our budget unattainable) repair. Some materials are so brittle that the mere act of handling them is sufficiently hazardous as to bar the extra destruction of photocopying. Exposure to the ultraviolet radiation in light is also a known risk to books and papers. Sometimes referred to as scholarly "dues-paying," copying by hand is a time-honored practice that ensures that the information is not just copied but absorbed and contemplated.

"No, this is not a general reading room." Special Collections is a high-security area where many rare or even unique materials are made available to students and scholars under careful supervision to ensure their preservation for generations to come. Close observation of our users is compromised when outside materials are introduced into the reading room. All back-packs, briefcases, and other containers must be placed on the shelves provided. Our table space is limited and those not using materials from Special Collections will be asked to find another study location in the library.

But finally, *"Yes, we do realize that limitations on use are an inconvenience, but we have the difficult task of encouraging use of the materials while protecting them for future users."* This is an often uneven compromise, but we are sure you will recognize and appreciate that these materials are here for your use because others in years past made the effort to preserve them for you. Thank you for your understanding and cooperation.

Special Collections & Archives
University of Idaho Library
PO Box 442351
Moscow, Idaho 83844-2351 USA
(208) 885-7951

Figure 7-5 Registration at the Library of Congress

Researchers must register in person at the Reader Registration Station; the Library cannot accept registrations via mail, telephone or the Internet.

Upon completion of a simple computerized self-registration process, the station attendant will check the information, take an identification photo, have the reader provide a digitized signature, and issue the printed plastic photo card to the reader. A Reader Identification card is good for two years and must be renewed in person when it expires.

Library Security, Reader Registration, http://www.loc.gov/rr/security/readerreg.html.

been informed about rules, copyright provisions, and other such legal concerns. Most repositories require users to show picture identification and acknowledge the rules for using materials. Some repositories keep the researcher's identification card during the time he or she spends in the repository.

Registration forms also enable the archivist to elicit information about topics and intended use of information. Such information helps the archivist give better service, provides the basis for analyzing how well the repository meets the needs of its users, and documents the nature and amount of use. Archivists also use registration information to build constituencies, to reach users for follow-up evaluations, and to inform them of new materials, additional services, or public programs.

Depending on its physical facilities, a repository may need different levels of user registration and identification. Many repositories have areas that require less security because users do not handle unique materials, such as exhibits, a museum, a microfilm reading room, or a reference library. Visitors to these areas may be asked simply to sign a visitors' log with their names and addresses so that the repository can count the number of visitors and where they came from. If visitors enter the reading room for archival and manuscript materials, they should complete more extensive registration.

The more detailed the registration process, the more it becomes a barrier to users. Repositories must balance their need for registration and the user's need to begin work. Before beginning an elaborate registration and interview, it may be useful to conduct a brief initial conversation to ascertain whether the repository is likely to contain materials to meet the user's needs. It is sometimes helpful to separate the purely administrative elements of registration and identification from the reference interview, both to save the time of the reference archivist and to separate reference assistance from security. All staff, however, must be trained to respond warmly and appropriately to all visitors.

Frequency of Registration

Frequency and evidence of registration are handled in several ways. Registration for each research topic gives a more detailed and accurate picture of use, but it is time consuming for users who return frequently with new topics and projects. Registering each user for a period of time is expeditious, though less informative. Registration once a year is useful for verifying addresses, reminding users of the rules, and compiling annual report data. Some repositories issue a reader card that must be presented each time the user comes to do research; others check the registration card on file and issue a daily permit each day that the user signs in. Figure 7-5 shows the procedures at the Library of Congress.

Registration Form

Registration forms, as seen in the sample in figure 7-6, typically incorporate the following elements:

- Name, permanent address, e-mail address, and phone number; local address and phone number if visiting.
- Notation of at least one form of identification, preferably with a photograph, such as a driver's license.
- Institutional affiliation and status or occupation. Repositories that limit access to certain categories of users require this information. Other repositories collect it to aid in evaluation

Figure 7-6 Sample Registration Form

I apply to use the Archives

Name _____ Date _____

Permanent Address (Street, City, State, Zip)   Permanent phone no.

_____ _____

Local Address (Street, City, State, Zip)   Local phone no.

_____ _____

E-mail address _____

Research Affiliation and Status (choose one)

Parent Institution	University/College	Work related	Personal
a. Department	a. Name	a. Employer	a. Genealogy
_____	_____	_____	b. Other
b. Position	b. Position	b. Position	_____
_____	__ Faculty	_____	
	__ Staff		
	__ Graduate Student		
	__ Undergraduate		
	c. Department		
	_____		

Statement of Research Topic

Intended Product from this Research (check all that apply)

__Professional report	__Radio Report	__Book	__Film
__Genealogy	__TV Report	__Article	__Video
__Slide presentation	__Personal Interest	__Thesis	__Exhibit
__Web publication	__Term Paper	__Dissertation	__Speech

Other _____

Use of Information About You

May we tell others of the subject of your research? ___yes ___no

May we tell others which materials you used? ___yes ___no

May we contact you by mail, e-mail, or phone as part of user studies? ___yes ___no

(continued)

Figure 7-6 continued

How did you learn about this repository? (check most important)

__ References or footnotes in published articles or books   __ Brochure

__ Teacher, professor, colleague, or friend   __ General knowledge, assumption

__ Archivist or librarian   __ Visit to exhibition

__ General search engine   __ Repository Web page

__ Published guides to archives   __ Television, radio, newspaper

__ Presentation by archives staff

__ Information from historical, professional, or genealogical organization

__ Databases __RLIN __OCLC __Library catalog ___NUCMC

Other _____

Before your first visit on this project, did you write, e-mail, or telephone to get information?

__ yes __no __ don't know

I have read the Rules for Use of Materials and agree to abide by them

Signed _____

Identification _____   Archivist _____

and planning. Lists of the most common types of affiliation and of status or occupation, each with an "other" category, can be provided with check-off boxes to facilitate entering and collating information.

- A brief statement of research topic.
- Statement of intended use of research. The most common products (book, article, dissertation, thesis, term paper, speech, genealogy, film, videotape, or exhibit) can be listed with check-off boxes, with space left to write in others.
- Statement of how the user learned of the repository. Although optional, this element is valuable for evaluating the usefulness of external finding aids and outreach activities. Check-off

boxes can list the most common descriptive tools (such as Web site, published guide, NUCMC, RLIN, OCLC, library catalog, or brochure) and the most common referral sources (such as teachers or librarians).

- Application for admission. Whether the user is asked to apply for admission depends on the access policy of the repository.
- Acknowledgment of the rules for using materials. Users sign the registration form to acknowledge that they have received and read a statement of the procedures for using documents and that they agree to follow them. This signature can protect the institution if the researcher commits an actionable offense, such as theft or copyright infringement, having signed an agreement not to do so.
- Statement regarding use of research information. Users indicate whether archivists may share the general nature of their research with other researchers working in the same subject area. Some repositories also ask whether they may inform others of materials used and request permission to contact the user for future user studies.
- Name of staff member and date of registration.

Daily Log

Daily use is also recorded. Most commonly, in addition to their initial registration, all visitors sign a daily log when they come in; some logs also have space to record the departure time. Other repositories record each daily visit on the registration form. A signed and dated record of visitors in their own handwriting is an important security tool. Beyond security, a record of daily use documents weekly, monthly, or seasonal patterns of reference demand and is useful for planning staffing and services.

Protecting Information about Users

In registering users, repositories collect personal information that must be protected. Registration information is exactly that sought by identity thieves, additionally so if credit card information is collected

Lockers provide a safe place for researchers to stow their personal items and let the archives control what materials enter the reading room. Photograph courtesy Cushing Memorial Library and Archives, Texas A&M University.

to pay for copies. Access to such information must be restricted to staff members who have a need to know. Drivers' licenses and other personal ID cards, if held, should be kept in a secure area, preferably locked and accessible only to staff. Credit card information should be destroyed as soon as payment is complete. Some states have laws regarding library patron information and its uses.

Personal Belongings in the Reading Room

Limiting personal materials in the reading room is an important security measure to protect documents from being concealed and removed in briefcases, books, handbags, coats, or other belongings. Most repositories allow only note cards, pencils, and laptops in the reading room; a few supply note paper and pencils for researchers to use. See figure 7-7. Although repository policy limits what is brought into the reading room, some users do need to bring in reference materials to collate materials or to compare information from various sources. Some researchers prefer to use notebooks, which may be quite bulky, rather than note cards. Such exceptions should be authorized only for good cause and decided on a case-by-case basis. It is helpful to list any materials a researcher is allowed to take into the reading room so that they can be checked out at the reference desk when the researcher leaves. Most repositories examine all materials removed from the reading room.

Figure 7-7 List of Prohibited Items in Reading Room at Library of Congress

Items that may not be brought into these rooms include, but are not limited to, the following:
- Audio devices (radios, CD or cassette players, etc.)
- Briefcases
- Cases for equipment
- Cellular telephones and audible pagers
- Computers larger than laptop size
- Containers larger than 9.5" x 6.25" (includes paper bags, boxes, backpacks, shopping bags, sleeping bags, etc.)
- Drinks (includes bottled water)
- Food
- Food or drink containers
- Handbags or purses larger than 9.5" x 6.25"
- Luggage
- Musical instruments and their cases
- Newspapers
- Outerwear (such as raincoats and overcoats)
- Pets
- Photocopiers larger than hand-held
- Scissors or other cutting implements
- Televisions
- Umbrellas

Library Security, http://www.loc.gov/rr/security/belongings.html.

Ideally, researchers should be able to store personal belongings in lockers or cabinets, and hang coats and outerwear in a coat room or coat rack. Commercially available lockers may use coins, but can be set so that the coin is returned to users when they retrieve belongings, or they may use keys that can be kept by users during the day. A table or shelf near the lockers is an added convenience for users as they remove belongings from lockers. If lockers are not available, a locked cabinet behind the reference desk may suffice, but this solution does not give the sense of privacy and control many users desire when leaving handbags or other personal belongings; it also increases the archivist's work and exposes the staff to accusations of theft. The least satisfactory alternative is a table for belongings in view of users and staff.

Managing Materials in the Reading Room

Call Slips

All users, including staff, should fill out and sign request forms, also called *call slips* or *pull slips,* for materials that they want to use. Likewise, staff should fill out request slips and separation forms when they withdraw material for copying, processing, preservation, filming, loan, or exhibition. These forms fulfill several needs and must be designed to meet them effectively. Signed request forms identify material to be retrieved and establish a user's responsibility for it. They also are used to control movement of material in and out of the storage area. Data from request forms can be evaluated to identify heavily used materials, assess acquisition policies and arrangement and description programs, and contribute to decisions about shelving, preservation, microfilming, publication, or outreach priorities.

Carbonless call slips that create multiple copies are particularly helpful. One copy is kept at the reference desk, filed by name of researcher or number of the table or cart on which the material is kept while in use, so that all material issued to a researcher is readily identifiable. A second copy is left in place of the withdrawn item. Some repositories keep a third copy with materials in use or give it to users for their records. Staff members should initial and date all copies when retrieving and reshelving materials.

Retrieving Materials

Once a request form has been filled out, a staff member checks that the user has signed and dated it and that enough information is included to identify the materials to be retrieved. When material is retrieved, a withdrawal flag with a copy of the request form is left in its place; this enables other staff members to know where the material is and also helps reshelving in order. A large, brightly colored cardboard square with a pocket for the request forms is a useful withdrawal flag.

Some repositories have over half their collections stored off-site. Repositories must let researchers know about collections in off-site storage at every available opportunity. For example, prominent notes about location, retrieval procedures, and retrieval times are posted in the reading room, in finding aids, and on the repository Web site. Reference staff should undertake periodic evaluation of collections stored off-site, based on user transaction records, staffing levels, on-site storage of held materials, and adequacy of finding aids for facilitating accurate retrieval. In responding to remote requests archivists themselves will encounter use of off-site materials. In some cases, a separate reading room, adequately staffed, may permit use of materials at a storage facility.

To prevent accidental mixing of materials, most repositories limit the amount of material delivered to a researcher at one time and further limit the amount in actual use. In general, researchers are asked to use only one folder or volume at a time.

Deciding how much material to deliver to a user at one time can be a problem: one folder, one volume, one box, or one cart? For most repositories, issuing one box at a time works well; but if sufficient space is available for each user to have a cart parked next to a table, more can be delivered on the cart, as long as the user has only one box open on the table. In setting limits, the archivist again balances the needs of users against the needs of the records and the capacity of the staff. Very low limits, such as issuing one folder at a time, slow research and require considerable staff time for many small retrievals and refiles; very large amounts make visual surveillance difficult and increase the danger of misfiling or misuse. To a large extent, the limits depend on the nature of the materials. It is unreasonable to apply the same rules to modern organizational records as to thirteenth-century manuscripts. Both records and users have different needs.

The quantity that may be made available also depends on the precision of the finding aids and the nature of the research problem. In some cases, the user and archivist can pinpoint the exact folder or item needed; in other cases the user must examine a large number of items, folders, or boxes to search for documents or information. Users engaged in negative searches to determine that certain documents or information do not exist may scan a large amount of material in a short time. Other users, tracing a particular statistic or name through a long time series, may move quickly from volume to volume or box to box.

Returning Materials

Users who leave materials even for a short time should return all materials to the proper box and close all volumes and containers. When leaving the research room, researchers should inform a staff member what is to be done with materials charged to them. Materials on hold for users returning later are best separated from materials in use and materials to be reshelved, and request forms and other control documents so marked.

When a user has finished with material, a staff member returns it to the stacks promptly, initialing and dating the request forms. To the extent possible, he or she should inspect the material before and after use. As materials are reshelved, staff members can keep a running tally of the number of boxes, volumes, folders, reels, or other units used. Such statistics, if regularly maintained, are useful when planning staff assignments and responsibilities.

After the materials have been reshelved, one copy of the form may be filed by name of collection or its control number, and the other by name of user. If a third copy is retained, it can be filed by date. Thus, request forms grouped by collection can be employed to track down problems with holdings, and to answer questions about who used materials and when. Call slips grouped by researcher name can help users identify and cite collections and help staff track collections used by problem patrons.

The Bentley Historical Library at the University of Michigan uses a distinctive out card to indicate the original location of the item being used. Photograph courtesy Bentley Historical Library, University of Michigan.

How long should a repository keep request forms? In general, the longer the better. The primary reason for long-term retention is security; archivists may not discover theft or abuse for some time. Request slips require storage space, and their filing is time consuming. If request forms are not organized, however, the value of retaining them is drastically reduced.

General Rules for Handling Records

Rules for use of materials are tailored to the needs of the holdings, but there are prudent standards of care common to all. Both researchers and staff must be taught to handle materials with care. All should be instructed to use only one box at a time, to take only one folder from a box at a time, and to handle documents only by the edges while providing enough support from underneath. Users should be instructed not to make marks on documents, trace them, or rest an arm or notepaper on the materials. Smoking, eating, drinking, and the use of ink are prohibited. Many repositories provide brightly colored cardboard markers to mark the place where a folder has been removed from a box and some add handling and retrieval guidelines to these markers as point-of-use instructional tools. The Bentley Historical Library provides heavy distinctive markers for folders or volumes withdrawn from a box. Each card carries a photograph drawn from the collections and supplies information about citation and handling collections.

Rules for use of materials should be posted prominently in the research room or on cards on research tables. Instructions for handling fragile or nontextual materials might also be printed and distributed with these materials. Such instructions would indicate how to turn pages of large or brittle volumes, how to remove a photographic enclosure from the photograph, or how to support a photograph.

Users should be directed to keep materials in their current order and to call apparent misfilings to the attention of the staff. If an archivist moves a misfiled item to another location, he or she should replace it with a withdrawal form to indicate the new location in case previous users cite it in its misfiled location.

Taking Information from Records

Users take information from records in many ways. Some use pencil and paper to take notes; a few may still use typewriters, cameras, or tape recorders. Increasingly, users expect to use laptop computers, scanners, or digital cameras. Most repositories allow laptops and tape recorders if they can be used without disturbing other researchers. Noise absorbing pads or shields can be used to muffle the sound of typewriters or laptops. Cases that house typewriters or computers should be stored outside the reading room and inspected after the machines are packed before the user leaves. The use of cameras and scanners is usually restricted in accordance with rules for photocopying, which will be discussed in the next chapter.

Forms

Administering reference services often appears to create "forms, forms, and more forms," but the administrative role goes beyond this daily routine.[228] Designing forms has become somewhat simpler with the publication of the *Sample Forms for Archival and Records Management Programs* and the ready availability of forms on repository Web sites.[229]

Automation of Registration and Retrieval Procedures

Archival registration and retrieval systems are ideal for automation. Since standard information is collected from each user, updated frequently, and aggregated for periodic reports, collecting data in an on-line database promises savings of staff time and enhanced use of visitor data. Database management software systems can be adapted to collect and manipulate such data. Initially, staff members may have to enter data, but software systems can be adapted so that users enter information themselves. Eventually, archivists might combine such a registration system with interactive software that informs users about the facilities, services, and procedures of the repository. Request forms and other elements of the retrieval system could also be automated. After materials are identified in the repository database, request slips could be printed as needed.

Most libraries use barcodes on each volume to manage the flow of materials in use. Fewer archival repositories use them because it is more difficult to link them to description in a meaningful way, although some archival repositories place barcodes on boxes, volumes, or other storage units.

Archivists envision collection management systems that integrate information about use of holdings as well as descriptive information and information for collection management. As users and archivists discover new information in holdings, it could be added to enrich the database.

Electronic Records

As in the case of other records, access to electronic archives is often seen as the last function in the life cycle of records. Advances in technology are changing the nature of reference service for electronic records. Archives are beginning to meet the objective of providing information about or from records where it is wanted, when it is wanted, and in the format in which it is wanted.[230]

Making electronic records available for research differs in significant ways from providing reference services for traditional analog records; that is, reference services for records that are "born digital" differ from those for traditional formats and digital surrogates of them. Electronic records can be copied quickly, and copies are identical to the original. Electronic records can be transmitted off-site without disrupting the original. Therefore, originals need not be made available for use. The customary rules for preserving and using textual records are not needed, but other questions arise. "Successful practices must consider changes to access mechanisms, as well as rights management and security requirements over the long term."[231]

Electronic records have been available for research for several decades now. Initially, most users manipulated and analyzed data sets on time-sharing mainframe computers. Most repositories provided users with a copy of the data on tape and a copy of the documentation describing the data. Most charged for the cost of the tape, or provided copies of the tape to members of research networks. Some, however, also provided programming assistance and statistical analysis. Among the best-known organizations to collect and distribute machine-readable data to members is the Inter-University Consortium for Political and Social Research (ICPSR), headquartered in Ann Arbor, Michigan. It now provides means to download data through the Internet. It also provides a useful on-line *Data Use Tutorial*.[232]

Making electronic records accessible over the Internet requires technical documentation as well as the data files themselves. For example, the New York State Archives and Records Administration makes electronic records available through its anonymous FTP server.[233] Web interfaces allow access to databases that have been kept in a variety of formats. As archives become part of on-line networks themselves, users are able to tap directly into electronic databases managed by the archives, though not necessarily held by it. Margaret Hedstrom suggests that making electronic records accessible on-line may be more cost effective for the repository than retrieving data from off-line data sets, then making copies and sending them to users. It certainly makes access to records easier for users.[234]

The National Archives recently inaugurated the Access to Archival Databases System (AAD). It provides a Web interface with on-line search and retrieval access to some 50 million historic electronic records created by more than twenty federal agencies; the ability to search for records with specific information; contextual information, including code lists; and explanatory notes from archivists. In addition to this new interactive searching capability, copies of electronic files from the National Archives can be ordered through the Electronic and Special Media Records Services Division reference staff. Before an order can be processed, the Division requires payment in advance and technical specifications submitted in writing.

Records created in recent years will be a combination of paper files and digital files. They may be parallel series, each mirroring the other. More likely, however, they will be filed according to completely different systems. The James J. Duderstadt Papers, 1963–1997, at the Bentley Historical Library, provide an example of personal papers in both paper and digital form. The entire collection comprises nineteen linear feet and 2,144 digital files (160.5 mb). The subgroup of digital documents dates from 1986 to 1997 and is comprised of Duderstadt's own writings, similar to the personal notebooks and speech files found in paper in earlier collections. The scope note reports that

> At the time of the . . . accession the Macintosh operating system version 8.0 was in use. The original organization and arrangement of Duderstadt's digital files has been preserved. Duderstadt maintained seven archival directories: Speeches, Idea Files, Strategy, Position Papers, Presentations, Write Files, and Legacy.

The Library adds a note on how to use the site, a statement of the conditions of use, and system requirements.

In the case of electronic records, only records that are used will be preserved and available to the future. "As digital materials are increas-

ingly acquired it will become obvious that not all can be equally preserved and used. Digital materials vary in how they are constructed,
organized, and described, and these factors will play a huge role in determining preservation and access possibilities—even when advanced systems, technologies, and techniques are available to repositories."[235]

Conclusion

Providing physical access to archives and manuscripts means negotiating a balance between the needs of users, records, and staff.
Planning for security and preservation must be integrated with planning services to meet users' needs. Providing physical access primarily
means setting administrative policies, but these policies have important consequences for the ability of users to perform their work efficiently. When users begin to use materials, they often request copies of

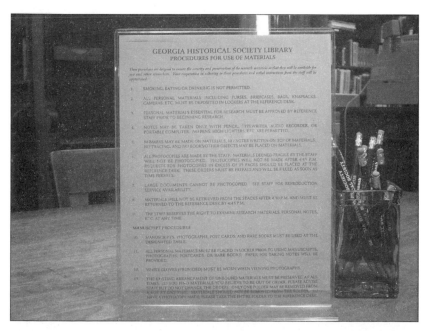

In house rules as seen at the Georgia Historical Society Reading Room. Prominent
display of the rules for using the archives reminds users what is expected.
PHOTOGRAPH COURTESY GEORGIA HISTORICAL SOCIETY, SAVANNAH.

them. Responding to requests for copies is a significant part of reference service and is the subject of the next chapter.

Further, many potential users find it difficult to come to a repository to carry on their research. Archivists must respond to requests from individuals unable to visit personally for information from their holdings and for research services. An important part of extending physical access is providing copies and loans. Archivists also develop programs for making collections of documents available to the general public.

CHAPTER 8

Providing Information from Archives: Copies and Loans

To use information found in archives, users note it, copy it, or borrow the documents in which it is found. They request copies for research use, legal use, publication, and exhibition. Chapter 5 considered the human dimensions of responding to individual requests for information *from* holdings rather than *about* holdings. Some requests for such information can be provided by the reference archivist, but most such requests are answered by providing copies. Archivists also copy to preserve information in fragile or deteriorating documents.

Electrostatic copying, microfilming, and photographic copying have been most common in archival settings, but researchers increasingly request digital copies or expect to make their own digital copies. Copyright law and document condition informs most decisions about copying archival documents, but repository policies and procedures are needed to administer copying services. Repositories also publish documents both in analog and digital forms. Although most archival materials do not circulate, loans are made for exhibition and research use.

Copying Documents

Requests for Copying

Copying for Research

Many archivists remember when researchers took notes by hand or by typewriter. But since note taking is slow, tiring, and prone to error, researchers eagerly embraced tools to ease it. Microfilming and photostatic reproduction were available by the first half of the twentieth century but had a small impact on research patterns because these processes are expensive and require skilled technicians. Microfilm also requires a reading machine.

In contrast, the advent of electrostatic (xerographic) copying in the 1960s, which made inexpensive facsimile copies, revolutionized both recordkeeping in offices and research in archives. Facsimile copies guarantee accuracy in transcription and allow users to consult the original text repeatedly at their convenience.[236] Remote users also want materials to be made available off-premises and frequently request copies by phone, mail, and e-mail.

With copying readily available, many users do not bring note cards or paper to the research room nor do they read and extract information from documents at the repository. They copy any document that appears relevant for later reading and reference. Users expect to be able to make not only copies of textual materials but of sound recordings, photographs, motion picture film, and videotape. Researchers also request copies of electronic records, a trend that will surely increase. Today researchers increasingly look for records to be digitized and available on-line. Or they request that the repository scan documents of interest and e-mail them to them. When they come to archives they bring their digital cameras or portable scanners.

Copying for Publication

Users request reproductions for publication. Archivists are accustomed to requests for reproductions of graphic materials to illustrate articles, books, popular magazines, and brochures, usually as 8 x 10 inch glossy black-and-white photographic prints, or color transparencies or slides. Users increasingly request digital copies for analog publications as well as for Web publication or PowerPoint presentations.

Copying for Exhibition

Copies also are used in exhibitions. Copies of historic photographs decorate restaurants, airports, and other public places. Repositories themselves may profit from selling high-quality copies, suitable for framing, of particularly attractive items such as the first panoramic photograph of a town or the charter of the parent institution.

Copying for Performance

Copies are also widely used in videotapes and television and film productions. They are also used in slide shows and PowerPoint presentations.

Copying for Legal Use

Archivists are occasionally required to produce copies for legal evidence. For copies to be acceptable in court, archivists must certify the copies of documents from their repositories. Unlike authentication, in which the archivist attests that the document is what it purports to be, certification of a copy is simply a statement that it is a true copy of the document.[237]

Copying for Preservation

Reformatting materials is also an important preservation measure. For repositories unable to undertake a systematic preservation survey, a request for copying may provide the first occasion for staff to examine closely the physical condition of an item. If it is so fragile that copying threatens its safety, future use also may endanger it. An appropriate means of copying, usually microfilming, will meet the needs of both user and repository. Preservation copying must meet the highest technical standards. The American National Standards

Institute (ANSI) has established standards for the technical quality of microfilm, photographic, and electrostatic copying technologies.

If all or part of a collection or series is heavily used and photocopies are frequently requested, the repository might consider microfilming the collection, series, or volume in its entirety and making copies available for purchase or interlibrary loan. The guidelines for determining policies for copying adopted by the Society of American Archivists encourage "orderly microfilming of archives and entire manuscript collections, together with appropriate guides" to improve access as well as to assure preservation.[238]

Ideally, copying for researchers and reformatting for preservation can be complementary and accomplished simultaneously. Unfortunately, reformatting for preservation requires more functionality, longevity, and fidelity than does copying for researchers, and it costs more than many researchers can or will pay. Copying for preservation aims at a stable copy that can replace the original for most purposes, but researchers usually do not require that kind of longevity. [239]

Copying Policies

Because of the number and complexity of copying requests, administering copying services can come to dominate reference service. In most cases, copying can be handled by paraprofessional staff. Adequate policies and procedures ensure that copy services meet users' needs and can be accommodated by staff.

Using Outside Vendors

Most repositories require that copying be done by their staff or by approved laboratories. Some repositories with extensive microfilming or photographic copy work maintain their own laboratories, but most contract with reputable service bureaus or professional photographers to supply copies. Few repositories maintain copy facilities for reproducing motion picture films, videotapes, or sound recordings, relying instead upon outside laboratories to perform such work. Users should be informed that they are contracting with an outside laboratory to perform copying and that the repository cannot guarantee the work of the lab. In some cases, a user has established relationships with another laboratory, and the archivist may wish to add it to the approved list after inspection.

In all circumstances, archivists must ensure the safety and preservation of original photographs, negatives, or audiovisual materials. Archivists should visit laboratories on a regular schedule, not less than once a year, to verify that originals are properly treated while in custody of the laboratory. Photographers, whether in the laboratory or in the repository, must demonstrate that they value historical originals by their sensitive treatment of them. The staff must also ensure that negatives to be retained by the repository are technically sound. Meeting ANSI standards helps ensure photographic quality and preservation standards.

Materials must be secure in transit as well as in the laboratory; staff members or bonded couriers hired by the repository, not users, should transport materials to off-site processors. Materials must be carefully packaged and protected from rain, rough handling, or extremes of temperature and humidity.

MANAGEMENT OF INTERMEDIATE COPIES

An "intermediate" is a copy of an original archival document from which other copies are made. Creating the negative or intermediate copy is usually the most expensive part of reproduction; subsequent duplicate negatives or positive copies are less expensive. When reproduction does not create a negative, such as in audio- or videotaping, a repository may require that two copies be made, one for the user and one for the repository so that the duplicate becomes an intermediate copy to be used for future copying.

Repositories should always retain the negatives of microfilm and photographs so that additional copies can be made from the negative and the original need not be subjected to the stress of repeated copying. The copy negative is linked to the original item by notations made on the envelope housing the original and in the finding aid, indicating that a negative is available. The negative must be identified and filed in a logical sequence. The sequence of copies may parallel the arrangement of the originals, or it may be a numerical sequence created as negatives are added. Lists of existing photographic negatives of popular subjects available and of publications on microfilm make useful reference and outreach tools, published both on paper and on the Web site.

In most repositories, the first researcher to order a copy is charged for both the user copy and the intermediate copy even though the archives retains it. And when two copies are made, as in audio or video copies, the cost of both is charged to the user. Users may protest paying for negative or intermediate copies that they do not keep, especially when, as in the case of microfilm or motion picture film, the repository requires that an entire volume, series, or reel be filmed when a user has requested only a part of it. This policy also means that researchers who do original research and locate items that have not been copied before pay more than researchers who use only materials that have already been copied. Those doing original work subsidize publishers and others who note their citation and use the intermediate copy that they paid for.

There is no easy solution to this problem; repositories seldom have the resources to reproduce extensively either for preservation or for use. Archivists may explain to users that such copying is one way of preserving originals. Users may also benefit from being able to copy from intermediate copies made by previous users. Larger repositories might set up a revolving fund, charging a prorated fee to the first user and charging part of the cost of the master negative to users who later request a copy from it.

Self-service Copying

In some repositories, users may make copies themselves on repository equipment. At the National Archives, for example, researchers may make paper copies of many textual and some audiovisual records at self-service electrostatic copiers, currently at the cost of fifteen cents per page. Paper copies made from microfilm or microfiche with microform reader-printers are thirty cents per page. In the Still Picture Research Room at Archives II, copies may be made on color electrostatic copiers at ninety-nine cents per page. In the Motion Picture, Sound, and Video Research Room at Archives II, a dubbing station is available for rent. In all cases, the researcher must show reference staff the records they propose to copy and the request must be approved before copying can begin.[240]

Users are sometimes allowed to bring equipment to the repository to make copies themselves. Often photographers and documentary film or video producers ask to bring their own equipment to copy still photographs. To accommodate these requests, copy tables are needed that adequately support items to be copied. Only available light should be used, and all copying must be done under supervision. Any materials copied are listed on the regular order form so that the repository can track use of copies. If these conditions cannot be met, these users should request and pay for photographic copies like other users.

The National Archives allows patrons to use their own scanners under some circumstances. A flatbed scanner may be used if the reference staff determines that it meets the standards set by the NARA Preservation Unit. Furthermore, sufficient space to use the equipment properly must be available, and the staff must determine that the documents are suitable for copying. Documents must be placed in polyester sleeves before scanning so that the scanner does not come into direct contact with them. As a general rule, hand-held scanners, flatbed scanners with automatic feeders, or personal copiers may not be used.[241]

The National Archives also allows researchers to use their own equipment to copy unrestricted video materials in the stations for viewing and listening to videotaped material in ¾-inch (U-Matic) or ½-inch VHS/S-VHS formats. Similarly, stations are provided for listening to nonrestricted audiotaped material in cassette or reel-to-reel formats, and users are allowed to make copies with their own equipment. Patrons may view 16 mm and 35 mm motion picture film and may use their own video camera to shoot the image directly off the viewing screen. Users may rent video duplication machines to dub a VHS, S-VHS, or ¾-inch tape onto a VHS tape purchased from the National Archives. Users purchase a videotape and time needed to duplicate nonrestricted videotapes.[242]

SETTING FEES FOR COPYING

Although few repositories charge for use of holdings, nearly all charge for copies. As recommended in the SAA guidelines, most repositories keep fees low to facilitate research. Many also believe that the ready availability of copies discourages theft. Some repositories, however, set fees high enough to discourage indiscriminate copying. The repository must decide how much of its costs are justified to recover. The direct costs of equipment and supplies may be readily calculated, but such indirect costs as staff time and overhead are more difficult to estimate. Many repositories set a minimum charge per order to cover indirect costs. The National Archives charges a flat fee per item to cover the cost of preparing orders for the outside vendors that they use.

Staff may also need to set priorities among copying orders, especially for large orders or in busy seasons. It is not fair, for example, for one large order to overwhelm copy staff for days or weeks while smaller orders are not copied. The repository must specify procedures for payment or billing, delivery or mailing. The use of credit cards has eased the burden of handling billing and paying.

SETTING LIMITS ON COPYING

Although archivists and curators limit photocopying under certain conditions, the archival profession is committed to encouraging the use of archival materials to the greatest extent possible. The guidelines for copying adopted by the Society of American Archivists state unequivocally, "It is the responsibility of a library, archives, or manuscript repository to assist researchers by making or having made reproductions of any material in its possession for research purposes. . . ."[243] Archivists and curators often have mixed feelings about copying: they recognize the importance of copying for the use and dissemination of archival information, but see dangers in unlimited copying, some real and some imagined.

Although recognizing that copying may need to be limited under certain circumstances, the SAA guidelines do not adequately address the question of limits on the number of photocopies. Copying may be limited, as explained above, for valid legal restrictions on reproduction, such as copyright. Many repositories go beyond copyright restrictions to limit the number of photocopies that they will make for one user or from one collection. Archivists must determine why the volume of copies is a problem. Is preservation of the originals the issue? Is copying too great a burden on the staff? Or is it that archivists lose control over information? Let us consider each of these questions in turn.

First, copying may harm documents, and the SAA policy states that copying may be limited if the physical condition of the originals would be unacceptably harmed by it. Copying may irreparably damage tightly bound volumes, brittle paper, and oversize scrapbooks. A repository may specify the type of reproduction that can be made, requiring, for example, microfilm rather than electrostatic photocopies for large numbers of copies, for substantial portions of a collection, if the physical condition is poor, or if awkward size precludes use of a photocopy machine. If copies are frequently requested for some records, staff might make a photocopy master to be used for copying instead of the original.

In many repositories, staff members, not users, make copies. They can judge whether physical condition permits copying and ascertain copyright status. Staff copying also reduces the possibility of careless handling, misfiling, or loss. Rather than removing items from collections, users flag documents to be copied to ensure their location and fill out an order form identifying the documents to be copied. Thus, if preservation is the concern, policies and procedures developed to protect documents from unacceptable damage are the solution.[244]

Second, handling copying requests, preparing materials for copying, and the copying itself consume staff time. Some users request many more copies than they will use; they may read only enough to identify material of potential interest, or they may request copies of entire folders on the basis of folder titles. If staff costs are not recovered in the price set for copying, or if money from copying services is not returned to reference, unlimited copying can distort reference priorities. One way to discourage indiscriminate copying is to set a low fee for small numbers of copies and considerably higher fees for large orders. Thus, if the burden of copying on the staff is the concern, full recovery of costs from users is a better solution than artificial limits on the number of copies.

Third, some archivists and curators object to losing control over access to materials in their custody and believe that unlimited copying means that the contents of archival holdings are scattered, sometimes out of context. Copies of manuscripts purchased at considerable expense have later been given to other repositories, which in turn made the materials available to users for the cost of reproduction. Thus, some archivists fear, perhaps justifiably, that making copies readily available will reduce the number of researchers coming to their repository, thereby lowering the use statistics that justify funding. For these reasons, some archivists limit the number of copies or refuse to photocopy at all, especially if rare or expensive manuscripts are involved. Posting images on the Web at very low resolutions makes them available for research but limits their further use for publication. Such images can also be watermarked.

It is important to note that repositories lose control over the use of *any* information made available to users, whether it is taken from the repository in copies, notes, or the researcher's head. Control is more an issue of access to information than it is an issue of the volume of copying. If information should not be disseminated, it should not be open for research.

In large measure, archivists can control this problem. Repositories should not accession copies from other institutions without permission from the institution owning the original. Likewise, they should require users to acknowledge that copies will not be given to another individual or repository without permission, and they should require all copies to bear the name of the repository. Requests for copies and citations to materials can be used to supplement the number of researcher registrations as measures of repository effectiveness. Citation is the key issue here. Accurate and complete citation and acknowledgement of an archives' holdings, rather than the interpretation or re-use of the material, should be the reference archivist's focus.

Thus, limits on copying may be needed for copyright protection or for preservation, and full costs of copying should be recovered, but archivists should not seek to control the flow of information by arbitrary limits on the number of photocopies they make.

COPYING FOR REMOTE REQUESTS

Many users assume that the ready availability of copying means they can write, e-mail, fax, or phone to order copies. The SAA guidelines acknowledge that such requests can overwhelm repository resources.

As noted in chapter 5, a repository is justified in refusing to supply copies if the request requires research by the staff or subjective judgments about the value of material for the user. Repositories should develop guidelines about the amount of time that can be devoted to finding items for users. Since such off-site users also must acknowledge required copyright notices before copies are supplied, the necessary form must be sent to the user, signed, and returned before copies are sent. If charges are to be assessed for searching or copying, users also should be informed of estimated costs and billing procedures before work is performed.

Copying Procedures

INFORMATION FOR USERS

Handouts explaining copying policies and copyright law save staff time and help users. Handouts explain

- the types and costs of reproduction available,
- procedures for requesting copies,
- procedures for identifying and flagging documents to be copied,
- billing,
- delivery or mailing of copies,
- the amount of time needed to process orders, and
- the costs and procedures for rush orders, if they can be accommodated. It is best to be very clear about the time required to process orders and to indicate if delays are likely.

ORDER FORMS

Order forms for copying may be simple or complex. In small repositories with limited copying options, one form may suffice. If, however, the repository contracts with several outside laboratories for different types of copying, a separate order form for each may be required. Although handouts may explain to users which forms are appropriate, it is likely that staff assistance will be required to identify the best type of reproduction and to supply all information requested on the form.

Order forms are also useful after copying is completed. The repository retains the original signed order form. One copy of the form is sent to the user with the copies; this helps the user identify the copies and cite them correctly. If a user misuses copies, signed forms may be important evidence that the repository informed the user of copyright and other use provisions. Since photocopy order forms are an item-level list of selected documents in collections, they can be used to prove ownership in later cases of theft. Order forms also can be used to study how users actually evaluate and select documents during the research process. Order forms are usually filed by name of user. Storing order forms takes space, but they should be kept for as long as the copies are likely to be in active use, at least five years.

Typical order forms include the following elements:

- Identification of documents to be copied. Space is provided for collection or series title, file unit, title or description of each item, its location in the file, and its page count.
- Type of reproduction to be made. List the types available to aid researchers in their selection.
- Copyright notice. The required statement must be printed on all order forms to conform to the law and to ensure that all researchers are warned of their obligations.
- Agreement for use of copies. Users acknowledge that copyright is not transmitted with copies, that they will abide by the law, that they will not transfer the copies to another individual or institution without permission of the repository, and that they will cite the repository as the location of the originals in any exhibit or publication using the materials.
- Information about price, payment, and delivery. Indicate the total number and cost of copies, method of payment, and method of delivery.
- Name, address, phone number, and signature of the requester.
- Date of request, date of completion, name of staff member receiving the order.

Handling, Billing, and Delivery of Copies

The widespread use of credit cards has made it much easier to handle payment for copy orders. Although the repository pays a fee for this convenience, this cost may well be offset by a reduction in the amount of staff time required to handle cash or checks. For orders paid in cash, policies and procedures for handling cash are needed, such as providing receipts, having enough change but not so much to tempt thieves, and transporting cash for deposit. Most repositories require payment in advance, or a deposit before making copies. Procedures may also be needed to handle foreign orders.

The repository will also need to establish procedures for delivery of copies, whether they are to be picked up in person, or sent by United States Postal Service or by commercial services such as Fed Ex and UPS.

Types of Copies

Photocopies

Researchers who want copies in lieu of note taking most commonly request photocopies, also known as electrostatic copies or xerographic copies, because they can be made inexpensively and quickly, read without equipment, marked up, and easily collated with other materials. Photocopying is most suitable for unbound documents selected from various parts of a collection or from several collections; it is not recommended for many bound volumes.[245]

Oversize records, such as architectural records, charts, and maps, present additional problems. Engineering copiers can copy large-format unbound materials, such as architectural drawings and cartographic records, but cannot copy bound volumes. A good source for assistance may be a printer or company that prepares material for printing.[246]

For photocopying, most repositories organize their own copying services because of the volume of copying, the relatively low cost of equipment, and the convenience of its ready availability. The user can largely prepare an order for photocopying, with assistance from staff if needed. If users flag documents properly and list items clearly on the order form, a staff member can copy items, box by box, folder by folder, efficiently and accurately. Some repositories allow users to photocopy unbound materials themselves. See the chapter 7 for the security and preservation considerations in making this decision. A good basic rule: if the copying mechanism doesn't physically touch the documents (camera vs. scanner) it is less likely to cause damage. If such copying is allowed, it is still wise to require the user to fill out the order form listing the items copied and to obtain the necessary agreements for use of the copies. It is useful to remind users that this will give them accurate citation information for their copies. Copyright notices must appear on all copies of materials protected by copyright.

In any case, original records should be placed by hand on the surface of the copy machine, not fed through an automatic feeder. Photocopying bound documents often damages the spine, especially when pages are forced against a flat platen to get a clear copy of text near the gutter.

Microform

Microfilming is a photographic process in which a negative film copy is first made, from which additional negative and positive copies are then produced. It is useful for research, preservation, and publication. Paper copies can be made from an entire roll of microfilm, and individual frames can be copied on a reader-printer. Microfilming selected documents from one or more collections for one user is not recommended since the selection will seldom be of use to other users. At some point, if many documents are to be copied from a series or collection it is better to film the entire group, rather than make electrostatic copies, since the microfilm can be used both for preservation and for reference by others.

Microfilming is also preferable to electrostatic copying for orders encompassing all or a substantial portion of a collection or series and for orders containing large numbers of oversize documents, such as maps or blueprints, or large numbers of photographs. Fragile or bound materials that would be damaged by electrostatic copying are excellent candidates for microfilming. Heavily used volumes, collections, and series are often better microfilmed than subjected to repeated use and electrostatic copying.

Microfilming is less damaging than electrostatic copying because materials are supported while open under an overhead camera. It produces a better image in a stable medium, and, most importantly, the negative film can be used to make unlimited numbers of additional copies. Light from repeated electrostatic copying can damage archival materials. Although some volumes may have to be unbound to microfilm them, having a permanent preservation copy may be an acceptable tradeoff. The unbound volume can then be placed in a suitable box and withdrawn from regular use. For oversize records, 105 mm microfiche with one image per fiche is sometimes used. It provides excellent resolution, with a much smaller ratio of reduction than 35 mm microfilm, and it can accommodate very large images in one frame.[247]

Microfilming should meet legal standards for admissibility as evidence, scholarly standards for use, and physical standards for permanence.[248] The National Historical Publications and Records Commission (NHPRC) has established scholarly standards for microfilm projects. Preparing an order for microfilming is usually more time consuming than responding to a request for electrostatic copying. Staff must prepare a table of contents for each roll and a table of contents for the entire project if it exceeds one roll. Filming the inventory of the collection is a good way to provide necessary information. Eye-legible targets are needed at the beginning of each roll of film and of each logical section of material. Items to be microfilmed must be in the correct order. Folded documents must be opened and flattened. Missing pages or damaged documents must be noted. Bindings may need to be loosened. Consultation with the camera operator and with a conservator ensures a good copy and reduces stress to the documents. When complete, the film should be checked, frame by frame, against the original materials.[249]

PHOTOGRAPHIC

Photographic copies can be made of historic photographs and of textual and printed materials as well. Users most often request 4 x 5 inch copy negatives and black and white prints in standard sizes: 4 x 5, 5 x 7, 8 x 10, 11 x 14, and 16 x 20 inches. Some occasionally request larger sizes. They may also request 35 mm slides and color transparencies.

Photographing historic photographs and documents requires a professional photographer and a copy stand set to allow the original to remain flat. Full-size reproductions of oversize documents can be made through the fixed-line silver halide process, though the process is very expensive.[250]

Audio

Sound archives have been recorded on a staggering variety of formats by a variety of commercial technologies beyond the scope of this book. Most are short-lived, vulnerable because of the inherent vice of the materials on which they were recorded. Each format requires specific equipment to use and copy it. Christopher Ann Paton provides a short course helpful in identifying types of audio recordings and making copies of the most vulnerable. She analyzes and compares analog and digital copying technologies and provides a list of sources for audio supplies.[251] Another useful source is the Association for Recorded Sound Collections (ARSC). Founded in 1966, it is "dedicated to research, study, publication, and information exchange surrounding all aspects of recordings and recorded sound."[252] In 2000, Congress established the National Recording Preservation Board in the Library of Congress "to maintain and preserve sound recordings and collections of sound recordings that are culturally, historically, or aesthetically significant."[253]

The National Archives states that all orders for broadcast quality copies require the use of intermediates. NARA loans intermediates to the vendor only if NARA staff can confirm that the item(s) is/are not restricted and that intermediates exist. Some sound recordings held by NARA have intermediate copies, and others do not. Intermediates are not required for nonbroadcast quality copies.

Moving Images

Moving images may be film or videotape, and they may be analog or digital. Reformatting is required for preservation and for use. The Association of Moving Image Archivists (AMIA) Web site provides links to helpful fact sheets.[254] Preparing motion picture film for reproduction is beyond the capabilities of most repositories. Usually, film is cleaned with an approved ultrasonic cleaner and splices repaired before copying. Copying for broadcast quality requires a skilled technician who may need to vary the light settings for different parts of the film and employ specialized techniques to enhance the picture or sound, such as wet gate film projection or electronic scratch removal. As a general rule, the technician supervises the copying of the entire roll. At the National Archives, if an intermediate copy does not exist, the user must defray the cost of producing a digital Betacam intermediate video copy that becomes the property of the National Archives, as well as pay for the customer copy. In addition, the entire roll of film, not specific portions, must be copied onto the intermediate and customer copy videocassette.

DIGITAL

To meet the demand for digital copies, repositories are establishing in-house laboratories for digital reproduction or sending materials to approved digital laboratories. Perhaps the first decision to make is whether master copies of all materials will be digitized to the most robust standard possible. Copies can then be produced as necessary. The "full informational capture" aims "to match the conversion process to the informational content of the original—no more, no less."[255] Alternatively, the repository may scan and produce digital images on demand and not retain a master copy. In either case, the repository needs to attach metadata that identifies the image, the digital format, the caption, and the credit information.[256] Repositories must protect legal rights in the underlying content.[257]

Copyright

In most cases, federal copyright law governs the making of copies. Congress adopted the *Copyright Act* in 1976, although it took effect in 1978, and has amended it several times in recent decades.[258] Legislation and court decisions in the years since the first edition of this manual reflect a greater awareness of the value of intellectual property rights. At the same time, personal copying of intellectual property has increased because of the availability and ease of electrostatic and digital copying. Reference archivists must understand the concepts applicable to archival copying and inform users of their responsibilities toward copyright holders. Likewise, archivists should not themselves knowingly violate copyright through unauthorized copying.[259]

Two principles form the basis of copyright law. First, the creator of a work that embodies unique expression has the right to benefit from the work. Second, the public and the advancement of knowledge will benefit by giving a limited grant for the exclusive right of this expression. Article 1 of the Constitution grants Congress the power "To promote the progress of science and useful arts, by securing for limited times to authors and inventors the exclusive right to their respective writings and discoveries." Copyright is a "cultural bargain" that encompasses rights for the creator, for users, and for the public. The copyright owner has rights enumerated in the law for a period of time. Ultimately, all works fall into the public domain, and certain limitations on the rights of ownership allow some uses even during the term of copyright protection.[260]

Ownership of Copyright

The copyright owner has the exclusive right to

1. reproduce the work;
2. make derivative works from it;
3. distribute copies of it;
4. perform it publicly; and
5. display it publicly.

Note that the law grants the right to make copies to the copyright owner and does not distinguish between making one copy and many. Publication is defined as distributing copies.

Under current law, copyright protection applies to any original work of authorship that is fixed in any tangible form, regardless of format. It includes, therefore, all documentary materials likely to be found in archival and manuscript repositories: manuscripts, photographs, drawings, audiovisual works, sound recordings, and electronic text.[261] The law protects the unique expression of ideas—that is, the exact words or images of the creator—but does not protect the ideas expressed or mere reported facts. Documents created by federal government agencies are not protected by copyright and can be copied and published by anyone; state and local governments may copyright materials they create, although state laws, regulations, and court opinions are often exempt from copyright by states.

Ownership of the copyright in a work is distinct from ownership of the item itself. Ownership of copyright also depends upon the circumstances under which the item was created. Copyright generally belongs to the creator of the work or to his or her heirs. For a work made by an employee in the scope of his or her work, however, copyright generally belongs to the employer. Copyright in the work of a freelance artist generally belongs to the artist, not to the purchaser of the work. Copyright protection exists whether or not copyright is registered with the Library of Congress, and copyright can be registered at any time.

Because ownership of copyright is not synonymous with ownership of an item, a repository owns many manuscripts, photographs, and other documents for which it does not own copyright. Ownership of copyright must be expressly transferred in writing. Although a donor may retain copyright when giving material to a repository, most repositories ask donors to give their copyrights to the repository. Donors may give copyright in materials they have created, such as copies of their outgoing letters, diaries, drafts of writings, or photographs they have taken. Such a transfer must be expressly made in the deed of gift.

If donors do not own copyright, they cannot give it to the repository. For example, the donor typically does not own the copyright in incoming correspondence. A repository may well own, through a deed of gift from a donor, letters written to the donor by a noted author, but it does not own the copyright. Copyright in the letters belongs to the author or the author's heirs, regardless of the physical ownership of the letters. Ownership of photographic negatives does not necessarily mean ownership of copyright, as many people mistakenly believe. As with other works, copyright in photographs belongs to the photographer—or to the employer if the work was done as part of an employee's work.

Term of Copyright

Term of copyright is wonderfully complicated, and the "limited times" have expanded dramatically. In 1790, the term was limited to a total of twenty-eight years— an initial term of fourteen years plus a renewal term of fourteen years. Today, determining the term of copyright is complicated because it cannot usually be determined by the date of the item in hand, but depends on the length of the life of the creator. To determine the length of time a document is protected by copyright, one must first know when it was created and whether it is published or unpublished. These variables are helpfully outlined in figure 8-1.[262]

Created After 1 January 1978

According to the *Copyright Act* of 1976, all works of authorship created after 1 January 1978 are protected by copyright from the moment of creation, whether published or unpublished, and whether or not they are marked with copyright notice. At this writing, all works created after 1 January 1978 are protected for the life of the author plus seventy years.[263] When the law took effect in 1978, the term was the life of the author plus fifty years. In 1998, Congress extended the term of copyright for twenty years in response to major media corporations in the *Sonny Bono Copyright Term Extension Act.* Also in 1998, Congress enacted the *Digital Millennium Copyright Act* (DMCA), which expanded traditional rights of copyright holders in the electronic realm.[264]

Published Before 1 January 1978

In 1992, Congress amended Section 304 of Title 17 of the *Copyright Act* making copyright renewal automatic for works still in their first term on 1 January 1978. For pre-1978 works still in their original or renewal term of copyright, the total term is extended to ninety-five years from the date that copyright was originally secured. This amendment dramatically curtailed the entry into the public domain of works protected by copyright before 1978. United States works published between 1923 and 1964 may be in the public domain unless they were

Figure 8-1 When Works Pass into the Public Domain in the United States: Copyright Term for Archivists[1]

Unpublished Works		
Type of Work	Copyright Term	What became public domain on 1 January 2003 in the U.S.
Unpublished works	Life of the author + 70 years	Works from authors who died before 1933
Unpublished anonymous and pseudonymous works, and works made for hire (corporate authorship)	120 years from date of creation	Works created before 1883
Unpublished works created before 1978 that are published before 1 January 2003	Life of the author + 70 years, or 31 December 2047, whichever is greater	Nothing. The soonest the publications can enter the public domain is 1 January 2048.
Unpublished works created before 1978 that are published after 31 December 2002	Life of the author + 70 years	Works of authors who died before 1933
Unpublished works when the death date of the author is not known[2]	120 years from date of creation[3]	Works created before 1883[3]

(continued)

Figure 8-1 continued

Published Works

Time of Publication in the U.S.	Conditions	Public Domain Status
Before 1923	None	In public domain
Between 1923 and 1978	Published without a copyright notice	In public domain
Between 1978 and 1 March 1989	Published without notice, and without subsequent registration	In public domain
Between 1978 and 1 March 1989	Published without notice, but with subsequent registration	70 years after death of author, or if work of corporate authorship, the shorter of 95 years from publication or 120 years from creation
Between 1923 and 1963	Published with notice but copyright was not renewed[4]	In public domain
Between 1923 and 1963	Published with notice and the copyright was renewed[5]	95 years after publication date
Between 1964 and 1978	Published with notice	95 years after publication date

(continued)

Figure 8-1 continued

Published Works

Time of Publication in the U.S.	Conditions	Public Domain Status
Between 1978 and 1 March 1989	Published with notice	70 years after death of author, or if work of corporate authorship, the shorter of 95 years from publication or 120 years from creation
After 1 March 1989	None	70 years after death of author, or if work of corporate authorship, the shorter of 95 years from publication or 120 years from creation

1 These two charts are based in part on Laura N. Gasaway's chart, "When Works Pass Into the Public Domain," at <http://www.unc.edu/~unclng/public-d.htm>, and similar charts found in Marie C. Malaro, *A Legal Primer On Managing Museum Collections* (Washington, D.C.: Smithsonian Institution Press, 1998), 155-156.

2 These works may still be copyrighted, but certification from the Copyright Office is a complete defense to any action for infringement.

3 Presumption as to the author's death requires a certified report from the Copyright Office that its records disclose nothing to indicate that the author of the work is living or died less than seventy years before.

4 A 1961 Copyright Office study found that fewer than 15% of all registered copyrights were renewed. For textual material (including books), the figure was even lower: 7%.

5 A good guide to investigating the copyright and renewal status of published work is Samuel Demas and Jennie L. Brogdon, "Determining Copyright Status for Preservation and Access: Defining Reasonable Effort," *Library Resources and Technical Services* 41:4 (October 1997): 323-334.

renewed in their twenty-eighth year. Furthermore, a work published without copyright notice in the United States before 1978 is in the public domain, because the 1909 law required publication with notice to ensure copyright, although this is not true for foreign works published without notice.

Unpublished Works Created Before 1 January 1978

Works created before 1 January 1978 that have not been published nor registered for copyright are protected for the life of the author plus seventy years. Any work that was neither published nor registered as of 1 January 1978, and whose author died more than 70 years ago, entered the public domain on 1 January 2003. Thus, on 1 January 2003, a large number of unpublished materials came into the public domain.

For example, a Civil War letter written in 1864 by a soldier who died later that year was protected until 31 December 2002, but is now in the public domain. For an author who died less than seventy years ago, the work will be protected for seventy years after the author's death. For example, a World War II letter written in 1944 by a soldier who died later that year will be protected until 2014.

Limitations on Rights of Copyright Holders: Fair Use and Copying by Libraries and Archives

Although copyright holders own exclusive rights over reproduction and use, there are limitations on these rights.[265] One of the most notable, found in Section 107 of the *Copyright Act,* is "fair use" of the work for criticism, comment, teaching, research, news reporting, or scholarship. Archivists and librarians make works available for study in the repository principally under this section. The doctrine of fair use is not an "affirmative right or entitlement of users." It is actually "an affirmative defense that limits a copyright owner's rights." As William Maher says, "fair use is less a grant of a right to copy, and more a defense against a charge of infringement," although few look forward to finding themselves in court.[266]

Making copies or publishing quotations without permission from the copyright holder under the fair use provision depends on the context of the use. The fair use test is specific to each case. Four factors are used to determine if a use is "fair":

- the purpose and character of the use,
- the nature of the material used,
- the amount of material used in relation to the whole, and
- the effect of the use on the market for the work.

All four tests need to be considered to allow copying or quotation without permission of the copyright holder.

In Section 108 of the *Copyright Act,* another limitation on the rights of copyright holders provides exemption from liability for copyright violation to archives and libraries when they make copies of copyrighted materials, under certain circumstances. They are allowed to make copies of copyrighted works without seeking permission of the copyright holder for two broad purposes—for preservation of holdings and for private use of their patrons. All of the following three conditions must be met to allow copying under Section 108:

1. the holdings of the library or archives are open to the public;
2. the copies are not made for commercial purpose; and
3. notice is given on the copies that the work may be protected by copyright.

A copy of a small portion of a published work can be made for a user if the copy becomes the property of the user and notice of copyright is given. A copy of an entire work, whether published or unpublished, may be made if the work is not available at a fair price. Section 108b also allows archivists to copy an entire document for preservation or for deposit in another archives or library.

It is important to note that copying without permission of the copyright holder under Section 108 applies only to copying for private research purposes. If archivists have any reason to suspect that the purpose of use is publication or other commercial or public dissemination, they should not make copies without permission from the copyright holder. Section 108(i) excludes copying musical works (including sheet music), pictorial works, graphic works, sculpture, films, or audiovisual works without permission for any of the purposes, other than preservation, noted by this section. It can be argued, however, that the legislative history of Section 108(i) can be read as justifying library and archival copying of works listed in 108(i) for users if there is evidence the copying is for private study or is a "fair use."[267]

Copies for Private Study

Section 108 requires archivists, curators, and librarians to inform users about copyright law. They must post notice at the place where orders are taken and on order forms. The required notice is found in figure 8-2.[268] Most repositories imprint a copyright statement on copies and require users to sign a statement agreeing to the proper use of copies. It is simplest to place a screen on a copying machine in such a way that all photocopies bear the required copyright notice and the name of the repository, or to use photocopy paper with a notice printed on it. A more time-consuming alternative is to stamp a notice on each copy.

A critical question for archivists arises when users ask to copy some or all of an unpublished work to aid their study. Must archivists

Figure 8-2 Required Copyright Notice

The copyright law of the United Staes (Title 17, United States Code) governs the making of photocopies or other reproductions of copyrighted materials.

Under certain conditions specified in the law, libraries and archives are authorized to furnish a photocopy or other reproduction. One of these specified conditions is that the photocopy or reproduction is not to be "used for any purpose other than private study, scholarship, or research." If a user makes a request for, or later uses, a photocopy or reproduction for purposes in excess of "fair use," that user may be liable for copyright infringement.

This institution reserves the right to refuse to accept a copying order if, in its judgment, fulfillment of the order would involve violation of copyright law.

have permission from copyright holders to make copies to facilitate research by users? If the repository does not own the copyright, as is usually the case, do archivists require the user to obtain permission before the repository allows copying? For many works it would be difficult if not impossible to locate the copyright holder; is it necessary then to require the user to make a good faith effort to locate the copyright holder before copies are made? These issues become even more difficult in an on-line environment.[269]

In general, archivists read Section 108 literally and copy freely for users, as long as the repository meets the three conditions noted above. Archivists cite the provisions of Section 108 to argue that copies of entire unpublished manuscripts can be made to aid study without seeking permission of the copyright holder, since no copies are available through normal trade channels at a fair price.[270] Archivists argue that Section 108 clearly includes copying in archives and that copyright law no longer distinguishes between published and unpublished works. Since some formats, such as audiovisual works, are specifically excluded from Section 108, one might infer that by implication copying of other materials not excluded, such as textual records, is allowed.[271]

The application of fair use under Section 107 to unpublished archival materials is not as clear as archivists and their users might wish. Before the 1976 law was enacted, fair use was not supported by statute and federal copyright law did not apply to unpublished materials. After the law took effect in 1978, most archivists believed that fair use would apply equally to all copyrighted materials, whether published or unpublished.[272] At the time of the first edition of this manual, court cases suggested that courts might apply "fair use" differently to unpublished materials to the detriment of the users of archival materials.[273] Experience, however, has moderated this concern. In 1992, Congress passed legislation confirming that fair use applies to unpublished works,[274] and the findings of more recent court cases have alleviated some concern and provide support for common archival and scholarly practice.[275]

Archivists must monitor current copyright developments, for they may find themselves in court to test provisions of currently accepted archival reference practice. They must also monitor developments in technology, as creators turn to digital rights management systems to prevent the making of any copies, even for fair use or preservation. Kenneth Crews notes that "Copyright has become entangled with the laws of privacy and free speech" and that it is becoming a means to control use rather than profit from it. Heather Briston urges archivists to become a "voice for restoration of reasonableness—the balance between access and permitted uses and the rights of copyright holders."[276]

Most repositories make copies for research use, without requiring permission from copyright holders. To protect their repositories, their holdings, and themselves, archivists institute procedures to inform users of copyright law, and they require users to acknowledge their responsibilities. Some archivists are exploring other options to aid users, such as the expanded use of interlibrary loan.

Requests for Permission to Publish

Another dramatic change in the daily work of reference archivists since the last edition of this manual has been the exponential increase in requests for permission to publish. Most publishers, whether they are publishing in traditional forms, in audiovisual formats, or in electronic formats, now require the creators of such products to get permissions from all "content providers." Even if a scholar's use could be justified as "fair use," publishers, ever mindful of their risk-adverse legal counsel, often prefer to have a paper trail to defend themselves in court if they are sued for infringement. Most publishers have departments to handle rights and permissions, and many send their "standard" forms to repositories requesting, in essence, exclusive rights for all uses in perpetuity. Archivists should not sign such documents. Most repositories create a form for users requesting permission and use it or another form to respond to such requests.

Repositories have developed policies and procedures to handle questions of rights and permissions and find that they must spend an increasing amount of time responding to such requests. Answering such queries can be greatly eased if ownership of copyright has been determined during acquisition and stated in the deed of gift and in the finding aids. If, for example, a donor has assigned copyright to the public, any user may publish freely from the material.

If the donor owned copyright and deeded it to the repository, then the repository owns copyright in those documents in the collections. Most repositories do not grant exclusive rights to anyone, instead they grant the right to use the item for a specific publication at a specific time. Some repositories are exploring licensing as a means of managing these issues, especially if more than one-time use is required.[277]

The repository may handle requests to publish short quotations routinely, granting nonexclusive permission if the quotation is properly cited. Requests to publish entire works require more detailed consideration. For example, manuscript repositories may hold copyright for diaries, journals, autobiographies, or collections of letters that are attractive candidates for publication. In most cases, the repository will not profit monetarily from publication, but making materials more accessible through publication will redound to the credit of the repository. The access policy should specify whether the repository will give exclusive publication rights for such items. If so, will it grant such requests on a first-come, first-served basis, or will it require that conditions be met to ensure an editorially sound and attractive publication? Procedures spelling out the obligations of all parties should be explained in the policy. If an exclusive right to publish is given, a time limit should be written into the agreement so that publication rights to the materials are not tied up for an indefinite period.

Although many repositories ask donors to transfer their copyrights to the repository, in most cases, however, repositories do not own the copyright in documents their custody. They cannot give permission for rights they do not own. Copyright is frequently held by the author or the author's heirs. If such is the case, the archivist must instruct users to seek permission from the copyright owner.

Most repositories respond to such requests to publish by stating that they do not own the copyright in the item and that it is the responsibility of the user to identify the copyright holders and obtain permission from them. Archivists are not responsible for such research on behalf of users. They may supply any information that is readily available from the item itself, such as stamps on the back of photographs or information from collection files.

Researchers wishing to use material beyond the limits of fair use must seek permission from copyright holders to publish direct quotations from documents, to publish photographs, or to make public use of audiovisual materials in archival custody. Archivists must explain these issues to users and caution them to seek permission to publish. Archivists also educate users to provide the correct citation for all published materials. It should be mandatory for publications to provide full citations for all documents, including photographs, but many do not.

As owners of physical documents, most repositories also require users to obtain permission from them to publish documents from their collections. That is, they require permission as owners of an artifact.[278] First, this requirement gives the repository an opportunity to identify cases of known retention of copyright. Second, this procedure also provides an opportunity to provide the exact citation the repository requires so that future users can find the item. Third, it provides an opportunity to document the uses of the collections in publications and other products. The next chapter discusses how such documentation is useful in identifying the indirect uses of collections. Fourth, some repositories charge a publication use fee as owners of the physical property. Some charge the fee for use at the same time they charge for the reproduction. Others request the fee when the request to publish is received. Still others request a donation in lieu of a use fee.

The repository faces similar issues when it plans its own publication projects. If repositories decide to publish documents themselves, either on paper or the Web, they too must determine copyright status and address these thorny issues. In many cases, it does not own the copyright in documents it would like to publish. Like other users, it must undertake a comprehensive search to locate any known copyright holders and seek permission from them.[279] If, after due diligence the repository has been unable to find copyright owners and it decides to publish, it must be prepared to give evidence of its good faith effort and a plausible fair use justification. Documentation of its "good faith" effort to locate copyright holders should be created and retained in case of an infringement suit. If infringement is proved, the repository must pay what a court determines.

Publishing reproductions of many works in archival holdings is a matter of risk analysis. It is difficult, if not impossible, to ascertain the copyright holder for many documents and photographs. In the case of photographs, it is often difficult to ascertain whether a photograph has been published and, if it has, whether it was published with or without copyright notice. Archivists know only too well that photographs are frequently published without proper attribution. It is also difficult, if not impossible, to determine whether the copyright was registered.

Little monetary value could be realized from any use of most documents. To bring a charge of infringement, an individual would have to prove copyright ownership, establish a monetary loss, and go to court. For infringement of copyright in an unregistered work, the copyright holder can recover only actual damages; that is, only direct losses can be recovered. For some materials, however, a greater risk might be assumed. Recent works, made by identified creators, which have been registered, and for which a market exists, call for greater scrutiny. For infringement of a registered work, punitive damages can be assessed.

Publishing Documents

The private historical societies of the eastern seaboard began reproducing documents over two centuries ago. Publishing documents was one of the primary motivations for establishing these societies. The state historical societies of the Midwest followed suit. In 1792, the Massachusetts Historical Society began publication of its *Collections*. The impetus of this effort was summed up by Thomas Jefferson writing to Ebenezer Hazard in 1791, "The lost cannot be recovered; but let us save what remains: not by vaults and locks which fence them from the public eye and use, in consigning them to the waste of time, but by such a multiplication of copies, as shall place them beyond the reach of accident."[280]

This work continues today, often under the auspices of university presses, supported in part by the National Historical Publication and Records Commission.[281] The Association for Documentary Editing (ADE) provides a venue for information about documentary editing practice today.[282] In recent decades, collections of documents were more likely to be published in microfilm rather than as letterpress publications. In the last few years, documents are increasingly published in digital form.[283]

Providing intellectual access to historical documents published electronically requires the same level of access provided by the annotation and indexing of traditional documentary publications. Standards are emerging for such publications. Many electronic publishers employ the Standard Generalized Markup Language (SGML) or a modified version of it called the Extensible Markup Language (XML). These standards provide rules for marking text through the use of tags. Sets of tags may be defined by a community of interested users for types of documents. These are called document type definitions (DTD).[284]

The Model Editions Partnership has established a DTD for historical documents and associated annotation and indexing. This organization discusses "ways of creating editions of historical documents which meet the standards scholars traditionally use in preparing printed editions. Equally important is our goal of making these materials more widely available via the Web."[285] The DTD is encoded in the *Model Editions Partnership Reference Manual Tag Set Documentation.*[286] An example of the application of this standard is found at the George Perkins Marsh Research Center at the University of Vermont, which provides access to transcriptions and images of selected letters in Marsh's correspondence.[287]

In the Burlington Agenda, archivists identified an eight-point research agenda for understanding the issues of most concern to archivists in publishing historical documents.[288] Archivists might also monitor EDOCS "discussion list and web site for professionals involved in the production, distribution, and organization of historical documents on the Internet." The discussion centers on issues "relating to electronic texts, including access, transcription, quality control, copyright and other legal problems, document markup and annotation, teaching applications, and textual analysis."[289]

Providing Access to Digital Surrogates of Documents

Repositories are now able to provide digital surrogates of documents in their holdings, especially photographic images, on the Web. Archivists can now link descriptions of documents to digital images of them. In some ways, this capability might be considered the ulti-

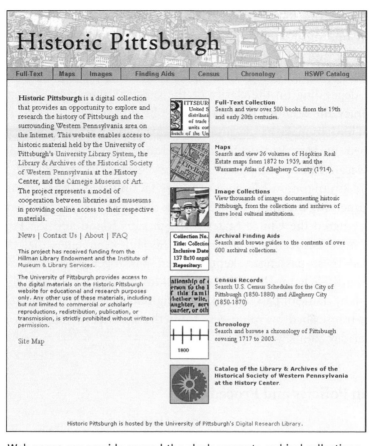

Web pages can provide around-the-clock access to archival collections.
IMAGE COURTESY HISTORIC PITTSBURGH, DIGITAL RESEARCH LIBRARY, UNIVERSITY OF PITTSBURGH.

mate in item-level description. For pictorial materials, providing a digital image provides a level of access not possible with the most detailed cataloging text. The Library of Congress American Memory Project serves as a prime example and offers useful advice for other repositories.[290]

Digital copies that are facsimiles of the original document differ from documents that are searchable. Facsimiles have been called "dumb files." They are, in essence, pictures of the document. They can be made "intelligent" in several ways so they may be searched. The least labor-intensive method is to embed indexing terms in the identification of the digital image. Linking the digital image to the finding aid is one means to do this. Second, typed or printed text can be scanned and converted to digital characters through Optical Character Recognition (OCR). This tool has varying degrees of accuracy depending on the clarity of the original characters. To ensure accuracy, the resulting digital text must be proofread.

Third, to make handwritten text searchable, it must be read, transcribed, and marked up for digital transmission. For example, the American Family Immigration History Center located in the Ellis Island Immigration Museum provides facsimiles of ships' manifests documenting the more than 22 million passengers and crew members who entered the United States through Ellis Island and the Port of New York between 1892 and 1924. The ship companies that transported these passengers kept detailed passenger lists, called "ship manifests." What makes this site useful for researchers is the ability to search by name of passenger. These original handwritten manuscripts were transcribed by volunteers from the Church of Jesus Christ of Latter-day Saints.[291]

Loan Policies and Procedures

Loans are the exception in archives and manuscript repositories, not the rule. Often there are acceptable substitutes for loans of original materials. For example, appropriate alternatives to a teacher's request to use original materials in a classroom might be inviting the class to visit the repository or providing multiple facsimile copies of materials for students to use in class. Other requests for loans can be met with copies, especially administrative requests.

Because they will receive loan requests for which no substitute will suffice and because loans are acceptable under certain circumstances, repositories must include loan policies in their access policy. A loan is a privilege, not a right; all requests for loans must meet the same standards and follow the same procedures. The archivist should review all loan applications. No matter how eloquent the user's plea or imminent the deadline, no shortcuts should be allowed in loan procedures. The three most common requests are for administrative use, research use, and exhibition. Some users also may ask to borrow records to make copies with their own copying equipment.

Loans for Administrative Use

Originating agencies may request the temporary return of records for administrative use or legal use. Donors may ask to borrow their materials for personal use. Institutional archivists may encounter demands from the legal department to give up records. Archivists should encourage such patrons to use records at the repository instead of having them returned, or they might provide copies, especially if the material is to be used for an extended period of time. The instruments documenting the transfer of the records to the archives, whether deed of gift, deposit agreement, or transfer agreement, should state in some detail the conditions under which records may be recalled, the people in the creating organization or agency authorized to request them, and how far in advance requests should be submitted.[292]

Loans for Exhibition

Exhibitions are important means of conveying information from archives to people unlikely to use them in person. Exhibitions also stimulate public appreciation of history and of the repository, and they encourage research use. Although copies often can be used for exhibition, the authenticity of original records captures public attention and interest. Museums, libraries, historical societies, or other cultural institutions request loans for exhibition; schools, businesses, or creating agencies may wish to borrow original records for public relations or educational functions. Donors of personal papers occasionally request loans for family reunions. Because of the importance of exhibitions and of the risks they entail, such loans require considerable scrutiny and careful preparation.[293]

Mary Lynn Ritzenthaler points out that archivists often, in effect, mount informal exhibits when they use attractive or valuable documents for show-and-tell orientation sessions for users, donors, or other visitors. Such use, if repeated frequently, may damage the documents most central to the repository mission. Repositories may protect such documents by keeping a record of their use and condition, encapsulating them, wearing gloves when handling them, or creating facsimile copies for demonstration.[294]

Loans for Research

Repositories should not loan archival materials to individual users, but the expanded use of interlibrary—or inter-repository—loan might considerably assist individual users and facilitate research. Use copies of microfilmed collections or series are obvious candidates for interlibrary loan. At this time, few repositories loan original materials through interlibrary loan, but more might consider it. Many collections that are neither heavily used nor fragile could be loaned for a limited time for use in another repository that follows the same level of professional care. Inter-repository loans might enable intensive use by an off-site user or group of students that would not occur in the home repository.

Some states have built networks through which original records are regularly transported to its members. Thirteen institutions partic-ipate in the Area Research Center network in Wisconsin, regulated by conditions established by the network. In 1998–1999, the network recorded over 1,000 loan transactions. More than 10,000 loan transac-tions have been completed in the more than thirty-year history of the program. A paraprofessional reference archivist manages the loan program, and a bonded interlibrary loan courier is used to transport the collections. Small repositories with limited hours lend collections to larger repositories so that researchers can take advantage of extended public use hours. Collections have been loaned to facilitate their use by students in a participating university. A similar network operates in Missouri.[295]

Loan Policies and Procedures

Requests for Loans

The repository loan policy should indicate how requests are to be for-mulated and submitted. Applications for loans should be made in writing and submitted in time to ensure proper preparation of materials. Requests for return of records for administrative use should be received at least two weeks in advance of the date of transmittal, and the application should explain why use of the documents in the archives or copies are not sufficient.

When possible, the archivist should work with exhibit designers to select materials and to ensure that appropriate preservation and security measures are incorporated into exhibition design. Six months advance notice is not too long to require for exhibition requests. Repositories may grant exceptions to the time stipulated for simple requests, but sufficient time is needed to respond to large or complicated requests.[296]

The repository's loan policy specifies the environmental conditions under which loaned items are to be used or exhibited. It is helpful to ask the borrower to complete a checklist describing its physical environment and security procedures. In addition to demonstrating acceptable levels of security, temperature, humidity, and lighting, the borrower for an exhibition must also guarantee safe and acceptable exhibition techniques. Staff of the lending repository may visit the site where the records will be used or exhibited. A facility report might be required before a loan is approved. The Registrar's Committee of the American Association of Museums publishes a standard form.[297]

A careful examination of requested materials should precede the decision to lend them. The archivist should make a detailed record of the condition of every item before it is loaned for exhibition, including photographic records of particularly valuable items. The National Park Service uses its Object Condition Report to record such information. Consultation with a conservator or with a museum accustomed to handling loan requests for exhibition may be warranted in some cases. Less detailed scrutiny is possible for larger groups of records returned for administrative use or for interlibrary loan, but their general condition should be noted and a complete list be made. If individual documents are to be removed from folders, it is useful to substitute a photocopy, as well as a separation sheet indicating the removal date, reason, and staff initials.

Some repositories prepare all materials loaned for exhibition and charge the borrowing institution for preparation costs and supplies. They encapsulate or mat items in physically and chemically stable materials and provide exhibit furniture, such as cradles to hold bound volumes.

The duration of the loan is related to the need of the borrower, the condition of the materials, and the physical circumstances of use. It should be as short as possible. As a general rule, only facsimiles, not original archival materials, should be permanently exhibited. Since damage from light exposure is cumulative, it may be necessary to withdraw heavily used items from exhibition.

The policy statement must also spell out how the materials will be packed, insured, and transported and who will carry out and pay for each of these functions. Many repositories pack and transport materials themselves and charge the expenses to the borrower. In some cases, staff members accompany the materials to their temporary location.

Loan Agreements

All conditions are recorded in a loan agreement. An appropriate agent of the borrowing agency signs it, verifying the conditions under which the materials will be used and the date of return. The loan agreement also specifies the names of authorized users, the method of transportation, whether copying is permitted, and exhibition techniques to be used. Loan forms must include agreement to meet the stated standards for use of the materials. Borrowers agree that they will not alter materials in any way and will retain original order. The loan policy and agreement should indicate the preferred citation for labels and acknowledgments.

Careful records must be kept of all loans, and the archivist should monitor their status on a regular basis. The repository should request copies of exhibition catalogs or other publications resulting from the exhibition.[298]

Conclusion

For many users, access to archival materials means obtaining copies or loans of them. While archival repositories are obligated to meet as many requests for copies as possible, policies and procedures are necessary to simplify the administrative costs of providing copies and to ensure that copyright law is observed. Copies can supply most needs for off-site use of records, but occasionally loans are necessary to meet continuing needs of creating administrators and to enrich exhibitions.

Previous chapters have examined user needs for intellectual, legal, and physical access to archives. Intellectual access is provided through finding aids and reference assistance. Legal access is defined in the access policy. Physical access is provided in the research room and through copies and loans. To meet these needs, repositories must organize, administer, and evaluate reference services. These topics are discussed in the next chapter.

CHAPTER 9

Managing Reference Services and Evaluating the Use of Archives

To meet users' needs, protect records, and use staff effectively, repositories organize, administer, and evaluate reference services. Staff qualified to provide reference services must be recruited, trained, supervised, and organized in reporting relationships conducive to meeting user needs. Managing reference services requires planning, policies, and procedures. Effective organization and management of reference services also depends on measuring and evaluating the use of archives through routine data collection and user studies. This chapter will discuss organizing and managing reference services and measuring and evaluating the use of archives.

Organizing Reference Services

Repositories typically organize reference staff in one of three models:

1. a curatorial organization, in which reference services are integrated with arrangement and description, often in a subject or format area;
2. a rotating organization, in which reference services are provided by all staff members in rotation; and
3. a functional organization, in which reference services are organized as a separate department.

The effectiveness of each of these arrangements depends on the size of the staff, the size and complexity of the holdings, and the nature of the finding aids. Each model has strengths and weaknesses.

Curatorial Organization

A curatorial organization recognizes that in provenance-based systems specialists who arrange and describe records can provide specialized and informed reference services for the records since they know how and why the records were created and organized. In a small repository, where one archivist provides all archival services, this ideal may be met. In larger repositories, it is impossible for any one person to be familiar with all holdings, so staff members are assigned responsibility for groups of records. Often they are organized on the basis of form, such as audiovisual records, or according to the source of records, such as legislative records.

From the user's point of view, reference services in the curatorial model are dispersed among divisions. Users depend on referrals to appropriate curatorial divisions, and their needs may be fragmented among them. If the subject specialist is absent, reference services may be unavailable. User needs may be dispersed and fragmented, and may not be identified or considered in overall repository planning.

When the curatorial pattern is followed, reference must be integrated with other work of the unit and adequately recognized. Staff development programs to train junior staff and to ensure continuity of reference services and subject expertise are important. Attention to the interpersonal nature of the reference interaction and review of reference services must be considered in overall repository management.

Rotating Reference Services

Many repositories rotate reference activities among staff members on a weekly, daily, or even hourly schedule. All staff members have the opportunity to interact with users and to discover how they pose queries and use finding aids and holdings. At the same time, users can benefit from the knowledge of those who acquire, arrange, describe, conserve, and promote the use of records. This model gives administrators maximum flexibility in scheduling work and may provide the staff with welcome diversity in work tasks.

Users, however, may find it difficult to develop rapport or continuing search strategies with a constantly changing staff. If staff fail to give sufficient attention to the substantive intellectual role of the archivist in guiding users, it may well devolve into providing only the administrative aspects of reference services. If all staff rotate, the staff member on duty may have had no experience with the records in use. Staff members are less likely to develop expertise or interest in reference activities when the period of service at the reference desk is limited and fragmented. Reference work may come to be seen as an interruption of one's "real" job and may be slighted in the press of other business. If everyone is responsible, it may be that no one is responsible.

Functional Organization

The functional pattern distinguishes reference and public service functions from other archival functions. Reference specialists offer continuity for users from initial interview to follow-up activities. This approach gives reference services an identity and makes reference staff members accountable for meeting user needs. Reference specialists can identify the research needs of major user constituencies and develop strategies to meet them. Reference staff can advocate user needs in institutional planning and relay information about user needs to repository staff responsible for acquisitions, processing, or public programs. In some repositories, reference services and public programs are combined in a public services department that systematically anticipates and answers user needs.

In a functional organization, reference staff members cannot, however, know holdings as well as those who acquire, arrange, and describe them; and, if the acquisitions or processing staff seldom see their work used, they may not understand user needs and perspectives. Because reference staff members deal with people all day, every day, they may experience "burnout" and find it difficult to respond imaginatively and patiently to repeated requests. Scheduling can also be a problem, since it may be difficult to staff the reference desk when

Evaluating collection resources and user needs is critical to the creation of collection development plans so that archives can provide the best resources and services.

reference archivists are away. Maintaining communications between technical services and reference staff is critical to making this arrangement work.

In a one-person repository, by necessity, the archivist becomes both subject specialist and reference specialist. In some large institutions, like the National Archives, models are combined: a reference consultant orients users, directs them to appropriate subject specialists, and maintains contact with them throughout research to ensure that all needed divisions are identified and all needed services are provided. In mid-sized repositories, the functional division may meet user needs better than staff rotation.

Staff Qualifications

No matter what pattern or combination of patterns is employed, service to users must be the foundation of all archival programs. It is critical to staff the reference desk with people capable of meeting both the intellectual and personal needs of users. Archival administration is a service profession, and *all* archivists should have a genuine spirit of public service. A real dedication to public service, however, is especially vital for reference staff, whether professional, paraprofessional, or clerical. A repository's image is largely shaped by the services provided to users. Reference staff members must be able to work with a wide variety of people, treating each request, no matter how mundane or routine, as a fresh question, mustering appropriate interest and assistance. Reference archivists must be particularly aware of the complicated dynamics of interpersonal relationships in archives. Patience, empathy, humor, and good temper are qualities especially important in staff members dealing with the public.

An ability to see process, not products, as the accomplishment of the day also is helpful for reference staff, for there are usually few tangible products to give meaning to each day's work. Instead, the "product" is the less tangible accomplishment of enabling others to pursue their work effectively. Reference staff must be able to adjust to a constantly changing set of priorities in daily responsibilities and be comfortable juggling many demands upon their time. They must be careful and consistent in handling archival materials under the stress of many demands for prompt service.

To give good service, reference staff members must also be knowledgeable about repository finding aids and holdings. They must understand the history, functions, record forms, and organizations of the records creators, and they must possess subject knowledge of the activities documented by repository holdings. Since appropriate referrals to other information sources are an important element of good service, a sense of the information universe is also necessary, as is familiarity with general reference tools and, increasingly, with on-line sources. Reference archivists must be familiar with laws and ethics relating to access and copyright. Stuart Strachan estimates that it can take up to five or six years for an archivist to learn the essentials necessary for good reference services in a large repository.[299]

Continuing education is important for all professionals, including reference archivists. Understanding the needs and research methods of major constituencies helps archivists understand their clients. Repositories need to give reference staff time and financial support to attend professional meetings of user groups as well as archival associations, to read new literature in both subject and professional fields, and to undertake user studies and research in repository holdings. Public service staff may also need training and support in stress management and in dealing with difficult patrons.[300]

Many administrative duties can and should be handled by paraprofessional and clerical staff. Repositories both large and small often employ paraprofessional reading room attendants to handle such services as registration, retrieval, reshelving, and copying. Although many repositories use support staff to filter users for referrals to appropriate professional staff for intellectual assistance, this arrangement often fails because of the intricacies of the initial interview. Many small repositories, and some large ones, rely on paraprofessional staff to provide more substantive reference services as well. With some supervision, they can instruct patrons in the use of finding aids, respond to directional questions, and answer simple factual questions. Likewise, experienced paraprofessionals may handle some substantive reference questions, particularly remote reference questions that allow for review by professionals. Carefully defined search protocols and reference procedures help this arrangement work.

Retaining good employees is important to the quality of reference service. Turnover is particularly damaging because certain kinds of knowledge about holdings can only be gained by experience in the same repository. Establishing clear expectations, helping all employees see how their tasks relate to the larger institutional mission, and acknowledging good work are important keys to staff retention. All positions, professional or paraprofessional, need written job descriptions outlining responsibilities, authority, and reporting requirements.

Reference services must not become a ghetto where archivists develop subject expertise but are unable to move up a career ladder of increasing administrative responsibility. In many repositories where promotions are based on increased administrative responsibilities, it is difficult to promote reference staff based on enhanced reference skills gained through study and experience. Repositories can resolve this problem by creating two career ladders, one for increased professional competence and another for greater administrative responsibility.[301]

Managing Reference Services

Managing reference services requires planning, establishing reference policies, implementing those policies in procedures, and administering these policies and procedures. It also requires advocacy and communication. These topics will be briefly discussed below.

Planning

Planning for reference services should be integrated into repository planning, both for strategic planning and annual planning. Reference staff should identify measurable goals and objectives for reference services. From these larger goals staff develop an annual work plan that details the activities to be undertaken, the individuals who will perform them, and the needed resources of equipment, money, and space.

Establishing Policies

Establishing policies for reference services rests on repository policies embodied in the access policy. As seen in chapter 6, policies must be established for access, restrictions to protect privacy and confidentiality, levels of reference services, levels of research services, security, preservation, fees, copying services, loans, and use of information.

Implementing Procedures

A procedures manual that outlines the details of reference procedures saves time and helps ensure consistent reference practices. A table of contents listing topics to be covered is shown in Appendix 4. Maintaining this manual in electronic form makes it easy to keep it up to date and accessible through repository networks to all staff.

Records Management

The numerous forms and responses to reference inquiries generated in providing reference services must be filed and appropriate retention periods determined for them. Most forms are retained in case the repository later discovers theft, abuse, or misuse. Reference records also are used to support requests for reference tools, equipment, staff, and finding aids; and such forms provide the basis for user studies.

Little guidance has been published on the scheduling and disposition of reference records. Researcher registration forms are usually filed by name of user in an annual file and kept for as long as possible. Request forms are filed and kept as long as possible to provide evidence in case of theft or abuse of records. The National Archives keeps both registration forms and call slips for twenty-five years. Photocopy request forms also are retained because they require a signature by which the user agrees to abide by copyright law. If later publication exceeds fair use, the repository will want to show that it informed the user. One repository keeps all reference letters for five years, filed in annual files, thereunder alphabetically by user. After five years, routine reference letters are destroyed; significant correspondence is kept indefinitely.

As reference services for off-site users are increasingly provided electronically, the repository may wish to file electronic copies of reference responses in a central directory so that the accumulated work of the reference staff can be accessible to all staff members, and easily and quickly searched.

Time Management

Time management in reference is difficult, but because of that very difficulty, it is vital. In the research room the time constraints of staff and users intersect and sometimes conflict. The larger the reference staff and the more numerous the users, the more complicated time management becomes. Time must be managed in the context of institutional mission and resources outlined in the access statement. Although regrettable, the reality is that no repository can be all things to all actual or potential users. Each repository must acknowledge its limitations of staff and budget and establish policies that serve the greatest number in terms of its overall mission. At the same time, the repository can work to identify unmet needs and seek resources to meet them. Priorities must be set as rationally as possible; it is unfair both to users and to reference archivists to make such decisions on an ad hoc basis.

Scheduling reference staff can be difficult because it is impossible to predict the volume of users and the complexity of their requests on any given day. Good recordkeeping through such tools as the registration form and daily log, however, enables the reference archivist to identify patterns in research volume and substance and to plan staffing allocations to meet them. With a large reference staff, a tracking system, as shown in figure 9-1, helps to monitor responsibility for each reference letter, e-mail inquiry, phone inquiry, or photocopy request. Each slip is filed by name of the staff member to whom the work is assigned.

Reference staff members seek ways to make best use of time and to make reference services more efficient and effective. One-to-one reference service may be the best way to meet certain user needs, but other solutions may be more effective to meet other needs. For example, if extensive and increasing reference assistance is needed for a particular body of records, allocating staff to create a folder title list or an index may decrease the need for reference assistance. If numerous new users need extensive assistance, increasing the number of staff members assigned to the reference desk is not the only solution and may not be the best. Developing educational programs such as Saturday workshops in research methods, creating brochures describing research strategies for common problems, or producing an introductory videotape or on-line tutorial may be a more effective use of time. Frequently requested information may be placed on the repository Web site.

Automation makes reference work more effective by capturing information kept largely in the heads of archivists, by freeing users from dependence on mediation by archival staff, and by allowing users to improve archival description. It can also be used to improve the management of reference services by creating standard responses

Figure 9-1 Tracking Requests

Directed to staff member (name) _____

Date directed _____

Name of researcher _____

Type of request

    Letter ___   E-mail ___   Phone Call ___   Copying ___

Notes_____

_____

_____

Courtesy Bentley Historical Library, University of Michigan.

to frequent requests. Automation can reduce the amount of time spent on routine administrative tasks such as registering users, keeping track of materials in the research room, and filing registration forms and request slips. Helen Tibbo describes a pilot user assessment system developed for the Manuscript Department at the University of North Carolina at Chapel Hill. It incorporates researcher registration, daily log, materials used by on-site patrons, and a user satisfaction survey, all kept in an integrated database.[302] A pilot on-line registration system has been developed for the James Duderstadt Papers at the Bentley Historical Library, University of Michigan.[303]

Advocacy and Communication

Reference archivists are advocates for the needs of users in repository planning, reporting regularly to repository management on use and user needs. Providing meaningful information to management is necessary to obtain adequate space and equipment, a sufficient number of well-trained staff members, usable finding aids, appropriate public programs, and useful publications. Reference archivists also communicate user needs to other staff members, especially those in technical services and acquisitions. Information should be exchanged with collecting staff on evolving user requests and research priorities.

In larger repositories, scheduled staff meetings of department heads provide for structured discussion of departmental needs. Reviewing the accessions log regularly keeps reference staff aware of new holdings; in turn, reference requests may suggest leads for possible acquisitions. Reference staff should read finding aids in draft and comment freely on them. In turn, processing staff members find that reading reference letters keeps them aware of user needs; they also might answer queries relating to their specialty.

Measuring and Evaluating the Use of Archives

"What is the use of archives?" Bruce Dearstyne has asked.[304] Many ask this question implicitly, if not explicitly. Sometimes the question refers to the activities of searching, reading, and noting information in archives.

More frequently, however, the question means, "What is the value of preserving historical records?" To respond to the question in either of its meanings, archivists measure and evaluate the use of archives at three levels: reference function level, repository level, and professional level.

At the level of the reference function, measuring the use of repository holdings is necessary to organize and manage reference services in the repository and to evaluate their effectiveness. Quantitative information about use and users is needed to allocate resources, plan staffing patterns, order equipment and supplies, plan programs to meet identified needs, and reward staff. Such information helps staff to determine whether the level of service is adequate, assess assumptions about reference services, and modify services to meet changing circumstances. Qualitative assessments of service outputs are needed to evaluate such attributes as promptness, thoroughness, courtesy, care, and adequacy of response. Meaningful evaluation of reference services compares performance with some standard—either repository objectives or professional standards.

At the repository level, understanding the use of the holdings is necessary to plan the work of the repository and to advocate support for it. Information about use of the repository is used to plan descriptive programs, set processing priorities, develop acquisition strategies, and plan public programs. Quantitative and qualitative measures are necessary to justify the value of archives to resource allocators.

At the broadest level, understanding and communicating the use of archives contributes to greater public understanding of the value of preserving them and the need to support archival and manuscript repositories. It also facilitates planning cooperative programs to carry out the archival mission, such as documentation strategies to preserve records of enduring value and national bibliographic systems to enhance accessibility. Examination of the uses of archives by all archivists will contribute to the development of standards of practice for the profession.[305]

Paul Conway suggests that archivists should measure and evaluate three aspects of the use of archives: quality, value, and integrity.[306] Conway's framework for studying the uses of archives, shown in figure 9-2, provides a useful structure for discussing evaluation. He defines this framework as follows:

1. QUALITY: How well do archivists understand and meet the information needs of users? To understand quality, archivists both measure user needs and evaluate the quality of reference services.
2. VALUE: What are the effects of use on individuals, groups, and society as a whole? To understand value, archivists assess the value of archival information to researchers and to indirect users beyond the repository.
3. INTEGRITY: How well do archivists balance their obligations to preserve materials against their obligations to make them available? The purpose of many of the forms used to manage reference service is security. Information gathered in them can be used, beyond security, to plan preservation and reproduction programs.

Since security and preservation have been considered in previous chapters, the following discussion will focus first on understanding user needs and evaluating the quality of reference service. Understanding the value of archives will be considered later in the chapter.

Evaluating Quality: Understanding User Needs

On the simplest level, understanding user needs begins with measuring the use of the repository. Developing quantitative measures of use is relatively straightforward for they are built into the daily work of the reference department. The many "forms, forms, forms" used in providing reference services generate a wealth of data to measure and evaluate them. Some data are supplied by users, for example, in registration forms. During the course of research visits, users supply information that can be analyzed to see how they structure their research at the repository. Request slips document what records are requested; requests for duplication suggest where users find useful information. Reference staff members supply other data, for example, in the phone log, from written responses to e-mail or mail requests, or from exit interviews.

In 1987 the Society of American Archivists and the National Association of Government Archivists and Records Administrators recommended keeping daily measures of users and of materials used,

Figure 9-2 Framework for Studying the Users of Archives

METHODOLOGY

OBJECTIVES	Stage 1 Registration (all users/always)	Stage 2 Orientation (all users at selected times)	Stage 3 Follow Up (sample users/selected times)	Stage 4 Survey (random sample)	Stage 5 Experiments (special groups)
Quality	Nature of Task • *Definition in terms of subject, format, scope*	Preparation of Researcher • *experience* • *stage of defined problem* • *basic/applied* Anticipated Service	Search Strategies and Mechanics • *search order* • *posing search*	Expectations and Satisfaction • *styles of research* • *approaches to searching* • *levels of service*	Access and Non-use • *frustration indexes* • *perceptions of use*
Integrity	Identification • *name* • *address* • *telephone* Agree to Rules	Knowledge of Holdings and Services • *written sources* • *verbal sources*	Intensity and Frequency of Use • *collections used* • *time spent with files*	Alternative to Physical Use • *value and use of microforms* • *value and use of databases*	Format Independence • *linkages with information creation* • *technology and information*
Value	Membership in Networks • *group affiliation* Can We Contact You? Can We Tell Others?	Intended Use • *purpose in terms of function and product*	Significant Use Significant Info • *importance of archives* • *other sources* • *valuable information* • *gaps in information*	Impact of Use • *increased use* • *citation patterns* • *decision-making*	Role of Historical Information in Society • *total potential demand* • *community network analysis*

Paul Conway, "Facts and Frameworks: An Approach to Studying the Users of Archives," *American Archivist* 49 (Fall 1986): 397.

copied, or loaned, and aggregating them monthly, quarterly, and annually. These measures, now updated, are shown in figure 9-3. Information also should be collected about the number of full-time equivalent employees (FTEs) devoted to reference activity including professional, paraprofessional, and clerical staff.[307]

Simply collecting data is not enough; it must be used. A repository can track statistical information to follow patterns of use within the repository. For example, graphing the number of daily visits over

Figure 9-3 Quantitative Measures of the Use of Archives

Counts of Users
- number of different persons using the repository
- number of daily visits (sum of the daily counts of users who spend all or part of any day in the repository)
- number of requests received by phone
- number of requests received by mail and e-mail
- number of hits on repository web page

Measurements of Materials Used
- number of retrievals
- number of collections/record groups/series used
- amount of material used, measured in feet or in number of volumes or containers
- number of pages downloaded from repository Web site

Measurements of Materials Copied or Loaned
- number of pages photocopied
- number of microform images duplicated
- number of photographs duplicated;, both analog and digital
- number of sound recordings duplicated (by type and unit)
- number of machine-readable storage units duplicated (by type and unit)
- number of loans and number of items loaned

a year helps to understand seasonal patterns of use and assists in assigning staff. Charting the total number of users over several years can indicate whether use is growing or declining. Knowing the number and types of copies is necessary to order equipment and supplies or to seek out new vendors.

Understanding user needs and the configuration of use in a particular repository, however, requires analysis of information beyond these numbers. Some demographic information collected from all users—in registration forms, call slips, photocopy forms, user evaluation forms, or exit interviews—should be aggregated and analyzed periodically in monthly, quarterly, and annual reports to provide a basis for studying user needs and the nature of use.

Regularly analyzed registration variables include the types of users, the organizations they represent, and their geographical distribution. Meaningful and discrete categories of users or queries to be analyzed must be carefully defined, and will vary according to repository mission. Categories can reflect occupational characteristics, such as staff from the parent institution, students from the parent university, or faculty from other universities. Institutional archives may wish to identify the departments using the archives, such as legal, corporate communications, or advertising. However structured, such analysis should identify user groups in terms of institutional mission and follow changes over time, so that archivists can measure how well they are meeting user needs.

For example, a large survey was conducted in British archives in 1998. One of its most interesting findings is that "22% of users were first time visitors to any archive in the u.k.," but that 70% of visits were by regular or intensive users who visited at least once a month. The study suggests considerable turnover among users. Ailes and Watt hypothesize that most first-time users do not return and the use statistics are generated by long-term users. As the authors note, one-time use might be satisfactory if such users found what they sought. If, however, they do not return because their experience was unsatisfactory, it is expensive for the repository, because outreach and promotion to build volume is expensive, as are "building understanding and relationships (where quality is an issue)." Most telling, "Reliance on a 'hard-core' of users is in business terms either a comfortable niche market or a dangerously narrow customer base."[308]

Photocopy forms at the Bentley Historical Library documented a significant growth in the demand for copying. This information was presented to management with a range of recommendations: take longer to complete orders for each user and let the backlog grow, charge more for copies, limit the amount of copies users can order, send more orders to microfilming, or hire more work-study students. The order forms also showed that microfilming was not a viable solution for the majority of requests.[309] More work-study students were hired.

In addition to the large amount of information collected directly from all users, it is helpful to seek other information periodically from all or from a random sample of users. For example, Conway suggests gaining additional information about sources consulted and research approaches used from samples of users.[310]

Information about use provides important feedback for other archival functions. Analyzing registration information to study how people find out about the repository, how they decide whether to visit, and what types of questions they ask can be used to evaluate effectiveness of descriptive programs. As use of on-line interfaces grows, it is important for archivists to understand "user presentation language," that is, the wording of the user's initial query.[311] This will enable archivists to design access interfaces with search capabilities that better meet user needs. Registration information about search categories, such as legislative history or genealogy, or about formats sought, such as textual records or visual materials, may be used to determine the effectiveness of acquisition programs or to structure public programs. Presentation of the dramatic increase in remote use should be used to advocate for support of these services; it will remind administrators that not all users actually visit the repository.

To reach new constituencies and better serve underrepresented ones, the repository must collect information from *potential* users. For example, institutional archivists have much indirect evidence at hand about potential users; they have an unparalleled opportunity to use their own holdings to analyze patterns of information creation, use, and transfer in the parent institution. Such research could be the basis for a focus group discussion with targeted administrators examining their needs and use of information and their perceptions of archival holdings and services. Such discussions could identify programs or specialized reference services that would enable administrators to make better use of archival holdings. Similarly, a historical society might develop focus group sessions with genealogists to identify their needs, or survey faculty of local university departments of history, political science, and sociology to determine both their research interests and teaching methods.

Evaluating Quality: Evaluating Reference Services

Both the performance of individual staff members and the performance of the repository must be considered in evaluating how well archivists meet the information needs of users.

DEVELOPING AND EVALUATING INDIVIDUAL PERFORMANCE

Developing and evaluating performance of individual reference staff members requires a set of goals and objectives for reference performance linked to behaviors that can be observed. Reference service rests on a set of professional competencies. In its *Role Delineation Statement for Professional Archivists,* the Academy of Certified Archivists has identified the knowledge necessary for archival work.[312] Additional insights can be gained from the library literature. For example, the American Library Association published *Professional Competencies for Reference and User Services Librarians* in 2003.[313] It has also published *Guidelines for Behavioral Performance of Reference and Information Services Professionals,* now under revision.[314] The Reference and Information Services Section of the International Federation of Library Associations has drafted *Digital Reference Service Guidelines,*[315] and the Virtual Reference Desk provides *Facets of Quality for Digital Reference.*[316] A repository can formulate checklists for both the behaviors and knowledge associated with good reference service, as in appendices 5 and 6. Such standards can be used for training reference staff and for periodically evaluating individual performance. [317]

EVALUATING REPOSITORY PERFORMANCE

Evaluating repository performance requires assessment of such qualitative factors as accessibility, quality of finding aids, comfort, quality of holdings, and accuracy of information provided. Quantitative measures can evaluate timeliness, costs, and other aspects of user satisfaction. This information can be obtained from users through exit interviews, evaluation forms, and follow-up surveys.

In the case of e-mails and letters, the repository may keep complete and accurate records of the questions asked, in the patrons' own words. Analysis of these questions may offer insights into users' natural language and provide guidance in structuring on-line resources. The repository can also capture the full text of the response, which can be used for evaluation and training.

Archivists need to structure meaningful measures of user satisfaction. In the survey of British archives in June 1998, Ailes and Watt found that 84 percent of the visitors surveyed found at least some of the information they sought. This study underscores again the importance of providing accurate information in advance of the visit. Of the unsatisfied visitors, 12 percent had gone to the wrong place or arrived too late.[318]

After a research visit, users can be asked to evaluate the quality of service. How well did archival reality meet initial expectations? How satisfactory were services, finding aids, and holdings? How well did the reference system perform in relation to user information problems? Such information can be requested directly from users during exit interviews, through user evaluation forms, or through other follow-up activities after the visit. See figure 9-4. The checklist reproduced in appendix 3 can also be used to assess repository performance.[319]

Setting measurable outcomes for service can be effective in setting goals for individual staff and documenting repository success or need for changes.

Understanding the Value of Use

Developing measures of the value of the use of archival materials and the information they contain is more problematic than evaluating the quality of reference service. To understand the effects of use on individuals, groups, and society as a whole, one must determine exactly what is to be measured and then how to measure it. It is dangerous to measure the value of archives only by the number of direct users

Figure 9-4 Follow-up Questionnaire for Users of Archives

1. Did you find the information that you sought? ____ yes ____ no
2. How important or significant was the information for your purposes?
   __ very important __ somewhat useful __ not at all useful
3. Was the information generally used:
   a. as illustration?
   b. to support one or more major points?
   c. to support several major parts of the project?
   d. as the basis for the entire project?
4. Did the information lead you to a new interpretation for the project?
   ____ yes ____ no
5. Did the information lead to other sources for your project?
   ____ yes ____ no
6. Did you submit the results of your research for publication?
   ____ yes ____ no
7. Was it published? ____ yes ____ no
   Article Title _____
       Publication_____
       Volume, date, page _____
   Book Title _____
       Publisher _____
       Place and date_____
8. Did you use it in an exhibit, film, or videotape? ____ yes ____ no
   Title _____
   Publisher_____
   Date _____
9. Did you take the information to a family reunion? ____ yes ____ no
10. Did you distribute it as a memo or report? ____ yes ____ no
11. Was it used in a lecture or speech? ____ yes ____ no
12. Was it used by a client?
    ____ yes ____ no
    If so, please explain _____
    _____
    _____

because archival and manuscript repositories will never be able to justify necessary support by quantitative comparisons to libraries, museums, or other public programs. Indeed, archivists must guard against measuring use of archives simply by activities in the reading room or direct inquiries to the repository because the indirect use of archives occurs in an unknown number of other settings.

Bruce Dearstyne has suggested two standards for evaluating the significance of use.[320] The first is the significance of the use in terms of the repository's mission and priorities. As seen in chapter 5, every repository should summarize its purpose and the types of research it is founded to support in a mission statement. The access policy is based on this statement. In determining repository policies, a publicly funded state archives must decide, for example, whether large numbers of citizens conducting genealogical research are more or less significant than a handful of nonresident scholars publishing research in specialized journals. It is important to repeat that, although level of services may vary, no one should be denied access to materials because of the nature of their research or their occupational status.

Dearstyne's second basis for evaluating the significance of use is the significance of the subject and the dissemination of its results. Here the focus is on the indirect uses of the information. Archivists can assess dissemination and use of archival information by asking users to identify the intended products of their research and by undertaking follow-up studies of the use of information. See figure 9-4. Archivists also can study the products of research to determine where information goes and how it is used after it leaves the archives through such tools as citation analysis.[321] Many repositories keep annual lists of these research products; in addition to their use as evaluative measures, they are useful as tangible results to present to administrators and funders.

User Studies

User studies can be used to gain greater understanding of quality, value, or integrity, and many repositories have the data and resources to undertake them systematically. Many archivists think that they do not have sufficient time to undertake user studies or that they do not know how to do so. Helen Tibbo, however, speculates that underlying these arguments is the belief that user studies are simply not worth the effort. She argues that archivists are content to rely on personal observation and anecdote, that "The digital revolution and unmediated access to finding guides and materials, however, makes user information essential and a centerpiece of repository knowledge if archivists are to effect optimized discovery, retrieval, evaluation, and use of archival materials."

Archivists must reprioritize their time. Conducting studies of users is as important as processing a collection or converting a finding aid to an electronic format. Tibbo challenges us:

> If archivists at each repository took the time required to process one collection. . . and spent that time on a study that told them who their users are, how they search for information, from what types of user education they would most benefit, and how archivists could design future finding tools to best facilitate research, would this not lay the foundation for significantly improved policies and practices at each repository?

She further challenges us to share the results with the profession.[322]

The British Public Services Quality Group noted the advantages of a cooperative survey of users across a number of archival repositories. First, repositories could learn more about their own users more cheaply by participating in a common study. Second, they could compare their results with the larger data set or with subsets of comparable repositories, and they could "benchmark" their results against "best practice" repositories. Third, repeating a common survey design at intervals can identify long-term trends. Fourth, the results could be used to gain resources from funding agencies at local and national levels.[323]

Repositories must acknowledge the centrality of reference services to their mission and determine the most effective means of organizing staff to provide necessary services to users. Evaluating reference services at both the individual and departmental level is important in maintaining and improving their quality and effectiveness. Measuring and assessing patterns of use in a given repository are important for planning and evaluating reference services and constitute an important part of repository planning and professionwide research. User studies also form the basis for planning public programs to promote the wider use of archives.

CHAPTER 10

Bibliographic Essay

In recent years, archivists have developed a sure sense of professional identity. I have been fortunate to participate in this development over the course of my professional lifetime. When I joined the staff of the Michigan Historical Collections some thirty years ago, archivists and manuscripts curators were quite separate and both found themselves on uncertain ground among records managers, historians, and librarians. Emerging professional identity is documented in the maturation (I might say explosion) of professional literature. When I entered the profession, only the *American Archivist* and a handful of monographs populated the shelf with the CD classification of the Library of Congress classification system.

I once thought that I could at least scan all archival publications and even some related publications in history, librarianship, and records management, but today I feel hard-pressed to keep aware of the archival literature, much less scan it or that of any of the related professions. Many one-volume overviews of the profession have been published in the past decade, and more specialized monographs are beginning to appear. The development of university-based archival education programs has provided a cadre of students and teachers engaged in research and writing about all areas of the archival enterprise.

General Works on Reference Services in Archives

Reference services were slower to develop an identity than other functions of archival administration. This comparative lack of research and writing on reference services may have resulted from the common assumption that reference services fall at the end of a continuum of activities that begins with the creation of the records in the originating office (shaped by records management), followed by appraisal, accessioning, arrangement, and description, and concluding with reference services and outreach activities. Driven by the need to manage and protect large quantities of records, archivists primarily thought of reference services as a series of administrative decisions made after records had been appraised, accessioned, arranged, and described. In recent years, however, archivists have begun to explore reference services. New interest has developed in part because of new research into the users of archives and in part because of the introduction of electronic access to archives.

In 1939, the ever-prescient Margaret Norton wrote "Archives and Libraries: Reference Work" *Illinois Libraries* 21 (August 1939): 26–28, reprinted in *Norton on Archives* (Carbondale, Ill.: Southern University Press, 1975), 101–5, one of the earliest and best discussions of reference service in archives. Most other early writings about reference services in archives focused on the externalities of the relationship between user and repository: administration, registration, security, paging, storage, retrieval, and copying. Early writing also dwelt on legal aspects of access such as privacy, restrictions, copyright, and even such topics as replevin. See, for example, Frank Evans, *The Administration of Modern Archives: A Select Bibliographic Guide,* rev. ed. (Washington: National Archives and Records Service, General Services Administration, 1968).

Few monographs are devoted to reference services in archives. The first American manual was Sue Holbert, *Archives & Manuscripts: Reference and Access* (Chicago: Society of American Archivists, 1977). Next came the first edition of this manual *Providing Reference Services for Archives and Manuscripts* (Chicago: Society of American Archivists, 1992). Hugh Taylor offered a broad overview in *Archival Services and the Concept of the User: A RAMP Study* (Paris: UNESCO, 1984; ERIC Document ED 246 906), and Michel Duchein offered an international perspective in *Obstacles to the Access, Use and Transfer of Information from Archives* (Paris: UNESCO, 1983).

Haworth Press published two useful collections of essays. Both appeared first as issues of *The Reference Librarian.* The first was edited by Lucille Whalen, *Reference Services in Archives* (New York: Haworth Press, 1986), and provided examples of reference services in a wide variety of settings. It includes, for example, Thomas Wilsted, "Establishing an Image: The Role of Reference Service in a New Archival Program"; and Frank A. Zabrosky, "Researching the Past: An Archivist's Perspective." Laura B. Cohen edited the second, *Reference Services for Archives and Manuscripts* (New York: Haworth Press, 1997). In it, James Cross provides a useful summary of changes in the decade since the earlier volume in "Archival Reference: State of the Art."

A history of reference service at the National Archives is found in Donald R. McCoy, *The National Archives: America's Ministry of Documents, 1934–1968* (Chapel Hill: University of North Carolina, 1978).

Other overviews of reference services appear as chapters in more general works. See, for example, T. R. Schellenberg, "Reference Service," in his *Modern Archives: Principles and Techniques* (Chicago: University of Chicago Press, 1956); Ruth B. Bordin and Robert M. Warner, "The Library and the Researcher" and "The Library and the General Public," in their *The Modern Manuscript Library* (New York: Scarecrow Press, 1966); Kenneth Duckett, "Uses of Collections," in his *Modern Manuscripts: A Practical Manual for Their Management, Care, and Use* (Nashville: American Association for State and Local History, 1975); and George Chalou, "Reference," and Mary Jo Pugh, "The Illusion of Omnicience: Subject Access and the Reference Archivist," in *A Modern Archives Reader: Basic Readings on Archival Theory and Practice,* edited by Maygene F. Daniels and Timothy Walch (Washington, D.C.: National Archives, 1984).

More recent examples include Sandra Hinchey and Sigrid McCausland, "Access and Reference Services," in the first edition of *Keeping Archives,* edited by Ann Pederson (Sydney: Australian Society of Archives, 1987), and Sigrid McCausland, "Access and Reference Services," in the second edition edited by Judith Ellis (Port Melbourne: Australian Society of Archivists, 1993); David R. Kepley, "Reference Service and Access," in *Managing Archives and Archival*

Institutions, edited by James Gregory Bradsher (Chicago: University of Chicago Press, 1988); Elizabeth Yakel, *Starting an Archives* (Lanham, Md.: Society of American Archivists and Scarecrow Press, 1994); Gregory S. Hunter, *Developing and Maintaining Practical Archives: A How-To-Do-It Manual* (New York: Neal-Schuman Publishers, 1997); and Bruce W. Dearstyne, "Services to Users," in his *Managing Historical Records Programs: A Guide for Historical Agencies* (Walnut Creek, Calif.: AltaMira Press, 2000).

The profession also provides essays on reference services in particular settings; see, for example, Cynthia Swank, "Life in the Fast Lane: Reference in a Business Archives," in *Reference Services in Archives,* edited by Lucille Whalen (New York: Haworth Press, 1986). Several essays in *The Records of American Business* (Chicago: Society of American Archivists, 1997) offer provocative perspectives, especially Francis X. Blouin, "Business and American Culture: the Archival Challenge," Michael Nash, "Business History and Archival Practice: Shifts in Sources and Paradigms," Marcy G. Goldstein, "The Evolving Role of In-House Business Archives: From Tradition to Flexibility," and Philip F. Mooney, "Archival Mythology and Corporate Reality: A Potential Powder Keg." Richard J. Cox discusses "Arranging, Describing, and Providing Reference in Institutional Archives," in his *Managing Institutional Archives: Foundational Principles and Practices* (New York: Greenwood Press, 1992); Frances O' Donnell explains "Reference Service in an Academic Archives," to academic library administrators in the *Journal of Academic Librarians,* 26 (March 2000): 110–18, and William Maher provides guidance for use in his *The Management of College and University Archives* (Metuchen, N.J.: Society of American Archivists and Scarecrow Press, 1992), especially 126–47 and 256–63.

Guides for researchers offer insights for reference archivists. Although written decades ago for the novice scholar, Philip C. Brooks, *Research in Archives: The Use of Unpublished Primary Sources* (Chicago: University of Chicago Press, 1969) still offers useful insights into reference services in archives. Ostensibly directed to beginning researchers, *Research and the Manuscript Traditions* by Frank G. Burke (Lanham, Md.: Scarecrow Press, and Chicago: Society of American Archivists,

1997) provides an idiosyncratic view of the uses of manuscript collections in the last forty years. *Teaching Bibliographic Skills in History: A Sourcebook for Historians and Librarians* edited by Charles A. D'Aniello (Westport, Conn.: Greenwood Press, 1993) includes, among others, Joyce Duncan Falk's review of databases and electronic sources in "Using Electronic Information Sources," which outlines the strengths and weaknesses of a number of databases and the processes for using them. Another guide for researchers is *Researcher's Guide to Archives,* edited by John C. Larsen (Hampden, Conn.: Library Professional Pubs, 1988). Of particular interest to reference archivists within that volume are Floyd M. Shumway, "The Ethics of Archival Research," Judith Ann Schiff, "General Use of Archives," and Christopher Densmore, "Archival Reference Tools."

On-line Works for Reference Services in Archives

Tanya Zanish-Belcher provides a useful overview in, "Archives and Special Collections: A Guide to Resources on the Web," *College & Research Libraries News* 64 (March 2003): 163–66.

Particularly noteworthy is the "Archivist's Toolkit" published by the Archives Association of British Columbia, designed "as a community resource for use by those working primarily in small and medium-sized archives in British Columbia." It includes Laura Coles, "Reference Services and Public Relations Activities," from its *Manual for Small Archives* (1988) and a number of forms and useful links to on-line repository policies and procedures. Visit http://aabc.bc.ca/aabc/toolkit.html.

Another example is found in "Museum Archives and Manuscript Collections" in appendix D: 45–56 in the National Park Service's *Museum Handbook,* vol. 2, and "Museum Collections Use," chapters 1 and 2 in *Museum Handbook,* vol. 3, both located at http://www.cr.nps.gov/museum/publications/handbook.html. All were written by archivist Diane Vogt-O'Connor, although not credited to her.

The Council for State Records Coordinators (COSHRC) provides links to technical information regarding education, how to use primary resources, and the status of state records programs, as well as professional field links to glossaries, resource directories, and archival organizations. Visit http://www.coshrc.org/.

Reference archivists may find the following sites useful for providing reference services or for their own research. American Law Sources On-Line (ALSO!) provides links to on-line sources of United States and Canadian law available without charge at http://www.law source.com/also/. See also, "Geographic Names Information System," found at http://geonames.usgs.gov/ and RootsWeb at http://www. rootsweb.com/, which provides assistance to genealogists.

The Academy of Certified Archivists maintains the *Role Delineation Statement for Professional Archivists,* which details the elements that encompass commonly accepted duties and responsibilities at http://www.certifiedarchivists.org/html/RoleDelineation.html.

David Mattison, "Images of History on the Web," *Searcher* 10 (May 2002), provides an excellent introduction to images on the Web. Visit http://www.infotoday.com/searcher/may02/mattison.htm. The Center for History and New Media at George Mason University "History Matters," at http://historymatters.gmu.edu/ provides links for teachers of American history.

Related Organizations

Library reference literature is helpful. Anyone charged with providing reference services must have access to the magisterial *Guide to Reference Books,* 11th ed. (Chicago: American Library Association, 1996). The twelfth edition will be titled *Guide to Reference Sources* and will be published on-line. The Reference and User Services Association (RUSA) of the American Library Association publishes *Reference & User Services Quarterly* (formerly titled *RQ*), as well as guidelines and standards.

The Association of College and Research Libraries publishes two journals, RBM: *A Journal of Rare Books, Manuscripts, and Cultural Heritage,* formerly known as *Rare Books and Manuscripts Librarianship,* and *College and Research Libraries,* as well as a newsletter, *College and Research Libraries News.* Its Web site also provides its standards and guidelines. RBMS Special Collections on the Web "contains links to indexes of special collections libraries and archival repositories, both general and specialized, around the world." Visit it at http://www.rbms.nd.edu/links/spec_colls_on_web.shtml.

The Special Libraries Association publishes the journal *Information Outlook*. It recently updated its *Competencies for Information Professionals of the 21st Century* in June 2003. See it at http://www.sla.org/content/learn/comp2003/index.cfm.

The Haworth Press publishes a number of journals in the area of reference services, most of which it also publishes as monographs.

The Internet makes it possible to scan the larger information universe. One of the most useful sites is the electronic journal D-LIB *Magazine* at http://www.dlib.org/, which publishes research articles and frequently includes writings on archival issues. RLG *DigiNews* publishes brief reports on research news at http://www.rlg.org/en/page.php?Page_ID=12081.

Keeping Up

The Society of American Archivists publishes the peer-reviewed journal the *American Archivist* and the newsletter *Archival Outlook*. A number of regional organizations publish substantial peer-reviewed journals, most notably, *Archival Issues*, published by the Midwest Archives Conference and *Provenance*, published by the Society of Georgia Archivists. Recently, two additional peer-reviewed journals have appeared, published by commercial presses. Kluwer Academic Publishers, based in the Netherlands, publishes *Archival Science* and Haworth Press has begun publication of the *Journal of Archival Organization*.

Archival journals from other English-speaking countries are also thought provoking, especially the excellent journal *Archivaria* by the Association of Canadian Archivists. Visit it at http://archivists.ca. See also the *Journal of the Society of Archivists* (United Kingdom) at http://www.archives.org.uk/; *Archives and Manuscripts: The Journal of the Australian Society of Archivists* at http://www.archivists.org.au/; and *Archifacts*, published by the Archives and Records Association of New Zealand at http://www.aranz.org.nz. Getting access to all of these journals is a problem for archivists outside major universities.

The International Council on Archives (ica) publishes serial publications, reports, and studies and provides useful links at http://www.ica.org/. The unesco "Archives Portal: An International Gateway to Information for Archivists and Archives Users" provides links to archival repositories and resources at http://www.unesco.org/webworld/portal_archives.

Understanding the Creation of Records and Archives

Interestingly enough, the advent of electronic communications networks has inspired new study of older communications systems. All reference archivists should read the first chapters of JoAnne Yates, *Control Through Communication: The Rise of System in American Management* (Baltimore: Johns Hopkins University Press, 1989) for its fine discussion of the history of organizational communication, information flows, information technology, and document forms. Bruce Breummer and Sheldon Hochheiser undertake a similar analysis of emerging organizations in *The High-Technology Company: A Historical Research and Archival Guide* (Minneapolis: Charles Babbage Institute, 1989). My introduction to these ideas was Hugh Taylor, "'My Very Act and Deed': Some Reflections on the Role of Textual Records in the Conduct of Affairs," *American Archivist* 51 (Fall 1998): 456–69, which remains worth reading.

Three review essays provide an archival context for recent monographs of interest to archivists. Margaret Hedstrom provides an archival framework for understanding records creation and electronic recordkeeping in her seminal article, "Understanding Electronic Incunabula: A Framework for Research on Electronic Records," *American Archivist* 54 (Summer 1991): 334–54; James O'Toole reviews recent research on literacy as it relates to the use of written records in "Toward a Usable Archival Past: Recent Studies in the History of Literacy," *American Archivist* 58 (Winter 1995): 86–99; and Peter J. Wosh reviews books relating to the postal service, "the first national information infrastructure," in relation to record making, recordkeeping, and communication patterns in the nineteenth century in "Going Postal," *American Archivist* 61 (Spring 1998): 220–39.

Ann Pederson, "Understanding Society through Its Records," is an effective on-line introduction to recordkeeping, and the use of records to ensure evidence and empower justice. Visit http://john.curtin.edu.au/ society/. A case study demonstrating the need to understand the creation of records to provide reference services for them is Naomi L. Nelson, "Taking a Byte Out of the Senate: Reconsidering the Research Use of Correspondence and Casework Files," *Provenance* 15 (1997): 37–62.

I found a number of new studies thought provoking: especially David M. Levy, *Scrolling Forward: Making Sense of Documents in the Digital Age* (New York: Arcade Publishing, 2001); Bernardo A. Huberman, *The Laws of the Web: Patterns in the Ecology of Information* (Cambridge, Mass.: MIT Press, 2001); and Abigail J. Sellen and Richard R. R. Harper, *The Myth of the Paperless Office* (Cambridge, Mass.: MIT Press, 2002).

Richard J. Cox, "Bibliography and Reference for the Archivist," *American Archivist* 46 (Spring 1983): 185–87; and Lawrence J. McCrank, "History, Archives, and Information Science," *Annual Review of Information Science and Technology* (1995) place archives in the larger information universe. Provocative and important is David Bearman, *Archival Methods*, Archives and Museum Informatics Report 9 (Pittsburgh: Archives and Museum Informatics, 1989). Kenneth E. Foote explores the relationship of archives, artifacts, and memorials in "To Remember and Forget: Archives, Memory, and Culture," *American Archivist* 53 (Summer 1990): 378–92. Francis X. Blouin explores how archivists shape archives in "Archives, Mediation, and Constructs of Social Memory," *Archival Issues* 24 (1999): 101–112.

Users of Archives

Early Views of Users

Systematic exploration of the uses and users of archives is a recent phenomenon. The elitism of the Historical Manuscripts Tradition persisted well into the twentieth century. See, for example, Howard Peckham, "Aiding the Scholar in Using Manuscript Collections," *American Archivist* 19 (July 1956): 221–28; and Jean Preston, "Problems in the Use of Manuscripts," *American Archivist* 28 (July 1965): 367–79. In contrast, the Public Archives Tradition, which became dominant in the past fifty years, emphasizes reference services to the general public. See, for example, Margaret Pierson, "Reference Services in the Indiana State Archives," and W. G. Ormsby, "Reference Service in the Public Archives of Canada," both in *American Archivist* 25 (July 1962): 341–51. Richard Berner describes these traditions in *Archival Theory and Practice in the United States: A Historical Analysis* (Seattle: University of Washington Press, 1983).

A considerable portion of the literature about archival reference services began as articles discussing the relationship between the user and the archivist. See, for example, Frank B. Evans, "The State Archivist and the Academic Researcher," *American Archivist* 26 (July 1963): 319–21; William F. Birdsall, "The Two Sides of the Desk: Archivist and Historian, 1909–1935," *American Archivist* 38 (April 1975): 159–73; and Dale C. Mayer, "The New Social History: Implications for Archivists," *American Archivist* 48 (Fall 1985): 388–99.

User-Centered Archival Administration

In the mid-1980s, some archivists urged the profession to be driven by the needs of users. Elsie Freeman Finch led this discussion and urged archivists to "begin to think of archives administration as client-centered, not materials-centered," in "In the Eye of the Beholder: Archives Administration from the User's Point of View," *American Archivist* 47 (Spring 1984): 111–23, and in "Buying Quarter Inch Holes: Public Support through Results," *Midwestern Archivist* 10 (1985): 89–97. Others promoting this perspective include Mary Jo Pugh, "The Illusion of Omniscience: Subject Access and the Reference Archivist," *American Archivist* 45 (Winter 1982): 33–44, reprinted in *Modern Archives Reader: Basic Readings on Archival Theory and Practice* (Washington, D.C.: National Archives, 1984); Hugh Taylor, *Archival Services and the Concept of The User: A RAMP Study* (Paris: UNESCO, 1984); William L. Joyce, "Archivists and Research Use," *American Archivist* 47 (Spring 1984): 124–33; David Bearman and Richard H. Lytle, "The Power of the Principle of Provenance," *Archivaria* 21 (1985): 14–27; Bruce Dearstyne, "What Is the Use of Archives? A Challenge for the Profession," *American*

Archivist 50 (Winter 1987): 76–87; Planning Group on the Educational Potential of Archives, Committee on Goals and Priorities, *An Action Agenda for the Archival Profession: Institutionalizing the Planning Process* (Chicago: Society of American Archivists, 1988); Lawrence Dowler, "The Role of Use in Defining Archival Practice and Principle: A Research Agenda for the Availability and Use of Records," *American Archivist* 51 (Winter and Spring 1988): 74–86; and Randall C. Jimerson, "Redefining Archival Identity: Meeting User Needs in the Information Society," *American Archivist* 52 (Summer 1989): 332–40.

Carolyn Heald, "Reference Services in Archives: Whither a Professional Ethos?" *CLJ (Canadian Library Journal)* 49 (October 1992): 353–59, believes that reference service is not part of the professional archival ethos. A student paper in a library journal, it offers a critical, albeit simplistic, analysis. Gabrielle Blais and David Enns, in "From Paper Archives to People Archives: Public Programming in the Management of Archives," *Archivaria* 31 (Winter 1990–91): 101–10, argue that public programming must recognize image, awareness, education, and use. Paul Macpherson argues that public user access must be part of the life-cycle continuum from the beginning and not tacked on at the end in "Public Access to Post-current Government Records," *Archives and Manuscripts* 30 (2002): 6–17.

Terry Cook, however, cautions archivists about wholesale adoption of corporate marketing strategies and customer analysis and argues instead that we must acknowledge the contextual nature of archives to enrich the user's experience in archives in "Viewing the World Upside Down: Reflections on the Theoretical Underpinnings of Archival Public Programming," *Archivaria* 31 (Winter 1990–91): 123–34. Barbara L. Craig furthers this Canadian perspective and argues that archival reference services must respect and promote provenance when reaching out to new users in "What Are the Clients? Who Are the Products?: The Future of Archival Public Services in Perspective," *Archivaria* 31 (Winter 1990–91).

User Studies

General Works

Archivists have called for user studies for several decades and frequently blame each other for not having done them, particularly in comparison with librarians, who have done thousands of them. Archivists, however, have done a fair number of studies. The problem is not the doing; the problem for both professions is using them to make changes. I cannot see that the studies of library users have done much to change the catalogs, indexes, and other tools used by librarians. The Library of Congress Subject Headings remain opaque to all.

Richard J. Cox in "Researching Archival Reference as an Information Function: Observations on Needs and Opportunities," *RQ* (Spring 1992): 387–39, groups research about archival reference into four areas: research about use in archival repositories, research into the accuracy and effectiveness of archival reference, studies of the impact of technology on research in archives, and research about the interaction between researcher and reference archivist.

Paul Conway has been instrumental in showing archivists the value and practice of studying users of repositories. In 1985, he found that most archives did not collect even the most rudimentary information about use, reporting his findings in "Perspectives on Archival Resources: The 1985 Census of Archival Institutions," *American Archivist* 50 (Spring 1987): 186–90. His article "Research in Presidential Libraries: A User Study," *Midwestern Archivist* 11 (1986): 35–56, is a practical study. Also useful is a 1987 paper, "User Models: Past, Present, Future: Enhancing Evaluation in the Automated Reference Environment." Another article, "Facts and Frameworks: An Approach to Studying the Users of Archives," *American Archivist* 49 (Fall 1986): 393–407, sets forth an intellectual framework that he tested and refined in his seminal research work, *Improving Access to the Nation's Archive: User Studies at the National Archives and Records Administration* (Pittsburgh: Archives and Museum Informatics, 1994).

Ann D. Gordon, *Using the Nation's Documentary Heritage: The Report of the Historical Documents Study* (Washington, D.C.: NHPRC, 1992) looked at the use of published historical documents. Richard

Cox's review of this report, "Archivists and the Use of Archival Records: Or, A View from the World of Documentary Editing," *Provenance* 9 (Spring-Fall 1991): 69–110, provides a thoughtful response to the study.

A compilation of user studies is found in *Midwestern Archivist* 11 (Summer 1986). It includes William J. Maher, "The Use of User Studies"; Jacqueline Goggin, "The Indirect Approach: A Study of Scholarly Users of Black and Women's Organizational Records in the Library of Congress Manuscripts Division"; Roy C. Turnbaugh, "Archival Mission and User Studies"; and Paul Conway, "Research in Presidential Libraries: A User Survey."

Other user studies include Clark Elliott, "Citation Patterns and Documentation for the History of Science: Some Methodological Considerations," *American Archivist* 44 (Spring 1981): 143–50; Fredric Miller, "Use, Appraisal and Research: A Case Study of Social History," *American Archivist* 49 (Fall 1986): 371–92; Bruce R. Bruemmer, "Keeping Track of Reference Use," *MAC Newsletter* (October 1988): 15–18; David Bearman, "User Presentation Language in Archives," *Archives and Museum Informatics* 3 (Winter 1989-90): 3–7; William J. Jackson, "The 80/20 Archives: A Study of Use and Its Implications," *Archival Issues* 22 (1997): 133–45; Kristina L. Southwell, "How Researchers Learn of Manuscript Resources at the Western History Collections," *Archival Issues* 26 (2002): 91–109; and Susan Hamburger, "How Researchers Search for Manuscript and Archival Collections," *Journal of Archival Organization* 2 (2004): 79–97.

Helen Tibbo and her students at the University of North Carolina have conducted important research in the use of archives. Master's theses include, for example, Marion Hirsch, *The Use of Manuscripts and Archives in Southern History: A Citation Study of Recent Articles from Bibliographies in the Journal of Southern History*, 1991; Elizabeth Ellis, *The Uses of Unpublished Materials by Literary Scholars: A Citation Study*, 1994; Jane Helen Ibl, *World Wide Web Pages and Academic Archives and Manuscript Repositories in North Carolina: A Survey and Recommendations for Standards*, 1996; and Shayera D. Tangri, *Evaluating Changes in the Methods by which Users of the University of North Carolina at Chapel Hill Manuscript Department Learn of the Holdings of the Department*, 2000. Tibbo challenges the profession to undertake systematic studies with "Learning to Love

Our Users: A Challenge to the Profession and a Model for Practice," Midwest Archives Conference, 4 May 2002, published in *Archival Issues*.

British archivists have begun systematic and shared user studies: Anthony L. Butler, "The Results of a Survey of Visitors to Warwickshire County Record Office," *Journal of the Society of Archivists*, 17 (1996): 175–81; Heather Forbes and Rosemary Dunhill, "Survey of Local Authority Archive Services: 1996 Update," *Journal of the Society of Archivists* 18 (1997): 37–53; and Jone Garmendia, "User" Input in the Development of Online Services: The PRO Catalogue, *Journal of the Society of Archivists* 23 (2002): 51–57.

Scholars

Avra Michelson and Jeff Rothenberg, "Scholarly Communication and Information Technology: Exploring the Impact of Changes in the Research Process on Archives," *American Archivist* 55 (Spring 1992): 236–315 is a good place to start. It is a major research study, providing many insights into the work of scholars and offering an extensive bibliography.

Relationships with scholars can be seen in Walter Rundell, Jr., *In Pursuit of American History: Research and Training in the United States* (Norman: University of Oklahoma Press, 1970); Fredric Miller, "Use, Appraisal, and Research: A Case Study of Social History," *American Archivist* 49 (Fall 1986): 371–92; Dale C. Mayer, "The New Social History: Implications for Archivists," *American Archivist* 48 (Fall 1985): 388–99; and Alonzo L. Hamby and Edward Weldon, *Access to Papers of Recent Public Figures: The New Harmony Conference* (Bloomington, Ind.: Organization of American Historians, 1977).

Examples of user studies focusing on traditional academic historical scholars start with Michael E. Stevens, "The Historian and Archival Finding Aids," *Georgia Archive* 5 (Winter 1977): 64–74; and Margaret Steig, "The Information of [*sic*] Needs of Historians," *College and Research Libraries* 42 (November 1981): 544–60. Later studies include Stephen E. Wiberley, Jr. and William C. Jones, "Patterns of Information Seeking in the Humanities," *College and Research Libraries* 50 (November 1989): 638–45; Diane Beattie, "An Archival User Study: Researchers in the Field of Women's History" *Archivaria*

29 (Winter 1989–90); and Donald Owen Case, "The Collection and Use of Information by Some American Historian: A Study of Motives and Methods," *Library Quarterly* 61 (1991): 61–82. Don C. Skemer, "Drifting Disciplines, Enduring Records: Political Science and the Use of Archives," *American Archivist* 54 (Summer 1991): 357–68, recommends studying trends in particular academic disciplines to identify new users and target outreach efforts. He notes that political scientists make little use of archival sources and discusses why this is so. Judy Reynolds reviews studies of the research habits of humanists in "A Brave New World: User Studies in the Humanities Enter the Electronic Age," *The Reference Librarian* 49–50 (1995): 61–81. See also Mary B. Folster, "Information Seeking Patterns: Social Sciences," *Library Users and Reference Services* (New York: Haworth Press, 1995): 83–93 and Charles Cole, "Name Collection by Ph.D History Students: Inducing Expertise," *Journal of the American Society for Information Science* 51 (2000): 444–55. Helen R. Tibbo shared her paper "Primarily History: Historians and the Search for Primary Source Materials," presented at JCDL in July 2002 and published in *American Archivist* 66 (Spring/Summer 2003): 9–50.

Ann D. Gordon studies legal historians in "A Portrait of Research in Legal History," in *Public Services Issues with Rare and Archival Law Materials,* edited by Michael Widener (New York: Haworth Press, 2001), also published as *Legal Reference Services Quarterly* 20 (2001): 5–16. Gari-Anne Patzwald and Sister Carole Marie Wildt discuss "The Use of Convent Archival Records in Medical Research: The School Sisters of Notre Dame and the Nun Study," *American Archivist* 67 (Spring/Summer 2004): 86–106.

STUDENTS

Michael Drake, of the Open University in the United Kingdom, nicely sums up the power of historical research to empower and liberate students and discusses means for structuring the experience for them in "The Democratisation of Historical Research: The Case for DA301," *Journal of the Society of Archivists* 17 (1996). Marian J. Matyn offers practical advice for structuring the student experience in "Getting Undergraduates to Seek Primary Sources in Archives," *History Teacher*

33 (May 2000): 349–55. This article also demonstrates how archivists can reach out to other audiences through their publications. Frank Manista and Jeanine Mazak also offer practical experience with "University Archives and Freshman Composition," *Reference Librarian* (1999) and www.msu.edu/Manistaf/archives.html.

There is a growing literature on using archives with students. See Elsie Freeman Finch, *Teaching with Documents: Using Primary Sources from the National Archives* (Washington, D.C.: National Archives, 1989); Mark A. Greene, "Using College and University Archives as Instructional Materials," *Midwestern Archivist* 14 (1989): 31–38; Marcus C. Robyns, "The Archivist as Educator: Integrating Critical Thinking Skills into Historical Research Methods Instruction," *American Archivist* 64 (Fall/Winter 2001): 363–84; and Anne J. Gilliland-Swetland, "An Exploration of K-12 User Needs for Digital Primary Source Materials," *American Archivist* 61 (1998): 137–57. Anne J. Gilliland-Swetland, Yasmin B. Kafai, and William E. Landis, "Integrating Primary Sources in the Elementary School Classroom," *Archivaria* 48 (Fall 1999): 89–116 is noteworthy as a research study that identifies methodologies for integrating primary sources in classrooms, reports on teacher perspectives, and suggests means for building partnerships between archivists and teachers.

Core research competencies for graduate students in history are discussed by Edwin Bridges, Gregory S. Hunter, Page Putman Miller, David Thelan, and Gerhard Weinberg, in "Toward Better Documenting and Interpreting of the Past: What History Graduate Programs in the Twenty-first Century Should Teach About Archival Practices," *American Archivist* 56 (Fall 1993): 730–49.

GENEALOGISTS

The literature relating to genealogists is scarce, especially considering the importance of this group. See Phebe R. Jacobsen, "'The World Turned Upside Down': Reference Priorities and the State Archives," *American Archivist* 44 (Fall 1981): 341–45. See also Peter W. Bunce, "Towards a More Harmonious Relationship: A Challenge to Archivists and Genealogists," and Elizabeth Shown Mills, "Genealogists and Archivists: Communicating, Cooperating, and Coping!" *SAA Newsletter*

(May 1990); Gail R. Redmann, "Archivists and Genealogists: The Trend toward Peaceful Coexistence," *Archival Issues* 18 (1993): 121–32; and Rosemary Boyns, "Archivists and Family Historians: Local Authority Record Repositories and the Family History User Group," *Journal of the Society of Archivists* 20 (1999): 62–74. R. Philip Reynolds in "Building User-Oriented Web Sites for Archives," *Provenance* 14 (1996): 49-71, provides a very helpful resource for building a Web site responsive to the needs of genealogists. A seminal research article is Wendy M. Duff and Deborah A. Torres, "Where is the List with All the Names? Information-Seeking Behavior of Genealogists," *American Archivist* 66 (Spring-Summer 2003): 79–95. In spite of his title, "Business Orientation and Customer Service Delivery: The Tyranny of the Customer," Bruno B. W. Longmore effectively describes how moving many of the services for genealogical research to the Web provided a business opportunity for archives and improved service for researchers in *Journal of the Society of Archivists* 21 (April 2000): 27–36.

Aprille Cook McKay, in "Genealogists and Records: Preservation, Advocacy and Politics," *Archival Issues* 21 (2002): 23–33, discusses strategies by which archivists and genealogists can build collaborative and cooperative relationships and forge alliances to advocate for preservation and access.

Diane K. Kovacs, *Genealogical Research on the Web* (New York: Neal-Schuman Publishers, 2001), gives a good introduction to the basics of genealogical research and an extensive annotated list of relevant Web sites. Another introduction is *The Genealogist's Handbook: Modern Methods for Researching Family History* (Chicago: American Library Association, 1995). The Board for Certification of Genealogists maintains a useful Web site at http://www.bcgcertification.org/.

Visual Researchers

A particularly thoughtful analysis of the uses of visual information in video productions is found in Kathleen Epp, "Telling Stories around the 'Electronic Campfire': The Use of Archives in Television Productions," *Archivaria* 49 (Spring 2000): 54–83. Elisabeth Kaplan and Jeffery Mifflin, "'Mind and Sight': Visual Literacy and the Archivist," *Archival Issues* 21 (1996): 107–27, review the concept of visual literacy and its application to the work of archivists. Joan M. Schwartz considers the uses of visual imagery in a thoughtful review essay, "Negotiating the Visual Turn: New Perspectives on Images and Archives," *American Archivist* 67 (Spring/Summer 2004): 107–122. Mary Lynn Ritzenthaler, Gerald J. Munoff, and Margery S. Long, *Administration of Photographic Collections* (Chicago: Society of American Archivists, 1984) is useful for archivists providing reference services for visual records. It is being revised by Mary Lynn Ritzenthaler and Diane Vogt-O'Connor, and will appear in 2005 as *Photographs: Archival Care and Management.*

See also Caroline R. Arms, "Getting the Picture: Observation from the Library of Congress on Providing Online Access to Pictorial Images," *Library Trends* 48 (Fall 1999): 379–409; and Karen Collins, "Providing Subject Access to Images: A Study of User Queries," *American Archivist* 61 (Spring 1998): 36–55.

The User's Point of View

Some archival users have described their experiences in print. Examples include Philip D. Jordan, "The Scholar and the Archivist," *American Archivist* 31 (January 1968): 57–65; and Laurence R. Veysey, "A Scholar's View of University Archives," *College and University Archives: Selected Readings* (Chicago: Society of American Archivists, 1979): 145–54. Page Putnam Miller explores viewpoints of more than fifty scholarly users of the National Archives in *Developing a Premier National Institution: A Report from the User Community to the National Archives* (Washington, D.C.: National Coordinating Committee for the Promotion of History, 1989). Barbara C. Orbach, "The View from the Researcher's Desk: Historians' Perception of Research and Repositories," *American Archivist* 54 (Winter 1991): 29–43, presents the views of ten historians and notes that citations, recommendations of colleagues, guides, and dialogue with repository staff are the most frequent means by which historians find relevant materials. Lois More Overbeck presents very practical and reasonable requests in "Researching Literary Manuscripts: A Scholar's Perspective," *American Archivist* 56 (Winter 1993): 62–69. Gillian North reports on the helpfulness of Internet resources in "Distance Researching via the Internet: A Researcher's Perspective," *Provenance* 16 (1996): 73-86.

Critical commentaries are Carl M. Brauer, "Researcher Evaluation of Reference Services," *American Archivist* 43 (Winter 1980): 77–79; and Mary N. Speakman, "The User Talks Back," *American Archivist* 47 (Spring 1984): 164–71. Michael R. Hill, *Archival Strategies and Techniques*, Qualitative Research Methods Volume 31 (Newbury Park, Calif.: Sage Publications, 1993) is a sobering indictment of how archival reference services look to a sociologist and demonstrates the gap between how archivists see themselves and how users see them. Gregory Hunter extrapolates these insights into charts contrasting the two perspectives in *Developing and Maintaining Practical Archives* (New York: Neal-Schuman Publishers, 1997): 190–91.

A conference on "How Does Society Perceive Archives?" was held in Marseilles, France, 13–16 November 2002. See http://www.archives-defrance.culture.gouv.fr/. A useful perspective from a related field is found in Mihaly Csikszentmihalyi and Kim Hermanson, "Intrinsic Motivation in Museums: What Makes Visitors Want to Learn?" *Museum News* (May/June 1995), which discusses the relationship of curiosity, interest, and the "flow experience" in engaging visitors in learning. Wendy Duff and Penka Stoyanova discuss the on-line display of archival information from the user's point of view in "Transforming the Crazy Quilt: Archival Displays from a User's Point of View," *Archivaria* 45 (Spring 1998): 44–67.

Users with Special Needs

The special needs of handicapped users have not been discussed widely in print. A good place to start is the *Americans with Disabilities Act* (ADA) Home Page at http://www.usdoj.gov/crt/ada/adahom1/htm. Recent articles include Andrew Whiteside, "Enhancing Provision of Archive Services for the Visually Impaired," *Journal of the Society of Archivists* 23 (2002): 74–86; and Mary Minow, "Welcome to. . . the Legal Responsibility to Offer Accessible Electronic Information to Patrons with Disabilities," *Libraries, Museums, and Archives: Legal Issues and Ethical Challenges in the New Information Era* (Lanham, Md.: Scarecrow Press, 2002): 113–57. Ronald L. Gilardi, "The Archival Setting and People with Disabilities: A Legal Analysis," *American Archivist* 56 (Fall 1993): 704–13; Lance J. Fischer, "The Deaf and

Archival Research: Some Problems and Solutions," *American Archivist* 42 (October 1979): 463–64; and Brenda Beasley Kepley, "Archives: Access for the Disabled," *American Archivist* 46 (Winter 1983): 42–51, remain useful as well.

Information Seeking

Research into information seeking crosses a number of disciplines. My interest was stimulated by several articles by Marcia J. Bates, beginning with "The Design of Browsing and Berrypicking Techniques for the Online Search Interface," *Online Review* 13 (October 1989):407–24. Her bibliography is extensive and her perspectives most recently summarized in "Toward an Integrated Model of Information Seeking and Searching," keynote address for the Fourth International Conference on Information Needs, Seeking and Use in Different Contexts, Lisbon Portugal, September 2002, on-line at http://www.gseis.ucla.edu/faculty/ bates/articles/info_SeekSearch-i-030329.html.

Gary Marchionini also introduced me to this field. He has an extensive bibliography, most notably, *Information Seeking in Electronic Environments* (Cambridge: Cambridge University Press, 1997). A useful introduction is his "Resource Search and Discovery," delivered at the Getty Art History Information Program in 1995, on-line at http:// www.ils.unc.edu/~march/getty.pdf.

A seminal review essay is Brenda Dervin and Michael Nilan, "Information Needs and Uses," *Annual Review of Information Science and Technology* 21 (1986): 3–33, followed by Helen Tibbo, "Information Systems, Services, and Technology for the Humanities," *Annual Review of Information Science and Technology* 26 (1991): 287–346; and William Sugar's review "User-Centered Perspective of Information Retrieval Research and Analysis Methods," *Annual Review of Information Science and Technology* 30 (1995): 77–109. A view of information seeking that is both organic and humane is found in Bonnie A. Nardi and Vicki L. O'Day, *Information Ecologies: Using Technology with Heart* (Cambridge: MIT Press, 1999).

The *American Archivist* published a special section on users and archival research in Volume 66 (Spring/Summer 2003), which came to hand as I completed copy-editing this manuscript. Its contents are important and should be read by all reference archivists: Helen R. Tibbo, "Primarily History in America: How u.s. Historians Search for Primary Materials at the Dawn of the Digital Age," 9–50; Elizabeth Yakel and Deborah A. Torres, "AI: Archival Intelligence and User Expertise," 51–78; Wendy M. Duff and Catherine A. Johnson, "Where is the List with All the Names? Information-Seeking Behavior of Genealogists," 79–95; and Barbara L. Craig, "Perimeters with Fences? Or Thresholds with Doors? Two Views of a Border," 96–101.

Reference Process

Intellectual Aspects of Reference Service

The intellectual functions of reference services in archives, especially the nature of mediation in provenance-based systems, have not been widely explored. Frank Burke succinctly described the indispensable role of the archivist in providing subject access in his deceptively titled, "The Impact of the Specialist on Archives," *College and Research Libraries* 33 (1972): 321–17. Richard Lytle identified and analyzed the two methods of access in "Intellectual Access to Archives: Provenance and Content Indexing Methods of Subject Retrieval," *American Archivist* 43 (Winter 1980): 64–75. Mary Jo Pugh elaborated these insights in "The Illusion of Omniscience: Subject Access and the Reference Archivist," *American Archivist* 45 (Winter 1982): 33–44, reprinted in *Modern Archives Reader.*

An excellent discussion of the intellectual aspects of the reference interaction in archives is found in American Management Systems, *Methodology for Developing an Expert System for Information Retrieval at the National Archives and Records Administration* (Washington, D.C.: National Archives and Records Administration, 1986). Frederick Stielow and Helen Tibbo offer a unique perspective in, "The Negative Search, Online Reference, and the Humanities: A Critical Essay in Library Literature," *RQ* 27 (Spring 1988): 358–65, whose insights about the usefulness of a negative search have not apparently received the attention they would appear to deserve.

William Saffady first noted the educational role of the reference archivist in "Reference Services to Researchers in Archives," *RQ* (Winter 1974): 139–44, followed more recently by Marcus C. Robyns, "The Archivist as Educator: Integrating Critical Thinking Skills into Historical Research Methods Instruction," *American Archivist* 64 (Fall/Winter 2001): 363–84. Recent literature notes the uses of archives in K–12 education. See Anne J. Gilliland-Swetland, "An Exploration of K–12 User Needs for Digital Primary Source Materials," *American Archivist* 61 (1998): 136–57; and Anne J. Gilliland-Swetland, Y. Kafai, and William Landis, "Integrating Primary Sources into the Elementary School Classroom: A Case Study of Teachers' Perspectives," *Archivaria* 48 (1999): 89–116.

Elizabeth Yakel argues for a new vision for reference services in the new millennium, particularly stressing the multiple roles organizational archivists might play as knowledge brokers, making archives part of knowledge management in organizations. See, for example, "Thinking Inside and Outside the Boxes: Archival Reference Services at the Turn of the Century," *Archivaria* 49 (Spring 2000): 140–59, and "Knowledge Management: The Archivist's and Records Manager's Perspective," *Information Management Journal* 34 (July 2000): 24–30. Richard M. Kesner makes a similar argument in "Information Resource Management in the Electronic Workplace: A Personal Perspective on 'Archives in the Information Society,'" *American Archivist* 61 (Spring 1998): 70–87.

Improving intellectual access through finding aids has been widely discussed in recent years, although this literature rarely examines the relationship of finding aids and the reference process. Seminal articles include David Bearman and Richard Lytle, "The Power of the Principle of Provenance," *Archivaria* 21 (1985–1986): 14–27; and "Archival Descriptive Standards: Establishing a Process for Their Development and Implementation. Report and Recommendations of the Working Group on Standards for Archival Description," *American Archivist* 52 (Fall 1989): 440–77. Most recently, Elizabeth Yakel examined arrangement and description as socially constructed practices in "Archival Representation," *Archival Science* 3 (2003): 1–25.

The development of the MARC format for archives and manuscripts prompted study of the implications of the use of the national bibliographic databases. See for example, David Bearman, "Archives and Manuscript Control with Bibliographic Utilities: Opportunities and Challenges," *American Archivist* 52 (Winter 1989): 26–39; Nancy Sahli, "National Information Systems and Strategies for Research Use," *Midwestern Archivist* 9 (1984): 5–14; and Avra Michelson, "Description and Reference in the Age of Automation," *American Archivist* 50 (Spring 1987): 192–208.

In the early 1990s, archivists studied the implementation of the MARC format. Robert P. Spindler and Richard Pearce-Moses asked, "Does AMC Mean 'Archives Made Confusing'? Patron Understanding of USMARC AMC Catalog Records," *American Archivist* 57 (Spring 1993): 330–341. Lyn M. Martin assessed the use of MARC in "Viewing the Field: A Literature Review and Survey of the Use of U.S. MARC AMC in U.S. Academic Archives," *American Archivist* 57 (Summer 1994): 482–97; and Helen R. Tibbo explored the consequences of subject searches in the national bibliographic databases in "'The Epic Struggle: Subject Retrieval from Large Bibliographic Databases," *American Archivist* 57 (Spring 1994): 310–26.

Tyler O. Walters explored "Automated Access Practices at Archival Repositories of Association of Research Libraries Institutions," *Archival Issues* 23 (1998): 171–89. Rita L. H. Czeck compared "Archival MARC Records and Finding Aids in the Context of End-User Subject Access to Archival Collections," *American Archivist* 61 (Fall 1998): 426–40.

Development of the Encoded Archival Description (EAD) proceeded apace as archivists began to implement MARC. Steven L. Henson reviewed these events in "NISTF II and EAD: The Evolution of Archival Description," *American Archivist* 60 (Summer 1997): 284–96. Jill M. Tatem outlined the difficulties with simply automating existing finding aids without understanding how users use them in "EAD: Obstacles to Implementation, Opportunities for Understanding," *Archival Issues* 23 (1998): 155–69. Recent research on electronic access to finding aids is found in Wendy Duff and Penka Stoyanova, "Transforming the Crazy Quilt: Archival Displays from a User's Point of View," *Archivaria* 45 (Spring 1998): 44–79. Two essays in *Encoded Archival Description on the Internet* (Binghamton, N.Y.: Haworth Press, 2001) assess the impact of EAD on reference services: Richard V. Szary, "Encoded Finding Aids as a Transforming Technology in Archival Reference Service," and Anne J. Gilliland-Swetland, "Popularizing the

Finding Aid: Exporting EAD to Enhance Online Discovery and Retrieval in Archival Information Systems by Diverse User Groups," which demonstrates how the finding aid might be linked with actual information-seeking behaviors. Michelle Light and Tom Hyry, "Colophons and Annotations: New Directions for the Finding Aid," *American Archivist* 65 (Fall/Winter 2002): 216–30, suggest that annotations be used to enhance description by reference archivists and users.

James Lambert, "L'archivistique au service des chercheurs: le respect des fonds et l'acces a l'information dans les services d'archives," *Archivaria* 45 (Spring 1998): 12–17, argues that both provenance and knowledgeable archivists are needed to compensate for the limitations of description, whether automated or not. Forthcoming in *American Archivist* but not yet at hand is Christopher J. Prom, "User Interaction with Electronic Finding Aids in a Controlled Setting."

Interpersonal Aspects of Reference Services

In contrast to the library literature, which is voluminous, little has been published about the interpersonal elements of the reference encounter in archives. The classic library text is William Katz, *Introduction to Reference Work,* especially part 3 on interview and search (Boston: McGraw-Hill, 2002). A practical and stimulating manual is *Conducting the Reference Interview: A How-To-Do-It Manual for Librarians,* by Catherine Sheldrick Ross, Kirsti Nilsen, and Patricia Dewdney (New York: Neal-Schuman Publishers, 2002).

An early discussion of reference services in archives that emphasized the human element is Robert Rosenthal, "The User and the Used," *Drexel Library Quarterly* (January 1975): 97–105. The best introduction remains Linda J. Long, "Question Negotiation in the Archival Setting: The Use of Interpersonal Communication Techniques in the Reference Interview," *American Archivist* 52 (Winter 1989): 40–51. Susan L. Malbin, "The Reference Interview in Archival Literature," *College and Research Libraries* 58 (January 1997): 69–80, provides a useful critique of the literature and a penetrating analysis of research needs. Helen Tibbo further elaborates the topic in "Interviewing Techniques for Remote Reference: Electronic versus Traditional

Environments," *American Archivist* 58 (Summer 1995): 294–310. For thought-provoking charts contrasting the perspectives of archivists and users, see Gregory Hunter *Developing and Maintaining Practical Archives, op. cit.* See also, Rhea Joyce Rubin, *Defusing the Angry Patron: A How-To-Do-It Manual for Librarians and Professionals* (New York: Neal-Schuman Publishers, 2000).

Reference Services on the Web

An excellent review of the paradigm shift in reference services is found in Carol Tenopir and Lisa A. Ennis, "A Decade of Digital Reference: 1991–2001," *Reference & User Services Quarterly* 41 (Spring 2002): 264–73. See also for a mid-decade view, "Reference Service in a Digital Age," by Guy Lamolinara and Ralf Grünke *LC Information Bulletin* (August 1998) at http://www.loc.gov/loc/lcib/9808/ref.html. The IFLA Reference and Information Services Section has drafted *Digital Reference Guidelines,* at http://www.ifla.org/VII/s36/pubs/drg03.htm. The Reference Section also has an annotated list of links at http://www.ifla.org/VII/s36/pubs/drsp.htm.

Archivists have begun to study interactions with off-site users, for example, Wendy M. Duff and Catherine A. Johnson, "A Virtual Expression of Need: An Analysis of E-mail Reference Questions," *American Archivist* 64 (Spring/Summer 2001): 43–60; Kristin E. Martin, "Analysis of Remote Reference Correspondence at a Large Academic Manuscripts Collection," *American Archivist* 64 (Spring/Summer 2001): 17–42; and Helen R. Tibbo, "Interviewing Techniques for Remote Reference: Electronic Versus Traditional Environments," *American Archivist* 58 (Summer 1995): 294–310.

The extraordinary growth of the World Wide Web can be seen in two articles published only three years after the first edition of this manual: David Wallace, "Museums and Archives on the Web: Resource Guidelines and the Emerging State of the Practice," *Archives and Museum Informatics* 9 (1995): 5–30; and William Landis, "Archival Outreach on the World Wide Web," *Archival Issues* 20 (1995): 129–47. Archivists quickly understood the importance of the Web. See, for example, papers given at the Berkeley Finding Aids Conference in April 1995, notably Patricia McClurg, "Access to Primary Sources:

During and After the Digital Revolution," and Daniel V. Pitti, "Settling the Digital Frontier: The Future of Scholarly Communication in the Humanities." See also Carole Prietto, "Spinning A (World Wide) Web," a paper delivered at the SAA meeting in September 1995. Michael O'Malley and Roy Rosenzweig also provide an early view of the use of the Web, "Brave New World or Blind Alley? American History on the World Wide Web," *Journal of American History* (June 1997): 132–55. Jean-Stephen Piche describes how the Web could provide linkages to archival information in a variety of formats, both for users and for staff in "Using the World Wide Web to Integrate Archival Functions," *American Archivist* 61 (Spring 1998): 106–22.

Studies of the use of on-line finding aids include Kathleen Feeney, "Retrieval of Archival Finding Aids Using World-Wide-Web Search Engines," *American Archivist* 62 (Fall 1999): 206–28. James M. Roth found, however, that most repositories mounting EAD finding aids had not developed formal evaluation systems to monitor their use in "Serving Up EAD: An Exploratory Study on the Deployment and Utilization of Encoded Archival Description Finding Aids," *American Archivist* 64 (Fall/Winter 2001): 220–21. Burt Altman and John R. Nemmers describe how they tested a Web site in the design phase and continued to monitor its use afterward in "The Usability of On-line Archival Resources: The Polaris Project Finding Aid," *American Archivist* 64 (Spring/Summer 2001): 121–31.

Design and evaluation of Web sites are considered in R. Philip Reynolds, "Building User-Oriented Web Sites for Archives," *Provenance* 14 (1996): 49–71; Carole Prietto, "Rare and Archival Law Materials in the World Wide Web: An Evaluation of Selected Sites," in *Public Services Issues with Rare and Archival Law Materials,* edited by Michael Widener (New York: Haworth Press, 2001): 67–70; Wendy Duff and Penka Stoyanova, "Transforming the Crazy Quilt: Archival Displays from a User's Point of View," *Archivaria* 45 (Spring 1998): 44–67; and Elizabeth Yakel and Jihyun Kim, "Midwest State Archives on the Web: A Content and Impact Analysis," *Archival Issues,* forthcoming.

The use of Web sites for instruction is noted in Diane E. Kaplan and William R. Massa, Jr., "Archival Insight via the Internet: Researcher Education When They Want It," *NEA Newsletter* 29 (April 2002): 4–7, with their example of a tutorial at "Using Manuscripts and Archives: A

Tutorial/An Instructional Tool for Finding Manuscripts and Archives at Yale and Beyond," at http://www.library.yale.edu/mssa/tutorial/.

Elizabeth H. Dow, et al., provide an overview of the issues when publishing full-text documents on the Web in "The Burlington Agenda: Research Issues in Intellectual Access to Electronically Published Historical Documents," *American Archivist* 64 (Fall/Winter 2001): 292–307.

Archivist Frederick Stielow has edited books for librarians that are helpful for archivists, including *Creating a Virtual Library: A How-To-Do-It Manual for Librarians* (New York: Neal-Schuman Publishers, 1999) and *Building Digital Archives, Descriptions, & Displays: A How-To-Do-It Manual For Archivists & Librarians* (New York: Neal-Schuman Publishers, 2003). Forthcoming is his *Automating and Displaying Archives on the Web* from the same publisher.

Bernie Sloan, "Digital Reference Services Bibliography" lists more than 600 citations at http://www.lis.uiuc.edu/~b-sloan/digiref.html. See also Joann M. Wasik, "Digital Reference Evaluation," 30 June 2003 Virtual Reference Desk at http://www.vrd.org/AskA/digref_assess.shtml.

Promoting the Use of Archives

Archivists have written extensively on the importance of promoting the use of archives. Elsie Freeman Finch, ed., *Advocating Archives: An Introduction to Public Relations for Archivists* (Lanham, Md.: Scarecrow Press, 1994) is an excellent place to start. It includes essays on public relations, fund-raising, media relations, marketing, anniversaries, volunteers, and friends. The introductory essay by Elsie Freeman Finch and Paul Conway goes far beyond its title, "'Talking to the Angel': Beginning Your Public Relations Program," and describes how to integrate public relations into all aspects of the reference process. See also Gabrielle Hyslop, "For Many Audiences: Developing Public Programs at the National Archives of Australia," *Archives and Manuscripts* 30 (2002): 48–59; and William Landis, "Archival Outreach on the World Wide Web," *Archival Issues* 20 (1995): 131–47.

Ann Pederson has led the way in showing how to promote the use of archives. Most recently, her "Understanding Society through Its

Records," is an effective on-line introduction to uses of records at http://john.curtin.edu.au/society/. Pederson's earlier works include a useful introduction to public programs, with Gail Farr, *Archives and Manuscripts: Public Programs* (Chicago: Society of American Archivists, 1982), and her "User Education and Public Relations," in *Keeping Archives* (Sydney: Australian Society of Archivists, 1987).

See also, Elsie Freivogel, "Educational Programs: Outreach as an Administrative Function," *American Archivist* 41 (April 1978): 147–53; Elsie Freeman, "Public Programs: What Alice Didn't Say," SAA *Reference, Access, and Outreach Newsletter* 2 (August 1987): 3–4; Barbara L. Craig, "What Are the Clients? Who Are the Products? The Future of Archival Public Services in Perspective," *Archivaria* 31 (Winter 1990–91) 135–141; Barbara L. Craig, "Old Myths in New Clothes: Expectations of Archives Users," *Archivaria* 45 (Spring 1998): 118–126; Angelika Menne-Haritz, "Access—The Reformulation of an Archival Paradigm," *Archival Science* 1 (2001): 57–82; and John J. Grabowski, "Keepers, Users, and Funders: Building An Awareness of Archival Value," *American Archivist* 55 (Summer 1992): 464–72.

Other exhortations include David B. Gracy, "Reference No Longer is a 'P' Word: The Reference Archivist as Marketer"; and Bruce W. Dearstyne, "Archival Reference and Outreach: Toward a New Paradigm," both in *Reference Services for Archives and Manuscripts* (New York: Haworth Press, 1997), 171–202.

For case studies in creating public programs, see *American Archivist* 54 (Summer 1991), which includes Raimund E. Goerler, "'Play it Again, Sam': Historical Slide Presentations in Public Programming—A Case Study," 378–88, and Michael F. Kohl, "It Only Happens Once Every Hundred Years: Making the Most of the Centennial Opportunity," 390–97. See also Joel Wurl, "Methodology as Outreach: A Public Mini-course on Archival Principles and Techniques," *American Archivist* 49 (Spring 1986): 184–86; and Sandra Myres, "Public Programs for Archives: Reaching Patrons, Officials, and the Public," *Georgia Archive* 7 (Spring 1979): 10–15. An excellent brochure is *Toward a Usable Past* (Albany: New York State Archives, 1984). For exhibits see *The Manual of Museum Exhibitions,* edited by Barry Lord and Gail Dexter Lord, (Walnut Creek, Calif.: AltaMira Press, 2002); and Gail Farr, *Archives and Manuscripts: Exhibits* (Chicago: Society of American Archivists, 1980), now dated.

George David Smith and Laurence E. Steadman present a well-reasoned argument for corporate archives "Present Value of Corporate History," *Harvard Business Review* 59 (November–December 1981): 164–75. John J. Grabowski, "Keepers, Users, and Funders: Building an Awareness of Archival Value," *American Archivist* 55 (Summer 1992): 464–72, discusses reaching out to genealogists, students, undocumented groups, and the media. Chauncey Bell expanded two papers and published them as "Remembering the Future: Organizational Change, Technology, and the Role of the Archivist," *Archival Issues* 25 (2000): 11–32.

Access

General

The "ALA-SAA Joint Statement on Access: Guidelines for Access to Original Research Materials" is found at http://www.archivists.org/statements/alasaa.asp. A good discussion of the history of access practices at the national level remains Raymond H. Geselbracht, "The Origins of Restrictions on Access to Personal Papers in the Library of Congress and the National Archives," *American Archivist* 49 (Spring 1986): 142–62. An international perspective is provided by Michel Duchein, *Obstacles to the Access, Use and Transfer of Information from Archives: RAMP Study* (Paris: UNESCO, 1983); and by Gabrielle Blais, *Access to Archival Records: A Review of Current Issues: A RAMP Study* (Paris: UNESCO, 1995).

Legal issues have frequently dominated discussions of reference service in archives. At this writing, the only discussion of all legal aspects of access for archives remains Gary M. Peterson and Trudy Huskamp Peterson, *Archives and Manuscripts: Law* (Chicago: Society of American Archivists, 1985), but the collection of excellent essays in *Libraries, Museums, and Archives: Legal Issues and Ethical Challenges in the New Information Era,* edited by Tomas A. Lipinski, updates the legal issues of most concern to archivists (Lanham, Md.: Scarecrow Press, 2002). It also identifies new issues. The essays were first presented at the Institute of Legal and Ethical Issues in the New

Information Era: Challenges for Libraries, Museums and Archives held in May 2000 at the University of Wisconsin-Milwaukee. Another collection of essays useful here is found in *Public Services Issues with Rare and Archival Law Materials,* edited by Michael Widener (New York: Haworth Press, 2001), particularly Menzi L. Behrnd-Klodt, who summarizes the legal process and the role of the archivist in "Lawyers, Archivists and Librarians: United or Divided in the Pursuit of Justice?" 113–33; and Akiba J. Covitz, "Providing Access to Lawyers' Papers: The Perils. . . and the Rewards," 151–80.

Thomas Elton Brown presents a case study, "The Freedom of Information Act in the Information Age: The Electronic Challenge to the People's Right to Know," *American Archivist* 58 (Spring 1995): 202–11. Richard J. Cox and David Wallace bring together a collection of case studies that demonstrate the relationship of recordkeeping and accountability in *Archives and the Public Good: Accountability and Records in Modern Society* (Westport, Conn.: Quorum Books, 2002). Jeannette A. Bastian, "Taking Custody, Giving Access: A Postcustodial Role for a New Century," *Archivaria* 53 (Fall 1999): 76, offers a concise but insightful historical analysis of access to archival records and argues that access is a primary responsibility of the custodian of records whether in a centralized or distributed environment. Kathryn Patterson, "The Archivist's Dilemma: Reconciling Individual Rights, Administrative Responsibilities and User Demands," *Archifacts* (October 1996): 158–172 is a thoughtful review of these issues in the New Zealand context that is stimulating for archivists in any country.

Student records are considered in Marjorie Rabe Barritt, "The Appraisal of Personally Identifiable Student Records," *American Archivist* 49 (Summer 1986): 263–75; and Charles B. Elston, "University Student Records: Research Use, Private Rights and the Buckley Law," *Midwestern Archivist* 1 (1976): 16–32. For the Buckley Amendment, see Mark A. Greene, "Letter to Editor," *American Archivist* 50 (Winter 1987): 3–4; Marjorie Barritt, "The Appraisal of Personally Identifiable Student Records," *American Archivist* 49 (Summer 1986): 263–75; Mark A. Greene, "Developing a Research Access Policy for Student Records: A Case Study at Carleton College," *American Archivist* 50 (Fall 1987): 570–79; and Charles B. Elston, "University Student Records: Research Use, Privacy Rights and the Buckley Law,"

Midwestern Archivist 1 (Spring 1976): 16–32, reprinted in *College and University Archives: Selected Readings* (Chicago: Society of American Archivists, 1979), 68–79. Most recently, Tamar G Chute and Ellen D Swain explored "Navigating Ambiguous Waters: Providing Access to Student Recrods in the University Archives," *American Archivist* 67 (Fall/Winter 2004) 212–33.

Discussions between archivists and scholars about the issue of access to contemporary records have produced an extensive bibliography. See, for example, *Final Report of the Joint AHA OAH Ad Hoc Committee to Investigate the Charges against the Franklin D. Roosevelt Library and Related Matters* (Washington, D.C.: American Historical Association, 1970); and Alonzo L. Hamby and Edward Weldon, *Access to Papers of Recent Public Figures: The New Harmony Conference* (Bloomington, Ind.: Organization of American Historians, 1977).

Writing access policies is considered by Anne Van Camp, "Access Policies for Corporate Archives," *American Archivist* 45 (1982): 296–98; Edie Hedlin, "Access: The Company vs. the Scholar," *Georgia Archive* 7 (Spring 1979): 1–9; Phyllis Barr, "Access to Church Records," *Provenance* 1 (1983): 40–48; and "Developing an Access Policy," *Keeping Archives* (Sydney: Australian Society of Archivists, 1987): 190–98. Administration of access is considered in Roland Baumann, "Administration of Access in State Archives," *American Archivist* 49 (1986): 349–69. Ian Mortimer, "Discriminating between Readers: The Case for a Policy of Flexibility," *Journal of the Society of Archivists* 23 (2002): 59–67, argues for providing greater levels of service for "serious" research.

Privacy and Confidentiality

An extended and thought-provoking discussion of the concept of privacy is found in Heather MacNeill, *Without Consent: The Ethics of Disclosing Personal Information in Public Archives* (Lanham, Md.: Society of American Archivists and Scarecrow Press, 1992), which addresses government archives and is an excellent introduction to the concepts. A shorter summary regarding British archives is found in Paul J. Sillitoe, "Privacy in Public Place, Managing Public Access to Personal Information Controlled by Archives Services," *Journal of the Society of Archivists* 19 (April 1998): 5–15. Recent legislation in Britain is considered by Jim Whitman, Julie McLeod, and Catherine Hare in "BIAP: Balancing Information Access and Privacy," *Journal of the Society of Archivists* 22 (2001): 253–74.

Margaret L. Hedstrom, "Computers, Privacy and Research Access to Confidential Information," *Midwestern Archivist* 6 (1981): 5–18 remains useful for privacy issues. A 1988 publication of the Mid-Atlantic Regional Archives Conference, *Constitutional Issues and Archives*, considers privacy and copyright issues. It includes Roland Baumann, "Privacy Act Expungements: A Necessary Evil?"; James Gregory Bradsher, "We Have a Right to Privacy"; and George Chalou, "We Have a Right to Know." See also, Alice Robbin, "State Archives and Issues of Privacy," *American Archivist* 49 (Spring 1986): 163–75; Harold L. Miller, "Will Access Restrictions Hold up in Court? The FBI's Attempt to Use the Braden Papers at the State Historical Society of Wisconsin," *American Archivist* 52 (Spring 1989): 180–90; James Gregory Bradsher, "Privacy Act Expungements: A Reconsideration," *Provenance* 6 (Spring 1988): 1–25; and Joan Hoff-Wilson, "Access to Restricted Collections: The Responsibility of Professional Historical Organizations," *American Archivist* 46 (Fall 1983): 441–47.

More recently, note Elena Danielson, "The Ethics of Access," *American Archivist* 52 (Winter 1989): 52–62; and Mark A. Green, "Moderation in Everything, Access in Nothing?: Opinions about Access Restrictions on Private Papers," *Archival Issues* 18 (1993): 31–41. Sara S. Hodson weighs the issues of access, restrictions, and the ethics of the donor relationship in a thoughtful essay, "Freeing the Dead Sea Scrolls: A Question of Access," *American Archivist* 56 (Fall 1993): 690–703. See also, her "Private Lives: Confidentiality in Manuscripts Collections," *Rare Books and Manuscripts Librarianship* 6 (1991): 108–18.

Ronald L. Becker, "The Ethics of Providing Access," *Provenance* 11 (1993): 57–77 and Bruce P. Montgomery, "Archiving Human Rights: A Paradigm for Collection Development," *Journal of Academic Librarianship* 22 (March 1999): 87–96, provide useful examples from collecting repositories. Diane E. Kaplan provides a case study in determining access policies in "The Stanley Milgram Papers: A Case Study on Appraisal of and Access to Confidential Data Files," *American Archivist* 59 (Summer 1996): 288–97. Jill Cariffe Cirasella, "At Odds?: Archives and Privacy," *Current Studies in Librarianship* 24 (Spring/Fall

2000): 88–92, argues for the privacy of writers. Jeannette Strickland, "Confidentiality Agreements," *Journal of the Society of Archivists* 23 (2002): 69–72, discusses agreements with users who are given access to records less than a hundred years old. Also of interest are Elena S. Danielson, "Privacy Rights and the Rights of Political Victims: Implications of the German Experience," and Sara S. Hodson, "In Secret Kept, In Silence Sealed: Privacy in the Papers of Authors and Celebrities," *American Archivist* 67 (Fall/Winter 2004): 176–211.

The Health Insurance Portability and Accountability Act, which came into effect in 2003, may present problems for some archivists, but little is written about it from an archival perspective. See Nikki Swartz, "What Every Business Needs to Know about HIPAA," *Information Management Journal* 37 (March/April 2003): 26–32.

Classification

In a review essay, David A. Wallace provides a wide-ranging and thoughtful overview of classification, declassification, and researcher access in "Archivists, Recordkeeping, and the Declassification of Records: What We Can Learn from Contemporary Histories," *American Archivist* 56 (Fall 1993): 794–814. Anne Van Camp discusses classification and declassification of State Department records in "Trying to Write 'Comprehensive and Accurate' History of the Foreign Relations of the United States: An Archival Perspective," *Archives and the Public Good* (Westport, Conn.: Quorum Books, 2002).

Copyright

Comprehending the details of copyright administration is daunting. SAA provides seminars on a regular basis. A number of Web sites provide ready access to information about this convoluted subject. Kenneth D. Crews maintains a leading copyright site called "Copyright Management Center" at http://www.copyright.iupui.edu. "Time-Line: A History of Copyright" is a helpful history of copyright with links to many pertinent documents, available through the Association of Research Libraries at http://www.arl.org/info/frn/copy/timeline.html. Also useful are American Library Association, "Copyright" at http://

www.ala.org/ala/washoff/WOissues/copyrightb/copyright.htm, and the University of Texas "Crash Course in Copyright" at http://www.utsystem.edu/ogc/IntellectualProperty/cprtindx.htm. Stanford University Libraries provides a useful bibliography relating to fair use with links to many documents at "Copyright and Fair Use" http://fairuse.stanford.edu/. See also the *Final Report to the Commissioner on the Conclusion of the Conference on Fair Use* at http://www1.uspto.gov/web/offices/dcom/olia/confu/confurep.htm.

Peter B. Hirtle, "When Works Pass Into the Public Domain in the United States: Copyright Term for Archivists," posted on-line by Cornell University at http://www.copyright.cornell.edu/Training/Hirtle_Public_Domain.htm, is a useful summary in table form. Also important is his "Archives or Assets?" *American Archivist* 66 (Fall/Winter 2003): 235–48, in which he challenges archivists to consider the financial barriers they place in the use of archival resources. A good summary for archivists is William J. Maher, "Between Authors and Users: Archivists in the Copyright Vise," *Archival Issues* 26 (2001): 63–75.

A comprehensive review is Kenneth D. Crews, "Fair Use of Unpublished Works: Burdens of Proof and the Integrity of Copyright," *Arizona State Law Journal* 31 (1999): 1–93. Crews joins Dwayne K. Butler in a review of the DCMA in "Copyright Protection and Technological Reform of Library Services: Digital Change, Practical Applications, and Congressional Action" in *Libraries, Museums, and Archives: Legal Issues and Ethical Challenges in the New Information Era* (Lanham, Md.: Scarecrow Press, 2002): 275–94. See also, William Maher, "Current Issues in Copyright Law and Archival Administration," *Archival Issues* 26 (2001): 63–75. Also useful is Christine Steiner, "The Double-Edged Sword: Museums and Fair Use," *Museum News* 76 (September/October 1997): 32–35, 48–49. Jodi L. Allison-Bunnell provides a case study in "Access in the Time of Salinger: Fair Use and the Papers of Katherine Anne Porter," *American Archivist* 58 (Summer 1995): 270–82. Thomas Mann grounds the debate in the real world of library reference in his "Reference Service, Human Nature, Copyright, and Offsite Service—in a 'Digitalage,'" *Reference & User Services Quarterly* 38 (1998): 55–61. A new and promising approach to the commercial uses of archival holdings is provided by Nancy E. Loe, "Avoiding the Golden Fleece: Licensing

Agreements for Archives," *American Archivist* 67 (Spring/Summer 2004): 58–85.

Electronic Records

Most discussion of electronic records focuses on their identification and preservation, and no body of literature on reference services for them yet exists. In 1988, RSR presented an issue devoted to reference services for machine-readable data files. Most notable for archivists are Edie Hedlin and Donald R. Harrison, "The National Archives and Electronic Data"; Katharine Gavrel, "National Archives of Canada: Machine-Readable Records Program"; and Margaret Hedstrom and Alan Kowlowitz, "Meeting the Challenge of Machine-Readable Records: A State Archives Perspective," RSR 16 (1988).

Discussion of reference services for electronic records is found in the few manuals for electronic records available, for example, William Saffady, *Managing Electronic Records*, 2nd ed., (Prairie Village, Kans.: ARMA International, 1998): 83–85. See also, Margaret Hedstrom, "Electronic Archives: Integrity and Access in the Network Environment," *American Archivist* 58 (Summer 1995): 270–82; Theodore J. Hull and Margaret O. Adams, "Electronic Communications for Reference Services: a Case Study," *Government Information Quarterly* 12 (1995): 297–308; and Theodore J. Hull, "Reference Services for Electronic Records in Archives," and Thomas J. Ruller, "Open All Night: Using the Internet to Improve Access to Archives: A Case Study of the New York State Archives and Records Administration," both in Laura B. Cohen, ed., *Reference Services for Archives and Manuscripts*, (New York: Haworth Press, 1997). See also, Margaret Hedstrom, "How Do Archivists Make Electronic Archives Usable and Accessible?" *Archives and Manuscripts* 26 (May 1998): 6–22 and "Electronic Archives: Integrity and Access in the Network Environment," in *Networking in the Humanities: Proceedings of the Second Conference on Scholarship and Technology in the Humanities held at Elvetham Hall, Hampshire, U.K., 13–16 April 1994: Papers in Honour of Michael Smethurst for his 60th Birthday* (London: Bowker-Saur, 1995), 77–95.

Administration of Reference Services

The administrative aspects of the initial interview are elaborated in Robert W. Tissing, Jr., "The Orientation Interview in Archival Research," *American Archivist* 47 (Spring 1984): 173–78. The SAA Forms Manual has made locating, evaluating, and adapting examples of the "forms, forms, forms" much easier. See *Sample Forms for Archival and Records Management Programs* (Lenexa, Kans., Chicago, Ill.: ARMA International and Society of American Archivists, 2002).

Security

This topic was initiated by Philip Mason, "Archival Security: New Solutions to an Old Problem," *American Archivist* 38 (October 1975): 477–92, and Timothy Walch followed with *Archives and Manuscripts: Security* (Chicago: Society of American Archivists, 1977). For an extended discussion of all aspects of security for archival holdings, see Gregor Trinkhaus-Randall, *Protecting Your Collections: A Manual of Archival Security* (Chicago: Society of American Archivists, 1995). The journal *Library and Archives Security* (New York: Haworth Press) is useful for recent developments. Jeremy Cauchi, "Access and Security: A Risk Management Approach," *Archifacts* (October 2000): 14–23, identifies security risks, and eight phases of security from anticipation, deterrence, prevention, detection, response, apprehension, recovery, and punishment.

See also, "Guidelines Regarding Thefts in Libraries," *C & RL News* (March 1988): 159–62; "ACRL Guidelines for the Security of Rare Book, Manuscript, and Other Special Collections," *C & RL News* (March 1990): 240–44; Vincent A. Totka, Jr., "Preventing Patron Theft in the Archives: Legal Perspectives and Problems," *American Archivist* 56 (Fall 1993): 664–72; and Bruce A. Shuman, "Seven Levels of Safety: Protecting People in Public Buildings," *Libraries, Museums, and Archives: Legal Issues and Ethical Challenges in the New Information Era* (Lanham, Md.: Scarecrow Press, 2002): 159–75.

Two case studies are Theresa Galvin, "The Boston Case of Charles Merrill Mount: The Archivist's Arch Enemy," *American Archivist* 53 (Summer 1990): 442–50; and Miles Harvey, *The Island of Lost Maps: A*

True Story of Cartographic Crime (New York: Random House, 2000), which details the thefts by Gilbert Bland.

Fees

Little has been written about fees in archival repositories. Claudia Landis, "Charging: A Limit to Access or a Means to Provide a Service?" *Archifacts* (April 1995): 26–31 weighs the issues. Gabrielle Blais, "'Pricing' the Corporate Memory: User Fees and Revenue Generation in a Public Archives," *Provenance* 13 (1995): 47–63, reports on a study at the National Archives of Canada that sought to determine what special benefits were given researchers and whether and how these benefits should be priced. She usefully defines and distinguishes between user fees and revenue generation, and between value-driven and market-driven approaches in public service agencies like archives.

Preservation

The relationship between preservation and the administration of reference services is found in Mary Lynn Ritzenthaler, *Archives and Manuscripts: Conservation* (Chicago: Society of American Archivists, 1983) and *Preserving Archives and Manuscripts* (Chicago: Society of American Archivists, 1993). See also, Committee on Preservation of Historical Records, National Materials Advisory Board, Commission on Engineering and Technical Systems, National Research Council, *Preservation of Historical Records* (Washington, D.C.: National Academy Press, 1986).

Facilities

Two recent publications are *Solid, Safe, Secure: Building Archives Repositories in Australia* by Ted Ling (National Archives of Australia, 1998) and "Guidance on Planning for a Research Space" Appendix D of *Museum Handbook* 3 *Museum Collections Use*, at http://www.cr.nps.gov/museum/publications/MHIII/mh3appd.pdf.

Reprography

Now outdated, but helpful for earlier processes is Carolyn Hoover Sung, *Archives and Manuscripts: Reprography* (Chicago: Society of American Archivists, 1982). Standards published by the American National Standards Institute (ANSI) are available from the Institute at 1430 Broadway, New York, NY, 10018; while Association for Information and Image Management (AIIM) standards are available from 1100 Wayne Ave, Silver Spring, MD, 20910. See the AIIM Web site at http://www.aiim.org/. An extensive discussion and list of standards are available in the National Park Service *Museum Handbook* 3 in Chapter 4: Two-Dimensional Reproductions at http://www.cr.nps.gov/museum/publications/MHIII/mh3ch4.pdf.

More detailed information can be found in Eastman Kodak, *Storage and Preservation of Microfilms, Kodak Publication* D-3 (Rochester, N.Y.: Eastman Kodak Company, 1996); Nancy Elkington, ed., *RLG Archives Microfilming Manual* (Mountain View, Calif.: Research Libraries Group, 1994) and *RLG Preservation Microfilming, Handbook,* (Mountain View, Calif.: Research Libraries Group, 1992); and Eastman Kodak, *Copying and Duplicating: Photographic and Digital Imaging Techniques* (Rochester, N.Y.: Kodak Publication M-1, CAT No. E152- 7969). Northeast Document Conservation Center (NEDCC) publishes technical leaflets: *Reformatting: Duplication of Historical Negatives,* and *Photographic Materials: A Short Guide to Nitrate Negatives: History, Care, and Duplication* (Andover, Mass.: NEDCC, 1994).

See also Steve Puglia, "Duplication Options for Deteriorating Photo Collections," in *Photograph Preservation and the Research Library* edited by Jennifer Porro (Mountain View, Calif.: Research Libraries Group, 1991), and *The Preservation of Acetate Film Materials: A Cost/Benefit Analysis for Duplication and Cool/Cold Storage* (College Park, Md.: National Archives and Records Administration, 1998); and Andrew Robb and Monique C. Fischer, *Guidelines for Care & Identification of Film-Base Photographic Materials* (Winterthur, Del.: University of Delaware Winterthur Museum, 1993).

Copying large materials is considered in Steve Puglia, *The Copying of Oversized Materials* (College Park, Md.: National Archives and Records Administration, March 1993, revised 1998), and Eleonore

Kissel and Erin Vigneau, *Architectural Photoreproductions: A Manual for Identification and Care* (New York Botanical Garden: Oak Knoll Press, 1999).

For film and videotape see Steven Davidson and Gregory Lukow, *The Administration of Television Newsfilm and Videotape Collections: A Curatorial Manual* (Los Angeles: American Film Institute, 1997).

For sound records see Association for Recorded Sound Collections, *Audio Preservation: A Planning Study,* (Silver Spring, Md.: Association for Recorded Sound Collections, 1987); Alan Calmes, "New Preservation Concern: Video Recordings," *Commission on Preservation and Access Newsletter* 22 (April 1990); Committee on *Preservation of Historical Records, Preservation of Historic Records: Magnetic Recording Media* (Washington, D.C.: National Academy Press, 1986); Alan Ward, *A Manual of Sound Archive Administration* (Trowbridge, Wiltsire, U.K.: Gower Publishing Company, 1990); Christopher Ann Paton, "Whispers in the Stacks: The Problems of Sound Recordings in Archives," *American Archivist* 53 (Spring 1990): 274–80; and "Preservation Re-Recording of Audio Recordings in Archives: Problems, Priorities, Technologies, and Recommendations," *American Archivist* 61 (Spring 1998): 188–219.

Digital Reproductions

Archivists and librarians try to cope with the implications of these new technologies. One place to start is Maxine K. Sitts, ed., *Handbook for Digital Projects: A Management Tool for Preservation and Access* (Andover, Mass.: Northeast Document Conservation Center, 2000), which includes chapters exploring all dimensions of digital projects. See it also at http://www.nedcc.org/digital/dman.pdf. Another introduction is Anne Kenney and Stephen Chapman, *Digital Imaging for Libraries and Archives* (Ithaca, N.Y.: Cornell University, 1996). See also Nancy E. Elkington, *Digital Imaging for Libraries & Archives* (Mountain View, Calif.: Research Libraries Group, 1994) and *Digital Imaging Technology for Preservation: An RLG Symposium* (Mountain View, Calif.: Research Libraries Group, 1994). A recent overview is Bertrand Lavédrine, *A Guide to the Preventive Conservation of Photograph Collections* (Los Angeles: Getty Conservation Institute, 2003). Another excellent resource is forthcoming, Mary Lynn

Ritzenthaler and Diane Vogt-O'Connor, *Photographs: Archival Care and Management* (Chicago: Society of American Archivists, 2005).

D-Lib Magazine, a monthly magazine on what's new in digital archives and library work, is a good mechanism for learning of new developments. See, for example, Stephen Chapman and Anne R. Kenney, "Digital Conversion of Research Library Materials: A Case for Full Informational Capture," *D-Lib Magazine* (October 1996); and Norman Paskin, "On Making and Identifying a 'Copy,'" *D-Lib Magazine* 9 (January 2003). Visit at http://www.dlib.org/.

See also Image Permanence Institute, *Recommendations for the Evaluation of Digital Images Produced from Photographic, Micrographic, and Various Paper Formats* (Rochester, N.Y.: Image Permanence Institute for the Library of Congress, May 1996), also available through http://memory.loc.gov/ammem/about/techIn.html. In 1996, the Commission on Preservation and Access and the Research Libraries Group sponsored *Preserving Digital Information: Report of the Task Force on Archiving of Digital Information*, available at http://www.rlg.org/ArchTF/tfadi.index.htm. The Commission on Preservation and Access joined with the Council on Library Resources to become the Council on Library and Information Resources, the administrative home to the Digital Library Federation (DLF) on-line at http://www.clir.org/.

Other on-line sources are "Future Directions in Access and Preservation Technologies and New Electronic Formats" by Colin Webb (October 1996) at http://www.nla.gov.au/nla/staffpaper/cwebb3.html; Library of Congress Technical Information and Background Papers at http://memory.loc.gov/ammem/about/techIn.html; NARA Guidelines for Digitizing Archival Materials for Electronic Access at http://www.archives.gov/research_room/arc/arc_info/guidelines_for_digitizing_archival_materials.pdf; National Library of Australia, "Preserving Access to Digital Information" at http://www.nla.gov.au/padi; Task Force on Digital Archiving, "Preserving Digital Information" at http://www.rlg.org/ArchTF/tfadi.index.htm; Research Library Group Preservation Program at http://www.rlg.org/preserv; and Society of American Archivists "Statement on the Preservation of Digitized Reproductions" at http://www.archivists.org/statements/preservation-digirepros.asp/.

EDOCS sponsors reviews of Web sites and software, distributes information about new developments in the field, hosts workshops and encourages collaboration among content producers, organizers, and publishers at http://history.furman.edu/edocs/.

Loans

A special issue of *Rare Books and Manuscripts Librarianship* 3 (Fall 1988) presented several papers on lending. Included are Thomas V. Lange, "Alternatives to ILL"; Thomas Hickerson and Anne R. Kenney, "Expanding Access: Loan of Original Materials and Special Collections"; and "RLG Guidelines for Lending." Timothy L. Ericson and Joshua P. Ranger, "'The Next Great Idea': Loaning Archival Collections," *Archivaria* 47 (Spring 1999): 85–113 also addresses this topic.

The National Park Service's *Museum Handbook* has a useful summary of the elements of a loan policy in volume 2 chapter 5, "Outgoing Loans." See it at http://www.cr.nps.gov/museum/publications/MHII/mh2ch5.pdf. It includes forms and checklists.

Education of Reference Archivists

Terry Eastwood, who established the model for archival education and has written widely about it, provides a detailed assessment of "Public Services Education for Archivists," in *Reference Services for Archives and Manuscripts,* edited by Laura B. Cohen (New York: Haworth Press, 1997): 27–38. See also, Janice E. Ruth, "Educating the Reference Archivist," *American Archivist* 51 (Summer 1988): 266–76.

Evaluation of Reference Services

Evaluation of reference services is addressed in Stuart Strachan, "How Good Are We?: Sketching the Parameters of Service Evaluation," *Archifacts* (April 1996): 50–54. See also, Diane G. Schwartz and Dottie Eakin, "Reference Service Standards, Performance Criteria, and Evaluation," *Journal of Academic Librarianship* 12 (1986): 4–8; Jane P. Kleiner, "Ensuring Quality Reference Desk Service: The Introduction of a Peer Process," *RQ* 30 (Spring 1991): 349–61; and Jennifer Mendelsohn,

"Perspectives on Quality of Reference Service in an Academic Library: A Qualitative Study," *RQ* 36 (Summer 1997): 544–57. Related professional organizations provide examples, such as the American Library Association, *Professional Competencies for Reference and User Services Librarians* (2003) and *Guidelines for Behavioral Performance of Reference and Information Services Professionals*.

Ethics

In 2005, the Society of American Archivists adopted an updated "Code of Ethics for Archivists." It is available at http://www.archivists.org/governance/handbook/app_ethics.asp. The International Council on Archives adopted its Code of Ethics on 6 September 1996, with commentary. See http://www.ica.org/biblio/spa/code_ethics_eng.html.

Heather MacNeil, *Without Consent: The Ethics of Disclosing Personal Information in Public Archives* (Lanham, Md.: Society of American Archivists and Scarecrow Press, 1992) probes the ethics of access. Elena Danielson has written extensively about the ethical dimensions of access issues. See "The Ethics of Access," *American Archivist* 52 (Winter 1989): 52–62; and "Ethics and Reference Services," in *Reference Services for Archives and Manuscripts* (New York: Haworth Press, 1997): 107–24.

Ethical issues are further explored in Nancy Lankford, "Ethics and the Reference Archivist," *Midwestern Archivist* 8 (1983): 7–13. Several essays in *Archives and the Public Good* present ethical issues, for example, Verne Harris, "'They Should Have Destroyed More': The Destruction of Public Records by the South African State in the Final Years of Apartheid, 1990–1994." Glenn Dingwall's review of codes of ethics received the Theodore Calvin Pease award, and was published as "Trusting Archivists: The Role of Archival Ethics Codes in Establishing Public Faith," *American Archivist* 67 (Spring/Summer 2004): 11–30. Karen Benedict examines every facet of archival work, including reference, in *Ethics and the Archival Profession: Introduction and Case Studies* (Chicago: Society of American Archivists, 2003).

ALA-SAA Joint Statement on Access to Original Materials in Libraries, Archives, and Manuscript Repositories

1. A repository[1] preserves collections[2] for use by researchers. It is the responsibility of a repository to make available original research materials in its possession on equal terms of access. Access should be provided in accordance with statutory authority, institutional mandate, the Code of Ethics for Archivists[3], the Standards for Ethical Conduct for Rare Book, Manuscript, and Special Collections Librarians[4], and this Joint Statement. A repository should not deny access to materials to any researcher, nor grant privileged or exclusive use of materials to any researcher, nor conceal the existence of any body of material from any researcher, unless required to do so by statutory authority, institutional mandate, or donor or purchase stipulation.

2. A repository is committed to preserving manuscript and archival materials and to making them available for research as soon as possible. At the same time, it is recognized that a repository may

---

This statement is available online at http://www.archivists.org/statements/alasaa.asp.

1 A *repository* is defined as an archives, manuscripts library, research center, or any other institution responsible for keeping primary research materials.

2 *Collections* are defined as individual manuscripts, archival or manuscript collections, fonds, or record groups found in repositories in any format.

3 *Code of Ethics for Archivists and Commentary* (Chicago: Society of American Archivists, 1992).

4 "Standards for Ethical Conduct for Rare Book, Manuscript, and Special Collection Librarians, with Guidelines for Institutional Practice in Support of the Standards," *College & Research Libraries News* 54 (April 1993): 207–215.

have legal and institutional obligations to protect confidentiality in its collections, and that private donors have the right to impose reasonable restrictions upon their papers to protect privacy or confidentiality for a reasonable period of time.

   a. It is the responsibility of the repository to inform researchers of the restrictions which apply to collections.

   b. The repository should discourage donors from imposing unreasonable restrictions and should encourage a specific time limitation on restrictions that are imposed.

   c. The repository should periodically evaluate restricted material and work toward the removal of restrictions when they are no longer required.

3. As the accessibility of material depends on knowing of its existence, it is the repository's responsibility to inform researchers of the collections in its custody. This may be accomplished through local, regional, or national catalogs; inventories and other internal finding aids; published guides; and the assistance of staff members.

4. To protect and insure the continued accessibility of the material in its custody, all materials must be used in accordance with the rules of the repository. Each repository should publish or otherwise make known to potential researchers its rules governing access and use. Such rules must be applied and enforced equally.

   a. The repository may limit use of fragile or unusually valuable materials, but should try to provide suitable reproductions to researchers in lieu of the originals.

   b. The repository may limit access to unprocessed materials, so long as the limitations are applied and enforced equally.

   c. The repository may, under special circumstances, loan or place on deposit with another repository part or all of a collection.[5]

---

5 Repositories wishing to participate in the interlibrary loan of materials may consult as a model the "Additional Guidelines for Access to Archives, Manuscripts, and Special Collections," Chapter 8 of the Research Libraries Group *Shared Resources Manual* (3rd ed., Stanford, CA: Research Libraries Group, 1987). The chapter is reprinted in *Rare Books & Manuscripts Librarianship* 3 (Fall 1988): 126–130. Repositories wishing to loan original materials for research or exhibitions may consult the RBMS "Guidelines for the Loan of

    d. The repository may refuse access to an individual researcher who has demonstrated such carelessness or deliberate destructiveness as to endanger the safety of the material, or to a researcher who has violated the policies and regulations of the repository.

    e. To protect its collections, a repository may, in accordance with statutory authority and institutional mandate, require acceptable identification of any individual wishing to use its materials, as well as a signature verifying the individual has read a statement defining the policies and regulations of the repository.

5. A repository should not charge fees for making available the materials in its holdings, except when required by statutory authority or institutional mandate. A repository should facilitate access to collections by providing reproduction services. These services can include electronic, paper, or photographic copies; microfilm; or other means of reproduction. All reproductions should be made in accordance with statutory authority, including copyright law, institutional mandate, and repository regulations. Reasonable fees may be charged for these copying or research services. A repository is not obligated to conduct copying or research services beyond those required by statutory authority or institutional mandate.

6. Each repository should publish or otherwise make available to researchers a suggested form of citation crediting the repository and identifying items within its holdings for later reference. Citations to copies of materials in other repositories should include the location of the originals, if known.

7. It is the researcher's obligation to satisfy copyright regulations when copying or using materials found in collections. Whenever possible a repository should inform a researcher about known copyrighted material, the owner or owners of the copyrights, and the researcher's obligations with regard to such material.

Rare and Unique Manuscript Materials," *College & Research Libraries News* 54 (May 1993): 267–269, or the "Guidelines for Borrowing Special Collections Materials for Exhibition," *College & Research Libraries News* 51 (May 1990): 430–434.

Statement on the Reproduction of Manuscripts and Archives for Reference Service

1. It is the responsibility of a library, archives, or manuscript repository to assist researchers by making or having made reproductions of any material in its possession, for research purposes, subject to certain conditions. Manuscript and archival materials may be reproduced if:

   a. The condition of the originals will permit such reproduction.

   b. The originals have no gift, purchase, or legal restrictions on reproduction.

2. In the interest of making research collections more generally available, the orderly microfilming of archives and entire manuscript collections, together with appropriate guides, is to be encouraged, within the available resources of the repository.

3. The price of reproductions shall be set by the repository, which should endeavor to keep charges to a minimum.

4. Copies should be made for reference use as follows:

   a. Repositories which permit their manuscript and archival holdings to be reproduced in whole or in part must specify before the copies are made what restrictions, if any, have been placed on the use or further reproduction of copies.

    b. Repositories may require that purchasers agree in writing to abide by any restrictions.

    c. All reproductions should identify the source of the original manuscript collection or archival record group.

5. The repository should inform the researcher:

    a. When and under what conditions permission to make extensive direct quotation from or to print in full any reproduction must be obtained from the institution owning the originals.

    b. That in the case of material under copyright, the right to quote or print, beyond fair use, must also be obtained by the researcher from the copyright owner.

    c. That the researcher assumes legal responsibility for observing common law literary rights, property rights, and libel laws.

    d. Of known retention of literary rights.

6. A repository may decline to furnish reproductions when fulfilling mail requests requires subjective criteria for selection of material to be duplicated or the commitment of an unreasonable amount of staff time for extended research to identify the material.

7. In cases when researchers request the reproduction of large amounts of material which they have identified in the course of their research, the repository may prescribe a preferred method of copying (i.e., microfilm vs. Xerox) and may provide for a reasonable time period in which to produce the copies.

Checklist for Access Policies and Reference Services

Principles. "The archives must provide opportunity for research in the records it holds. The archives should be open for research use on a regular and stated schedule. It should provide adequate space and facilities for research use and should make its records available on equal terms of access to all users who should abide by its rules and procedures. Any restrictions on access should be defined in writing and should be carefully observed.

The archives should provide information about its holdings and assist and instruct users in their use. Staff members familiar with the holdings and capable of making informed decisions about legal and ethical consideration affecting reference work should be available to assist readers. The archives should report its holdings to appropriate publications so that potential users may know of their existence. The archives should assist users by providing reproductions of materials in its possession whenever possible."

Amplification. Any restrictions on access should be defined in writing and should be carefully observed. There should be regular and systematic review of restrictions to determine when they expire, and prompt opening of material upon expiration of restrictions.

An archives should protect and preserve materials used, including loans and materials used in reading rooms; so that they may survive for future use. It should keep records of the identity of all users and their use of materials to assess patterns of use, to trace previous research paths, and to support replevin of alienated materials. Rules and procedures for use should protect historical materials and legitimate interests of the archives. They should be stated clearly and posted for examination by all users. They should not unduly encumber access to sources.

An archives should comply with applicable laws, especially those related to proprietary rights (such as copyright), privacy and confidentiality, and freedom of information. An archives has a responsibility to inform users of laws and governmental or institutional regulations that affect their research.

YES   NO   N/A

___   ___   ___   1. Does the archives maintain hours of service on a regular and posted schedule?

___   ___   ___   2. Are the number of hours reasonably adequate for anticipated use?

___   ___   ___   3. Does the archives have a written policy on access?

___   ___   ___   4. Is the access policy equitable and consistent with the SAA Statement on Access?

___   ___   ___   5. Does the policy clearly define who may use the facility?

___   ___   ___   6. Are the records of restrictions well-maintained, clear, and easily and equitably administered?

___   ___   ___   7. Is there a systematic procedure for periodic review of restrictions and prompt opening of materials after restrictions expire?

YES   NO   N/A

___   ___   ___   8. Is there an adequate plan for deciding whether an unprocessed or partially processed collection shall be made available for research?

___   ___   ___   9. Is the policy regarding loans equitable and easily administered?

___   ___   ___   10. Are loaned records adequately protected?

___   ___   ___   11. Does the archives keep adequate records of materials loaned?

___   ___   ___   12. Does the archives provide for readers written guidelines containing information about policies affecting research use, such as access policies, rules for use of materials, security rules, sample citations, photocopy policies, copyright provisions, and other specific infor-mation?

___   ___   ___   13. Are the rules and procedures adequate to control and protect materials, provide a proper atmosphere for research, and yet not unduly impede access to materials?

___   ___   ___   14. Is the space provided for researchers (the reading room) adequate?

___   ___   ___   15. Is the reading room appropriately equipped for the records to be examined?

___   ___   ___   16. Is it adequately staffed?

YES   NO   N/A

____   ____   ____   17. Are staff supervision and surveillance sufficient to provide necessary assistance and to prevent theft or damage, including potential dangers from copying documents?

____   ____   ____   18. Does the archives answer written requests for information about its holdings?

____   ____   ____   19. Does the archives answer telephone requests for information about its holdings?

____   ____   ____   20. Are there appropriate guides to the archives?

____   ____   ____   21. Does the archives make finding aids available to readers?

____   ____   ____   22. Does the archives regularly report holdings and new accessions to major catalogs such as NUCMC and/or enter descriptive information about record groups and collections into on-line catalogs and databases?

____   ____   ____   23. Are the records of reference service adequate to permit analysis of reference needs, to provide protection in case of theft or abuse, and to permit planning for and evaluation of reference services?

____   ____   ____   24. Does the archives have a policy on informing readers of parallel research?

____   ____   ____   25. Is an adequate reference collection accessible?

____   ____   ____   26. Does the archives provide copying services to researchers?

YES   NO   N/A

___   ___   ___   27. Is the copying service convenient and are its charges/fees appropriate?

___   ___   ___   28. Are records adequately protected from harm during copying?

___   ___   ___   29. Does the archives refuse to provide copies when the copy process risks damage to the original?

___   ___   ___   30. Are staff members who deal with researchers well-informed about laws affecting research, especially copyright, privacy, and freedom of information laws?

___   ___   ___   31. Do staff members inform users of the implications of these laws for their research as appropriate?

Archives Planning and Assessment Workbook (Chicago: Society of American Archivists, 1989), 45–47.

Reference Procedures Manual— Suggested Contents

Overview of Reference Services
    Repository mission statement
    Access policy
    Hours and services

Administration
    Position descriptions for professional staff, support staff, and volunteers
    Checklists for orientation, training, and evaluation
    Scheduling staff for reference service
    Reporting relationships and procedures
    Collecting measurements of use: definitions and procedures
    Analyzing, evaluating, reporting on use
    Monitoring and ordering supplies
    List of all forms, their filing and disposition
    List of all brochures, maps, and other handouts
    Location of master copies of forms, handouts
    Instructions on giving directions to repository
    Area map
    Floor plan of repository
    Floor plan of research room, indicating finding aids, reference tools, equipment

Finding Aids
  Description and relationships of finding aids
  Location of finding aids
  Instructions for using finding aids

Registration
  Procedures

Interaction with Researchers in Reading Room
  Reference interview
  Continuing assistance
  Exit interview or other follow-up activities

Responding to Remote Inquiries
  Phone inquiries
  Written inquiries: postal or e-mail
  Loan requests
  Requests for permission to publish
  Responding to a subpoena
  Protocols for common questions

Security
  Control of belongings and outerwear
  Limits on amounts of material
  Observing and monitoring use
  Responding to suspected theft or abuse of materials

Restrictions
  Privacy and confidentiality
  List of restricted collections, series, items

Retrieval and Reshelving Procedures
  Procedures for requesting materials
  Control of materials in research room
  Control of materials to be copied
  Control of materials to be reshelved
  Reshelving procedures

Searching protocols for missing items
Searching protocols for common searches

Rules for Use of Materials

Rules for use by researchers
Rules for use by staff
Textual materials
Photographic materials
Microfilm
Special forms
Forms
Filing
Retention

Equipment

Using audiovisual or other special equipment
Maintaining equipment
Monthly fire extinguisher checks

Duplication

Electrostatic photocopying
Microfilming
Photographic copying
Audiovisual duplication
Digital duplication
Oversize duplication
Price lists and order forms

Emergency Response Plans

Lists of emergency contacts
Checklists for monthly management safety walkarounds
Fire
Power outage
Natural disasters, such as earthquake, tornado, flood
Medical emergency—staff or researcher
Disoriented or disorderly researcher

Public Programs
    Scheduling
    Preparing
    Conducting
    Evaluating
    Orientation sessions
    Exhibits
    Lectures
    Conferences

Examples of all forms and all handouts

Standards for Reference Archivists—Behaviors Associated with Good Reference Service

Approachability
- Defines the informational needs of users by such techniques as customer surveys and analysis of user requests
- Develops policies and procedures designed to serve the information needs of various user groups, based on evaluation of institutional mandates and constituencies, the nature of the collections, relevant laws and ethical considerations, and appropriate technologies
- Keeps abreast of current research trends and strategies
- Establishes a "reference presence" wherever users look for it
- Engages approaching patrons, stops other activities when patrons approach and focuses attention on the patrons' needs
- Acknowledges users who are waiting
- Establishes initial eye contact with users
- Acknowledges the presence of patrons through smiling and/or attentive and welcoming body language
- Acknowledges patrons through the use of a friendly greeting to initiate conversation, and/or by standing up, moving forward, or moving closer to them
- Remains visible to patrons as much as possible
- Roves through the reference area offering assistance whenever possible, approaches patrons and offers assistance with questions such as, "Are you finding what you need?" "Can I help you

with anything?" or "How is your search going?"

- Provides a visible link to reference services from the repository's website
- Alert to users needing help but not asking for it
- Demonstrates a friendly attitude, neither condescending nor didactic

Interest

- Appears unhurried during the reference transaction
- Faces patrons when speaking and listening
- Signals an understanding of patrons' needs through verbal or non-verbal confirmation, such as nodding of the head or brief comments or questions
- Acknowledges user e-mail questions in a timely manner
- States procedures and policies clearly in an accessible place on the Web, indicates scope of questions, types of services provided, and expected turnaround time
- Demonstrates positive response and attitude towards questions

Listening/Inquiring

- Uses a tone of voice and/or written language appropriate to the nature of the transaction
- Allows the patrons to state fully their information need in their own words before responding
- Rephrases the question or request and asks for confirmation to ensure that it is understood
- Seeks to clarify confusing terminology and avoids excessive jargon
- Uses open-ended questioning techniques to encourage patrons to expand on the request or present additional information
- Maintains objectivity and does not interject value judgments about subject matter or the nature of the question into the transaction
- Uses reference interviews or Web forms to gather as much information as possible without compromising user privacy
- Demonstrates ability to deal effectively with problem personalities
- Able to buy time when needed

Reference Skills
- Works with the patrons to narrow or broaden the topic when too little or too much information is identified
- Finds out what patrons have already tried, and encourages patrons to contribute ideas
- With patron, constructs a competent and complete search strategy
- Explains the search strategy and sequence to the patrons, as well as the sources to be used
- Explains how to use records when appropriate
- Recognizes when to refer patrons to a more appropriate guide, database, repository, archivist, or other resource
- Communicates effectively orally and in writing
- Communicates sense of determination to do a good job
- Employs all necessary resources: archival records in all formats, library resources, Internet resources
- Makes an appropriate response to user requests by providing information about records and papers, providing information from records and papers, providing access to records and papers, making copies, referring to other sources, or denying the requests for information

Follow-up
- Asks patrons if their questions have been completely answered
- Encourages the patrons to return if they have further questions by making a statement such as "If you don't find what you are looking for, please come back and we'll try something else."
- Consults other archivists when additional subject expertise is needed
- Facilitates the process of referring patrons to another repository or information agency through activities such as calling ahead, providing direction and instructions, and providing the other repository and the patron with as much information as possible about the amount of information required, and sources already consulted
- Creates, maintains, and periodically reviews records of user requests, for self-evaluation and planning purposes

Outreach, Advocacy, and Promotion

- Promotes the use of records and papers by identifying potential users and uses, by analyzing and describing the benefits of use, and through public and educational programs
- Develops an understanding of, and support for, the archival program among resource allocators, key constituents, potential donors, allied professionals, and within related functional areas (IT, library, etc.) of the archives' parent organization
- Participates in programs that draw directly on records and papers to support such activities as exhibitions, conferences, publications, and editorial projects
- Participates in efforts to publicize archival collections and repositories through print, electronic, and broadcast media

Academy of Certified Archivists, 2003 *Role Delineation Statement Revision* at www.certi-fiedarchivists.org/html/RoleDelineation.html; American Library Association, *Professional Competencies for Reference and User Services Librarians* at http://www.ala.org/ala/rusa/rusaprotools/referenceguide/professional.htm; and American Library Association, *Guidelines for Behavioral Performance of Reference and Information Services Professionals* at www.ala.org/ala/rusa/rusaprotools/referenceguide/guidelinesbehavioral.htm.

Standards for Reference Archivists—Knowledge Associated with Good Reference Service

Reference archivists know and can apply knowledge of:

Subject Matter

The subject areas of an institution's holdings, and how they relate to holdings in other repositories, including knowledge of records creators and their records, such as

- the functions of the parent organization and its changes through time
- the functions of record creators
- forms of recordkeeping in parent organization and donated collections
- recordkeeping technologies
- handwriting, dating conventions, terminology used in documents
- the influence of technology on the structure of information
- the scope of collections and acquisitions policy of the repository

Research Needs

Research strategies, needs, and past and current research interests and trends of genealogists, scholars, journalists, and other major users of records and papers including knowledge of

- information-seeking patterns and behaviors of primary constituencies
- communication principles involving interaction with users both in person and through other channels

Reference Services

Issues and elements of archives user services, including policies and procedures governing access, reference services, and reproduction, including knowledge of

- repository finding aids
- basic information tools, including on-line catalogs, search systems, databases, Web sites, journals and monographs in both printed and electronic formats, videos, and sound recordings
- equipment needed to use record forms
- how to use and preserve different record forms
- laws, regulations, and ethical principles governing copyright, freedom of information, privacy, confidentiality, security, and equality of access
- reference strategies based on varying holdings, formats, media, and user needs
- research methodologies and characteristics of queries of major constituencies of repository
- accepted best practices for safeguarding records and papers while in use and accommodating researcher-owned technical equipment in research rooms
- techniques for expediting the handling of repeated requests on the same or similar topics through such tools as reference files, reference reports, frequently asked question pages on web sites, or surrogates of actual documents

Outreach and Public Programs

The variety of uses of records and papers, the benefits of such uses, and methods of imparting this information to potential users, including

- the range of approaches that might be taken to advance public understanding of archival work and programs, such as news releases, Web sites, exhibitions, press kits, and curriculum packages
- methods of presenting archival records and papers, or information from or about them, in a user-friendly manner that encourages use of archives

- methods of articulating to resource allocators the benefits of establishing and supporting the continued operation of an archival program in an organization
- methods of collaborating with functional units within the archives' parent organization to enhance or further archival work

---

Academy of Certified Archivists, *2003 Role Delineation Statement Revision* at www.certified archivists.org/html/RoleDelineation.html; American Library Association, *Professional Competencies for Reference and User Services Librarians* at http://www.ala.org/ala/rusa/ rusaprotools/referenceguide/professional.htm; and American Library Association, *Guidelines for Behavioral Performance of Reference and Information Services Professionals* at www.ala.org/ala/rusa/rusaprotools/referenceguide/guidelinesbehavioral.htm.

Notes

1. Looking Backward, Looking Forward

1 Bernardo A. Huberman, *The Laws of the Web: Patterns in the Ecology of Information* (Cambridge, Mass.: MIT Press, 2001), 13–14.

2 Mihaly Csikszentmihalyi and Kim Hermanson, "Intrinsic Motivation in Museum: What Makes Visitors Want to Learn?" *Museum News* (May/June 1995): 36.

3 Hugh Taylor, *Archival Services and the Concept of the User* (Paris: UNESCO, 1984), 89.

4 David Bearman, *Archival Methods* (Pittsburgh: Archives and Museum Informatics, 1989), 1.

2. Reference Services in Archives

5 Elizabeth Yakel, "Listening to Users," *Archival Issues* 26 (2002): 111–23.

6 David M. Levy, *Scrolling Forward: Making Sense of Documents in the Digital Age* (New York: Arcade Publishing, 2001), 23.

7 Ibid., 27–28.

8 Ibid., 35.

9 JoAnne Yates, *Control Through Communication: The Rise of System in American Management* (Baltimore: Johns Hopkins University Press, 1989); Peter J. Wosh, "Going Postal," *American Archivist* 61 (Spring 1998): 220–39.

10 Levy, *Scrolling Forward*, 96.

11 Abigail J. Sellen and Richard R.R. Harper, *The Myth of the Paperless Office* (Cambridge, Mass.: MIT Press, 2002).

12 Megan G. Sniffin-Marinoff, "To Archive or Not to Archive? The Message of a (Somewhat) Meaningless Question," *Government Information Quarterly* 16 (1999): 199–202.

13 Frank Burke, "Similarities and Differences" in *Archive Library Relations,* edited by Robert L. Clark, Jr. (New York: R. R. Bowker Company, 1976), 31–35. This

theme is developed in Lawrence J. McCrank editor, *Archives and Library Administration: Divergent Traditions and Common Concerns* (New York: Haworth Press, 1986). See especially David Klaassen, "The Provenance of Archives under Library Administration," 37.

14 "The Information Family Tree" from Ann Pederson, "Understanding Society Through Its Records," http://john.curtin.edu.au/society.

15 Levy, *Scrolling Forward,* 30.

16 Constitution of the United States, Article I, Section 1.

17 Letter to W. T. Barry, 4 August 1822, in G. P. Hunt, ed., *The Writings of James Madison* ix (New York: G. P. Putnam's Sons, 1910), 103.

18 The mission statement and vision statement of the National Archives are found at http://www.archives.gov/.

19 Richard Berner, *Archival Theory and Practice in the United States: A Historical Analysis* (Seattle: University of Washington Press, 1983).

20 Howard Peckham stated in 1956 that the research library is not a public library. "If it should open its doors to competent scholars, then it should close them to those who are not competent," in "Aiding the Scholar in Using Manuscript Collections," *American Archivist* 19 (July 1956): 221–28.

21 Bruce W. Dearstyne, *Managing Historical Records Programs: A Guide for Historical Agencies* (Walnut Creek, Calif.: AltaMira Press, 2000), 102–21.

22 "'The Imperative of Challenging Absolutes' in Graduate Archival Education Programs: Issues for Educators and the Profession," *American Archivist* 63 (Fall/Winter 2000): 385.

23 Elizabeth Yakel, "Impact of Internet-based Discovery Tools on Use and Users of Archives," ica 2002, International Conference of the Round Table on Archives, at www.ica.org/new/citra.php?pcitraprogramid=24&plangue=eng.

24 Elsie Freeman Finch and Paul Conway, "Talking to the Angel: Beginning Your Public Relations Program," in *Advocating Archives: An Introduction to Public Relations for Archivists,* edited by Elsie Freeman Finch (Lanham, Md.: Scarecrow Press, 1994), 5–22.

25 *Code of Ethics for Archivists* (Chicago: Society of American Archivists, 2005), on-line at http://www.archivists.org/governance/handbook/app-ethics.asp; Elena S. Danielson, "Ethics and Reference Services," *Reference Services for Archives and Manuscripts* (New York: Haworth Press, 1997), 107–124. International Council on Archives *Code of Ethics* adopted on 6 September 1996, on-line at http://www.ica.org/biblio/spa/code_ethics_eng.html. Karen Benedict, *Ethics and the Archival Profession: Introduction and Case Studies* (Chicago: Society of American Archivists, 2003).

3. Identifying Uses and Users of Archives

26 "Declaration Breaks Records," *San Francisco Chronicle Review,* 4 March 1990, 15.

27 Trevor Livelton discusses this point in his *Archival Theory, Records, and the Public* (Lanham, Md.: Scarecrow Press, 1996), especially chapter 3.

28 *An Action Agenda for the Archival Profession: Institutionalizing the Planning Process* (Chicago: Society of American Archivists, 1988), 66.

29 *Action Agenda,* 66; also Paul Conway, "Facts and Frameworks, An Approach to Studying the Users of Archives," *American Archivist* 49 (Fall 1986): 396.

30 *Action Agenda,* 66.

31 Page Putnam Miller, *Developing a Premier National Institution: A Report from the User Community to the National Archives* (Washington, D.C.: National Coordinating Committee for the Promotion of History, 1989), 9.

32 Elsie Freeman, "Buying Quarter Inch Holes: Public Support through Results," *Midwestern Archivist* 10 (1985): 89–97.

33 Csikszentmihalyi and Hermanson, "Intrinsic Motivation in Museums," 34.

34 Colin Mick, "Human Factors in Information Work," *ASIS* 17 (1980): 21–23; David Bearman, "User Presentation Language in Archives," *Archives and Museum Informatics* 3 (Winter 1989–90): 3–7.

35 William L. Joyce formulates a similar distinction in "Archivists and Research Use," *American Archivist* 47 (Spring 1984): 124–33. Trudy Peterson and Nancy Bartlett shared unpublished works that explore this distinction.

36 Finch and Conway, "Talking to the Angel," 5–22.

37 Philip De Lancie, "Refreshing Media Management: Coca-Cola Turns Archives into Assets," *Econtent* 25 (May 2002): 18–22.

38 Thomas Wilsted, "Establishing an Image: The Role of Reference Service in a New Archival Program," *Reference Services in Archives* (New York: Haworth Press, 1986), 171.

39 Bearman, *Archival Methods,* 44; and Bearman and Richard H. Lytle, "The Power of the Principle of Provenance," *Archivaria* 21 (1985): 14–27.

40 http://libraries.mit.edu/archives/mithistory/histories-offices.html.

41 Elizabeth Yakel, "Thinking Inside and Outside the Boxes: Archival Reference Services at the Turn of the Century," *Archivaria* 49 (Spring 2000): 153; and "Knowledge Management: The Archivist's and Records Manager's Perspective," *Information Management Journal* 34 (July 2000): 24–30.

42 William L. Joyce, "Archivists and Research Use," *American Archivist* 47 (Spring 1984): 124–33; *Toward A Usable Past: Historical Records in the Empire State* (Albany: New York State Archives, 1984).

43 Robert Brent Toplin, "Introduction: Movie Reviews," *Journal of American History* 76 (December 1989): 1004; Kathleen Epp, "Telling Stories around the 'Electronic Campfire': The Use of Archives in Television Productions," *Archivaria* 49 (Spring 2000): 54–83.

44 Avra Michelson and Jeff Rothenberg, "Scholarly Communication and Information Technology: Exploring the Impact of Changes in the Research Process on Archives," *American Archivist* 55 (Spring 1992): 236–315.

45 Lawrence Dowler, "The Role of Use in Defining Archival Principle and Practice: A Research Agenda for the Availability and Use of Records," *American Archivist* 51 (Winter and Spring 1988): 79; Donald Owen Case, "The Collection and Use of Information by Some American Historians: A Study of Motives and Methods," *Library Quarterly* 61 (1991): 61–82.

46 Margaret Steig, "The Information of [sic] Needs of Historians," *College and Research Libraries* 42 (November 1981): 544–60; Michael E. Stevens, "The Historian and Archival Finding Aids," *Georgia Archive* 5 (Winter 1977): 64–74;

Mary B. Folster, "Information Seeking Patterns: Social Sciences," in *Library Users and Reference Services,* edited by Jo Bell Whitlatch (New York: Haworth Press, 1995), 83–93; Helen R. Tibbo, "Primarily History: Historians and the Search for Primary Source Materials" *American Archivist* 66 (Spring/Summer 2003): 9–50.

47 Laurence R. Veysey, "A Scholar's View of University Archives," *College and University Archives: Selected Readings* (Chicago: Society of American Archivists), 154.

48 Bianca Falbo, "Teaching from the Archives," *RBM* 1 (2000): 33–35; Marian J. Matyn, "Getting Undergraduates to Seek Primary Sources in Archives," *History Teacher* 33 (May 2000): 349–55; Laurie Lounsberry McFadden, "Making History Live: How to Get Students Interested in University Archives," *College & Research Libraries News* 59 (June 1998): 423–25.

49 "History is Primary, Man!" *The Bentley Historical Library* 8 (Spring 2003): 4.

50 David Kobrin, *Beyond the Textbook: Teaching History Using Documents and Primary Sources* (Portsmouth, N.H.: Heinemann, 1997).

51 William J. Maher, *The Management of College and University Archives* (Metuchen, N.J.: Scarecrow Press, Society of American Archivists, 1991), 259.

52 Edwin Bridges, Gregory S. Hunter, Page Putman Miller, David Thelan, and Gerhard Weinberg, "Toward Better Documenting and Interpreting of the Past: What History Graduate Programs in the Twenty-first Century Should Teach About Archival Practices," *American Archivist* 56 (Fall 1993): 730–49.

53 The Bentley Historical Library at the University of Michigan posts a list of suggested research topics to help students conceptualize archival research in fields such as black history, business, environment, politics, science and technology, wars, and women's history at http://www.umich.edu/~bhl/.

54 Elsie Freeman Finch, "Making Sure They Want It: Managing Successful Public Programs," *American Archivist* 56 (Winter 1993): 70–75, and *Teaching with Documents: Using Primary Sources from the National Archives* (Washington, D.C.: National Archives, 1989); Mark A. Greene, "Using College and University Archives as Instructional Materials," *Midwestern Archivist* 14 (1989): 31–38; Marcus C. Robyns, "The Archivist as Educator: Integrating Critical Thinking Skills into Historical Research Methods Instruction," *American Archivist* 64 (Fall/Winter 2001): 363–84; Anne J. Gilliland-Swetland, "An Exploration of K–12 User Needs for Digital Primary Source Materials," *American Archivist* 61 (1998): 136–57; Anne J. Gilliland-Swetland, Y. Kafai, and William Landis, "Integrating Primary Sources into the Elementary School Classroom: A Case Study of Teachers' Perspectives," *Archivaria* 48 (1999): 89–116; Ken Osborne, "Archives in the Classroom," *Archivaria* 23 (1986–87): 16–40.

55 For example, "Using Manuscripts and Archives: A Tutorial /An Instructional Tool for Finding Manuscripts and Archives at Yale and Beyond," on-line at http://www.library.yale.edu/mssa/tutorial/. See Diane E. Kaplan and William R. Massa, Jr., "Archival Insight via the Internet: Researcher Education When They Want It," *NEA Newsletter* 29 (April 2002): 4–7.

56 James J. Lorence, "Teaching History at Two-Year Institutions: A Status Report and View of the Future," The Organization of American Historians, 1999,

http://www.oah.org/pubs/commcoll/lorence.html. In 1990, OAH estimated that more than 30 percent of all history enrollments were in community colleges, *OAH Newsletter* (February 1990): 2.

57 Teaching American History Grant Program, Office of Innovation and Improvement, U.S. Department of Education, http://www.ed.gov/programs/teachinghistory/.

58 National Archives and Records Administration at www.archives.org/; Library of Congress American Memory at http://memory.loc.gov/; Valley of the Shadow Project at http://valley.vcdh.virginia.edu; and Minnesota Historical Society Educational Resources at http://www.mnhs.org/school/ .

59 http://www.ourdocuments.gov/;
and National History Day, Inc. at http://www. nationalhistoryday.org/.

60 Ian Mortimer, "Discriminating Between Readers: The Case for a Policy of Flexibility," *Journal of the Society of Archivists* 23 (2002): 59–67.

61 Commission on the Humanities, *The Humanities in American Life* (Berkeley: University of California Press, 1980), 137.

62 Adrian Ailes and Iain Watt, "Survey of Visitors to British Archives, June 1998," *Journal of the Society of Archives* 20 (1999).

63 Public Services Quality Group for Archives and Local Studies, "National Survey of Visitors to British Archives February 2001," on-line at http://www.nationalarchives.gov.uk/archives/psqg/.

64 *OAH Newsletter* (February 1991): 6.

65 Rosemary Boyns, "Archivists and Family Historians: Local Authority Record Repositories and the Family History User Group," *Journal of the Society of Archivists* 20 (1999): 61.

66 Phebe R. Jacobsen, "'The World Turned Upside Down': Reference Priorities and the State Archives," *American Archivist* 44 (Fall 1981): 341–45; Peter W. Bunce, "Towards a More Harmonious Relationship: A Challenge to Archivists and Genealogists," and Elizabeth Shown Mills, "Genealogists and Archivists: Communicating, Cooperating, and Coping!" *SAA Newsletter* (May 1990).

67 Margaret Mannix, "Plugging In To Your Roots," *U.S. News & World Report*, December 23, 1996, 73–74.

68 Nancy Shute, "Family History, Without the Dust," *U.S. News & World Report*, April 30, 2001, 48.

69 American Library Association, *Guidelines for a Unit or Course of Instruction in Genealogical Research at Schools of Library and Information Science* (1996), offers elements of knowledge needed by reference staff providing services for genealogists. See, for example, *Guide to Genealogical Research in the National Archives*, edited by Anne Bruner Eales and Robert M. Kvasnicka (Washington, D.C.: National Archives Trust Fund Board, 2000).

70 Boyns, "Archivists and Family Historians," 65.

71 The Statue of Liberty, Ellis Island Foundation, Inc., Web site at http://www.ellisisland.org/.

72 Boyns, "Archivists and Family Historians," 69.

73 This section began during my participation in the 1997 Research Fellowship Program for the Study of Modern Archives administered by the Bentley

Historical Library, University of Michigan, and funded by the Andrew W.
Mellon Foundation, the National Endowment for the Humanities, and the
University of Michigan.

74 Gary Marchionini, *Information Seeking in Electronic Environments* (Cambridge:
Cambridge University Press, 1995): 6–28. For an interesting application of
mental maps, see George Bain, "Visualizing the Archival Work Process: A
Survey and Interpretation," *Archival Issues* 21 (1996).

75 Marcia Bates, "The Design of Browsing and Berrypicking Techniques for the
Online Search Interface," *Online Review* 13 (1989): 407–424, on-line at
http://www.gseis.ucla.edu/faculty/bates/berrypicking.html.

76 This insight is mine, supported by Robert Lee Cross, "A Relational View of
Information Seeking" (dissertation, Boston University, 2001). See also, Marcia J.
Bates, "Toward an Integrated Model of Information Seeking and Searching"
(keynote address for the Fourth International Conference on Information Needs,
Seeking and Use in Different Contexts, Lisbon, Portugal, September 2002), on-
line at http://www.gseis.ucla.edu/faculty/bates/articles/info_SeekSearch-i-
030329.html.

77 Thomas Mann, *Library Research Models* (New York: Oxford University Press,
1993), 91. Early development of this section appeared in my article, "Information
Seeking in Organizations and Archives," crm *Cultural Resource Management* 21
(1998): 10–14, on-line at http://crm.cr.nps.gov/archive/21-6/21-6-3.pdf.

78 This observation also helps archivists understand why staff members are often
reluctant to send their records to the archives.

79 Ann D. Gordon, "A Portrait of Research in Legal History," *Public Services Issues
with Rare and Archival Law Materials* (New York: Haworth Press, 2001); also
published as *Legal Reference Services Quarterly* 20 (2001): 12.

80 Bates, "Berrypicking," 418.

81 Brian Friel, "Blackout," *Government Executive* (May 2002): 16–23.

82 Yakel, "Thinking Inside and Outside the Boxes," 147.

83 Mary W. Sprague, "Information-Seeking Patterns of University Administrators
and Nonfaculty Professional Staff Members," *Journal of Academic Librarianship*
19 (1994): 378, cited in William Brown and Elizabeth Yakel, "Redefining the Role
of College and University Archives," *American Archivist* (Summer 1996): 282.

84 Brown and Yakel, "Redefining the Role," 283.

85 Cross, "A Relational View of Information Seeking," 171.

86 Ibid., 174.

87 Paul Conway, *Partners in Research: Improving Access to the Nation's Archive*
(Pittsburgh: Archives and Museum Informatics, 1994).

88 Kristina L. Southwell, "How Researchers Learn of Manuscript Resources at the
Western History Collections," *Archival Issues,* 26 (2002): 91–109.

89 Elizabeth Yakel, "Listening to Users," *Archival Issues* 26 (2002).

90 Levy, *Scrolling Forward,* 112.

91 Barbara Craig, "Old Myths in New Clothes: Expectations of Archival Users,"
Archivaria 45 (Spring 1998): 122; Terry Cook, "Viewing the World Upside

Down: Reflections on the Theoretical Underpinnings of Archives Public Services," *Archivaria* 31 (Winter 1990-91): 123-34.

92 Craig, "Old Myths in New Clothes," 121–22; Laurie B. Crum, "Digital Evolution: Changing Roles and Challenges for Archivists in the Age of Global Networking," *Archival Issues* 20 (1995): 51–63; Bruno Delmas, "Archival Science Facing the Information Society," *Archival Science* 1 (2001): 25–37.

4. Providing Intellectual Access to Archives

93 For discussion of the principles underlying archival finding aids—provenance, original order, hierarchy of control, collective description, and progressive refinement of control—see Kathleen Roe, *Arranging and Describing Archives and Manuscripts* (Chicago: Society of American Archivists, 2005).

94 Elizabeth Shaw, "Designing Access and Delivery Systems: Thoughts of a Programmer on Making the Implicit Explicit" (paper delivered at the Society of American Archivists, 1999). Copy in possession of author.

95 Ibid.

96 Ibid.

97 Jennifer Davis Heaps, "Tracking Intelligence Information: The Office of Strategic Services," *American Archivist* 61 (Fall 1998): 287–308.

98 I started to use the term "pile management" when working with staff in my current position, but found that others have also used this term. See Malcolm Gladwell, "The Social Life of Paper: Looking for Method in the Mess," *New Yorker,* March 25, 2002. It is a useful term when helping staff members organize their records.

99 Victoria Irons Walch, *Standards for Archival Description: A Handbook* (Chicago: Society of American Archivists, 1994), 2.

100 "Report of the Working Group on Standards for Archival Descriptive," *American Archivist* 52 (Fall 1989): 441.

101 Richard Lytle, "Intellectual Access to Archives: Provenance and Content Indexing Methods of Subject Retrieval," *American Archivist* 43 (Winter 1980): 64. See also, David Bearman and Richard Lytle, "The Power of the Principle of Provenance," *Archivaria* 21 (1985–1986): 14–27; Michelle Light and Tom Hyry, "Colophons and Annotations: New Directions for the Finding Aid," *American Archivist* 65 (Fall/Winter 2002): 216–30.

102 Richard Berner calls this the public archives tradition in *Archival Theory and Practice in the United States: A Historical Analysis* (Seattle: University of Washington Press, 1983).

103 Mary Jo Pugh, "The Illusion of Omniscience: Subject Access and the Reference Archivist," *American Archivist* 45 (Winter 1982): 33–44.

104 American Management Systems, *Methodology for Developing an Expert System for Information Retrieval at the National Archives and Records Administration* (Washington, D.C.: National Archives, 1986).

105 Ruth Bordin and Robert Warner, *Modern Manuscript Library* (New York: Scarecrow Press, 1966).

106 Richard Berner has called these cataloging systems the historical manuscripts tradition in *Archival Theory and Practice in the United States: A Historical Analysis* (Seattle: University of Washington Press, 1983), 30.

107 Committee on Finding Aids, *Inventories and Registers: A Handbook of Techniques and Examples* (Chicago: Society of American Archivists, 1976).

108 The term "bridging tools" is from *Keeping Archives* (Sydney: Australian Society of Archivists, 1987), 164.

109 David Bearman, "Archives and Manuscript Control with Bibliographic Utilities: Opportunities and Challenges," *American Archivist* 52 (Winter 1989): 33. See also, Avra Michelson, "Description and Reference in the Age of Automation," *American Archivist* 50 (Spring 1987): 192–208; Alden Monroe and Kathleen Roe, "What's the Purpose? Functional Access to Archival Records," in *Beyond the Book: Extending MARC for Subject Access,* edited by Toni Petersen and Pat Molholt (Boston: G. K. Hall, 1990), 157–70; Helena Zinkham, Patricia Cloud, and Hope Mayo, "Providing Access by Form of Material, Genre, and Physical Characteristics: Benefits and Techniques," *American Archivist* 52 (Summer 1989): 300–319.

110 Steven L. Hensen, *Archives, Personal Papers, and Manuscripts: A Cataloging Manual* (Chicago: Society of American Archivists, 1989); David Bearman, "Authority Control: Issues and Prospects," *American Archivist* 52 (Summer 1989): 286–300. Standards for data values include the Library of Congress Subject Headings, Library of Congress Name Authority File (LCNAF) for personal names, the Getty Thesaurus of Geographic Names (TGN), and the Getty Art & Architecture Thesaurus (AAT).

111 Steven L. Hensen provides an overview of this history in "NISTF II and EAD: The Evolution of Archival Description," *American Archivist* 60 (Summer 1997): 284–96.

112 Daniel V. Pitti, "Encoded Archival Description: An Introduction and Overview," *D-Lib Magazine* 5 (November 1999), and "Encoded Archival Description: The Development of an Encoding Standard for Archival Finding Aids," *American Archivist* 60 (Summer 1997), later published in *Encoded Archival Description: Context, Theory, and Case Studies* (Chicago: Society of American Archivists, 1998). The standard is maintained at www.loc.gov/ead. See also, http://jefferson.village.virginia.edu/ead.

113 Jill M. Tatem, "EAD: Obstacles to Implementation, Opportunities for Understanding," *Archival Issues* 23 (1998): 155–69.

114 Repositories of Primary Sources, http://www.uidaho.edu/special-collections/ Other.Repositories.html.

115 Archival Internet Resources, http://www.tulane.edu/~lmiller/ ArchivesResources.html.

116 http://www.nagara.org/websites.html; http://www.unesco.org/webworld/portal_archives/pages/Archives/.

117 *Directory of Archives and Manuscript Repositories in the United States,* 2nd ed. (Phoenix: Oryx Press, 1988).

118 Proquest UMI, Archives USA, http://archives.chadwyck.com/.

119 American Association for State and Local History, http://www.aaslh.org/.

120 American Library Association, Fact Sheet Number 3, gives information about the *American Library Directory 2004–2005*, 57th ed.; see http://www.ala.org/ala/alalibrary/libraryfactsheet/alalibraryfactsheet3.htm. The directory is published by Information Today, Inc.; see http://www.books.infotoday.com.

121 Berkeley Digital Library, *LibWeb Library Servers via www*, http://sunsite.berkeley.edu/Libweb/.

122 Compiled by Lee Ash and William G. Miller, 7th ed. (New Providence, N.J.: R.R. Bowker, 1993).

123 Farmington Hills, Mich.: Gale, 2002.

124 Hilary and Mary Evans, 6th ed. (London and New York: Routledge, 1996).

125 Edited by Andrew H. Eskind, Greg Drake, Kirsti Ringger, Lynne Rumney (New York: G.K. Hall, 1996).

126 Edited by Richard Prelinger, Cyndy Turnage, Peter Kors, Celeste R. Hoffnar (New York: Prelinger Associates, 1989 and New York: Second Line Search, 1997). See Footage.net at www.footage.net.

127 Greg Colati, "Like Magic: Creating a Sustainable Internet Presence" (paper delivered at the New England Archivists Fall Meeting, 21 October 1995); Terry Abraham, "Net Worth: Adding Value to the Archival Web Site," Society of American Archivists, Annual Meeting, 30 August 1996.

128 Elizabeth Yakel and Jihyun Kim, "Midwest State Archives on the Web: A Content and Impact Analysis," *Archival Issues*, forthcoming.

129 Dearstyne, *Managing Historical Records Programs*, 116–18. A useful and accessible guide to designing Web sites is Patrick J. Lynch and Sara Horton, *Web Style Guide: Basic Design Principles for Creating Web Sites*, 2nd ed. (New Haven: Yale University Press, 2002) at http://www.webstyleguide.com/. Jakob Nielsen maintains an on-line column about making Web sites more usable at http://www.useit.com/.

130 Helen R. Tibbo and Lokman I. Meho, "Finding Finding Aids on the World Wide Web," *American Archivist* 64 (Spring/Summer 2001): 77.

131 Washington, D.C.: United States Government Printing Office, 1995. See the National Archives and Records Administration Web site at http://www.archives.gov.

132 Thomas E. Powers and William H. McNitt, *Guide to Manuscripts in the Bentley Historical Library* (Ann Arbor: University of Michigan, 1976); Robert M. Warner and Ida C. Brown, *Guide to Manuscripts in the Michigan Historical Collections of the University of Michigan* (Ann Arbor: University of Michigan, 1963), see http://www.umich.edu/~bhl/.

133 Richard C. Davis, *North American Forest History* (Santa Barbara, Calif.: Clio Books, 1997); Andrea Hinding, et al., *Women's History Sources: a Guide to Archives and Manuscript Collections in the United States* (New York: Bowker, 1979); and J. Albert Robbins, *American Literary Manuscripts: a Checklist of Holdings in Academic, Historical, and Public Libraries, Museums, and Authors' Homes in the United States* (Athens: University of Georgia Press, 1977).

134 National Union Catalog of Manuscript Collections at http://www.loc.gov/coll/nucmc/.

135 Research Library Group at http://www.rlg.org.

136 Online Computer Library Center at www.oclc.org.

137 ProQuest Company at http://www.proquestcompany.com/.

138 ProQuest, ArchivesUSA at http://archives.chadwyck.com/.

139 Burt Altman and John R. Nemmers, "The Usability of On-line Archival Resources: The Polaris Project Finding Aid," *American Archivist* 64 (Spring/Summer 2001): 121–31; Tibbo and Meho, "Finding Finding Aids," 66; James M. Roth, "Serving Up EAD: An Exploratory Study on the Deployment and Utilization of Encoded Archival Description Finding Aids," *American Archivist* 64 (Fall/Winter 2001): 220–21.

140 Lists of sites can be found at the EAD Round Table of the Society of American Archivists at http://www.iath.virginia.edu/ead/sitesann.html and at Encoded Archival Description Official Website at http://www.loc.gov/ead/eadsites.html.

141 Online Archive of California at www.oac.cdlib.org.

142 Cynthia Swank, "Life in the Fast Lane: Reference in a Business Archives," *Reference Services in Archives* (New York: Haworth Press, 1986), 82.

143 Charles M. Dollar, "Archival Theory and Practices and Informatics: Some Considerations" paper delivered at the University of Macerata, Italy, (7 September 1990), 18.

144 Angelika Menne-Haritz, "Access—The Reformulation of an Archival Paradigm," *Archival Science* 1 (2001): 57–82. See also, Bearman, *Archival Methods.*

145 Board for Certification of Genealogists, 1307 New Hampshire Avenue, N.W., Washington, D.C. 20036, at http://www.bcgcertification.org/.

146 Bearman and Lytle, "The Power of the Principle of Provenance," 25.

147 Bearman, "Authority Control Issues and Prospects," 286–99.

5. The Reference Process

148 Bonnie A Nardi and Vicki L. O'Day, *Information Ecologies: Using Technology with Heart* (Cambridge, Mass.: MIT Press, 1999), 104.

149 American Management Systems, "Methodology for Developing an Expert System for Information Retrieval at the National Archives and Records Administration," (Washington, D.C.: National Archives and Records Administration, 1986).

150 Nardi and O'Day, *Information Ecologies,* 85.

151 Linda J. Long, "Question Negotiation in the Archival Setting: The Use of Interpersonal Communication Techniques in the Reference Interview," *American Archivist* 52 (Winter 1989): 40–51; Susan L. Malbin, "The Reference Interview in Archival Literature," *College and Research Libraries* 58 (January 1997): 69–80; Gregory S. Hunter, *Developing and Maintaining Practical Archives,* (New York: Neal-Schuman Publishers, 1996), 190–91.

152 Finch and Conway, "Talking to the Angel," 5–22.

153 Joanna Lopez Munoz, "The Significance of Nonverbal Communications in the Reference Interview," *RQ* 16 (Spring 1977): 220.

154 Catherine Sheldrick Ross and Patricia Dewdney, "Negative Closure: Strategies and Counter-Strategies in the Reference Transaction," *Reference & User Services Quarterly* 38 (Winter 1998): 151–63.

155 Finch and Conway, "Talking to the Angel," 5–22.

156 Ailes and Watt, "Survey of Visitors," 177–94.

157 Michael R. Hill, *Archival Strategies and Techniques,* vol. 31, *Qualitative Research Methods,* (Newbury Park, Calif.: Sage Publications, 1993), 41–42.

158 Ross and Dewdney, "Negative Closure," 151–63.

159 Ross and Dewdney, "Negative Closure."

160 Ralph Gers and Lillie J. Seward, "Improving Reference Performance: Results of a Statewide Study," *Library Journal* 110 (1 November 1985), quoted in Ross and Dewdney, "Negative Closure."

161 Ibid.

162 Robert S. Tissing, Jr., "The Orientation Interview in Archival Research," *American Archivist* 47 (Spring 1984): 173–78, focuses almost exclusively on the administrative elements of the initial interview.

163 Ailes and Watt, "Survey of Visitors."

164 Interview with Nancy Bartlett, 2 July 1997.

165 Sara K. Weissman, "E-ref Characteristics," 18 October 2002, at http://www.gti.net/weissman/character.html.

166 Kristin E. Martin, "Analysis of Remote Reference Correspondence at a Large Academic Manuscripts Collection," *American Archivist* 64 (Spring/Summer 2001): 17–42; Wendy M. Duff and Catherine A. Johnson, "A Virtual Expression of Need: An Analysis of E-mail Reference Questions," *American Archivist* 64 (Spring/Summer 2001): 43–60.

167 Barbara Pearson, posting on LIBREF-L, 24 July 2003. LIBREF-L is a moderated discussion of issues related to reference librarianship at http://www.library.kent.edu/libref-l/.

168 Carolyn Buck, "Electronic Mail Reference Services," 3 December 1999, at http://www.slais.ubc.ca/courses/libr500/fall1999/www_presentations/C_buck/ref_interview.htm.

169 Helen R. Tibbo, "Interviewing Techniques for Remote Reference: Electronic Versus Traditional Environments," *American Archivist* 58 (Summer 1995): 294–310.

170 Danna Bell-Russel, Archives List Serv, 8 Aug 2002, at listserv@listserv.muohio.edu.

171 Mary Margaret Bell, "Managing Reference E-mail in an Archival Setting: Tools for the Increasing Number of Reference Queries," *College and Research Libraries News* 63 (February 2002). The on-line version is at http://www.ala.org/ala/acrl/acrlpubs/crlnews/backissues2002/february/managingreference.htm.

172 Thomas J. Ruller, "Open All Night: Using the Internet to Improve Access to Archives: A Case Study of the New York State Archives and Records Administration," in *Reference Services for Archives and Manuscripts,* edited by Laura B. Cohen (New York: Haworth Press, 1997), 161–70; Michael O'Malley and Roy Rosenzweig, "Brave New World or Blind Alley? American History on the World Wide Web," *Journal of American History* 84 (June 1997): 132–55.

173 Duff and Johnson, "A Virtual Expression of Need," 43–60.

174 Mary Minow, "Welcome to . . . the Legal Responsibility to Offer Accessible Electronic Information to Patrons with Disabilities," in *Libraries, Museums, and Archives: Legal Issues and Ethical Challenges in the New Information Era,* edited by Tomas A. Lipinski (Lanham, Md.: Scarecrow Press, 2002): 113–57. Federal electronic accessibility standards are found in Section 508 of the *Rehabilitation Act,* Fed. Reg. 63 (31 March 2000) at http://www.access-board.gov/508.htm.

175 Kristin E. Martin, "Analysis of Remote Reference Correspondence at a Large Academic Manuscripts Collection," *American Archivist* 64 (Spring/Summer 2001): 17–42; Craig, "Old Myths in New Clothes," 125.

176 Bruno B. W. Longmore, "Business Orientation and Customer Service Delivery: The Tyranny of the Customer," *Journal of the Society of Archivists* 21 (April 2000): 27–36.

177 Caroline R. Arms, "Getting the Picture: Observations from the Library of Congress on Providing Online Access to Pictorial Images," *Library Trends* 48 (Fall 1999): 379.

178 Bentley Historical Library, Access and Reference Services, Genealogy page at http://www.umich.edu/~bhl/bhl/refhome/genie.htm.

179 R. Philip Reynolds, "Building User-Oriented Web Sites for Archives," *Provenance* 14 (1996): 49-71; Carole Prietto, "Rare and Archival Law Materials on the World Wide Web: An Evaluation of Selected Sites," in *Public Services Issues with Rare and Archival Law Materials,* edited by Michael Widener (New York: Haworth Press, 2001): 67–70; Wendy Duff and Penka Stoyanova, "Transforming the Crazy Quilt: Archival Displays from a User's Point of View," *Archivaria* 45 (Spring 1998): 44–67.

180 Elizabeth Yakel, "Impact of Internet-based Discovery Tools on Use and Users of Archives," ICA 2002, International Conference of the Round Table on Archives, at www.ica.org/new/citra.php?pcitraprogramid=24&plangue=eng.

181 Tibbo and Meho, "Finding Finding Aids," 61–77.

182 Kathleen Feeney, "Retrieval of Archival Finding Aids Using World-Wide-Web Search Engines," *American Archivist* 62 (Fall 1999): 206–28.

183 See, for example, New York State Archives at http://www.archives.nysed.gov/aindex.shtml.

184 Bernie Sloan, "Digital Reference Services Bibliography," 20 September 2004, Graduate School of Library and Information Science, http://www.lis.uiuc.edu/~b-sloan/digiref.html. Suzanne Gray, "Virtual Reference Services: Directions and Agendas," *Reference & User Services Quarterly* 39 (Summer 2000): 365–75. *The Virtual Reference Desk* (VRD), sponsored by the United States Department of Education, seeks the "successful creation and operation of human-mediated, Internet-based information services" at www.vrd.org; IFLA Reference Work Section, "Digital Reference Service Guidelines,"at the Library of Congress Global Reference Network http://www.loc.gov/rr/digiref/digirefguidlines.html.

185 Buff Hirko, "Live, Digital Reference Marketplace," *Library Journal,* 15 October 2002, at http://newsroom.digi-net.com/PDFs/News/news_101502.pdf.

186 Finch and Conway, "Talking to the Angel," 5–22.

187 Tamar G. Chute, "Selling the College and University Archives: Current Outreach Perspectives," *Archival Issues* 25 (2000): 45.

188 John J. Grabowski, "Keepers, Users, and Funders: Building an Awareness of Archival Value," *American Archivist* 55 (Summer 1992): 464–72.

189 Michelle Light and Tom Hyry, "Colophons and Annotations: New Directions for the Finding Aid," *American Archivist* 65 (Fall/Winter 2002): 216–30.

190 Elsie Freeman, "Public Programs: What Alice Didn't Say," saa *Reference, Access, and Outreach Newsletter* 2 (August 1987): 3–4, and "Educational Programs as Administrative Function," *American Archivist* 41 (April 1978): 147–53.

191 Gabrielle Blais and David Enns, "From Paper Archives to People Archives: Public Programming in the Management of Archives," *Archivaria* 31 (Winter 1990–1991): 101–13; Kathleen Roe, "Public Programs," *Managing Archives and Archival Institutions,* edited by James Gregory Bradsher (Chicago: University of Chicago Press, 1989): 219–20; Csikszentmihalyi and Hermanson, "Intrinsic Motivation in Museums," 34.

192 Chauncey Bell, "Organizational Change and the Role of the Archivist," Society of California Archivists, Annual Meeting, May 1998; Grabowski, "Keepers, Users, and Funders," 464–72.

6. Determining Access Policies

193 Lewis Bellardo and Lynn Lady Bellardo, *A Glossary for Archivists, Manuscript Curators, and Records Managers* (Chicago: Society of American Archivists, 1991).

194 "Glossary," *Modern Archives Reader* (Washington, d.c.: National Archives, 1984), 339; Frank Evans, et al., "A Basic Glossary for Archivists, Manuscript Curators, and Records Managers," *American Archivist* 37 (July 1974): 415–33.

195 Gary M. Peterson and Trudy Huskamp Peterson, *Archives & Manuscripts: Law* (Chicago: Society of American Archivists, 1985), especially chapters 3 and 4; Heather MacNeill, *Without Consent: The Ethics of Disclosing Personal Information in Public Archives* (Lanham, Md.: Society of American Archivists and Scarecrow Press, 1992).

196 Akiba J. Covitz, "Providing Access to Lawyers' Papers: The Perils . . . and the Rewards," and Menzi L. Behrnd-Klodt, "Lawyers, Archivists and Librarians: United or Divided in the Pursuit of Justice?" both in *Public Services Issues with Rare and Archival Law Materials,* edited by Michael Widener (New York: Haworth Press, 2001).

197 "Standards for Access to Research Materials in Archival and Manuscript Repositories," *American Archivist* 37 (January 1974): 153–54. American Library Association/saa Joint Statement on Access to Original Research Materials Approved by the acrl Standards & Accreditation Committee, acrl Board of Directors, and the ala Standards Committee, February, 1994. This statement, slightly revised, was jointly promulgated by the American Library Association and saa. See http://www.archivists.org/statements/alasaa.asp.

198 Bearman, *Archival Methods,* 43.

199 Richard J. Cox discusses this quandary, but finds no easy solution in *Managing Institutional Archives: Foundational Principles and Practices* (New York: Greenwood Press, 1992), 148–50.

200 Tomas A. Lipinski, "Tort Theory in Library Museum and Archival Collections, Materials, Exhibits, and Displays: Rights of Privacy and Publicity in Personal Information and Persona," in *Libraries, Museums, and Archives: Legal Issues and Ethical Challenges in the New Information Era,* edited by Tomas A. Lipinski (Lanham, Md.: Scarecrow Press, 2002), 47–58.

201 Tomas A. Lipinski, "Legal Issues Involved in the Privacy Rights of Patrons in 'Public' Libraries and Archives," in *Libraries, Museums, and Archives: Legal Issues and Ethical Challenges in the New Information Era,* edited by Tomas A. Lipinski (Lanham, Md.: Scarecrow Press, 2002), 95–110.

202 (5 *u.s. Code* 552); House of Representatives, "A Citizen's Guide on Using the Freedom of Information Act and the Privacy Act of 1974 to Request Government Records," 2002, at http://www.fas.org/sgp/foia/citizen.html, pages 76–506.

203 National Park Service, *Museum Handbook* 2000, vol. 2, appendix D, 45–53 and vol. 3, chapters 1 and 2, at http://www.cr.nps.gov/museum/publications/handbook.html.

204 Anne Van Camp, "Trying to Write 'Comprehensive and Accurate' History of the Foreign Relations of the United States: An Archival Perspective," in *Archives and the Public Good: Accountability and Records in Modern Society,* edited by Richard J. Cox and David A. Wallace (Westport, Conn.: Quorum Books, 2002), 229–43.

205 National Archives and Records Administration, Washington, D.C. 20408.

206 20 *u.s. Code* Annotated 1232g.

207 Behrnd-Klodt, "Lawyers, Archivists and Librarians," 113–33; Jeannette Strickland, "Confidentiality Agreements," *Journal of the Society of Archivists* 23 (2002): 69–72.

208 Ronald L. Becker, "The Ethics of Providing Access," *Provenance* 11 (1993): 57–77; Bruce P. Montgomery, "Archiving Human Rights: A Paradigm for Collection Development," *Journal of Academic Librarianship* 22 (March 1999): 87–96.

209 Joseph L. Sax, "Not So Public: Access to Collections," *RBM* 1 (2000): 101–15. Also by Sax, *Playing Darts with A Rembrandt: Public and Private Rights in Cultural Treasures* (Ann Arbor: University of Michigan Press, 1999).

210 Covitz, "Providing Access to Lawyers' Papers."

211 Diane Kaplan, "The Stanley Milgram Papers: A Case Study on Appraisal of and Access to Confidential Data Files," *American Archivist* 59 (Summer 1996): 288–97.

212 See also, Association of College & Research Libraries "Guidelines for the Preparation of Policies on Library Access," prepared by the ACRL Access Policy Guidelines Task Force, *C&RL News,* December 1992. It is available on-line at http://www.ala.org/ala/acrl/acrlstandards/guidelinespreparation.htm. *Code of Ethics for Archivists* (Chicago: Society of American Archivists, 2005), on-line at http://www.archivists.org/governance/handbook/app_ethics.asp; "Standards for Ethical Conduct for Rare Book, Manuscript, and Special Collections Librarians, with Guidelines for Institutional Practice in Support of the Standards," *C&RL News* 54 (April 1993): 207–15.

213 Finch and Conway, "Talking to the Angel," 5–22.

214 Behrnd-Klodt, "Lawyers, Archivists and Librarians," 116–17.

215 Mortimer, "Discriminating Between Readers," 59–67.

216 "Statement on User Fees and Access," *SAA Newsletter* (January 1974).

217 Peter B. Hirtle, "Archives or Assets?" *American Archivist* 66 (Fall/Winter 2003): 235–248.

7. Providing Physical Access to Archives

218 *Americans with Disabilities Act,* Public Law 336, 101st Cong., (July 26, 1990). Americans with Disabilities Act (ADA) home page at http://www.usdoj.gov/ crt/ada/adahom1.htm; Ronald L. Gilardi, "The Archival Setting and People with Disabilities: A Legal Analysis," *American Archivist* 56 (Fall 1993): 704–13; Minow, "Welcome to," 113–57; Ronald L. Gilardi, "The Archival Setting and People with Disabilities: A Legal Analysis," *American Archivist* 56 (Fall 1993): 704–13.

219 Finch and Conway, "Talking to the Angel," 11–12.

220 "Guidance on Planning for a Research Space," *Museum Handbook,* vol. 3, appendix D, on-line at http://www.cr.nps.gov/museum/publication/hand-book/html.

221 Michael J. Kurtz, *Managing Archival and Manuscript Repositories* (Chicago: Society of American Archivists, 2004), 168.

222 Megan Spriggs, "Access to Oversize Records: Space Requirements and Reprographic Options for Architectural Archives," (paper, Society of American Archivists, 22 August 2002).

223 For reviews of equipment, see *Library Technology Reports* (Chicago: American Library Association), at https://www.techsource.ala.org/lt.

224 Gregor Trinkhaus-Randall, *Protecting Your Collections: A Manual of Archival Security* (Chicago: Society of American Archivists, 1995).

225 Vincent A. Totka, Jr., "Preventing Patron Theft in the Archives: Legal Perspectives and Problems," *American Archivist* 56 (Fall 1993): 664–72.

226 Bruce A. Shuman, "Seven Levels of Safety: Protecting People in Public Buildings," in *Libraries, Museums, and Archives: Legal Issues and Ethical Challenges in the New Information Era,* edited by Tomas A. Lipinski (Lanham, Md.: Scarecrow Press, 2002), 159–75.

227 Mary Lynn Ritzenthaler, *Preserving Archives and Manuscripts* (Chicago: Society of American Archivists, 1993).

228 Kathleen Marquis referred to the "forms, forms, forms" nature of archival reference service. Nancy Bartlett stimulated my thinking about the management of archival reference services.

229 *Sample Forms for Archival Records and Management Programs* (Chicago and Lenexa, Kans.: ARMA International and the Society of American Archivists, 2002).

230 Thomas Brown, "Standards for MRR Reference Service," *Archival Informatics Newsletter* 2 (Summer 1988): 33–35.

231 Gail M. Hodge, "Best Practices for Digital Archiving: An Information Life Cycle Approach," *D-Lib Magazine* 6 (January 2000) at http://www.dlib.org/dlib/january00/01hodge.html. An interesting framework is Kenneth Thibodeau, "Building the Archives of the Future: Advances in Preserving Electronic Records at the National Archives and Records Administration," *D-Lib Magazine* 7 (February 2001), at http://www.dlib.org/dlib/february01/thibodeau/02thibodeau.html.

232 See the ICPSR Web site at http://www.icpsr.umich.edu.

233 Theodore J. Hull, "Reference Services for Electronic Records in Archives," in *Reference Services for Archives and Manuscripts* edited by Laura B. Cohen (New York: Haworth Press, 1997), 147–160.

234 Margaret Hedstrom," How Do Archivists Make Electronic Archives Usable and Accessible?" *Archives and Manuscripts* 26 (May 1998): 6–22.

235 William G. LeFurgy, "Levels of Service for Digital Repositories," *D-Lib Magazine* 8 (May 2002) at http://www.dlib.org/dlib/may02/lefurgy/05lefurgy.html.

8. Providing Information from Archives: Copies and Loans

236 Archivists may also find these forms in their holdings. For a discussion of these earlier forms of reprography, consult Carolyn Hoover Sung, *Archives and Manuscripts: Reprography* (Chicago: Society of American Archivists, 1982); and Eleonore Kissel and Erin Vigneau, *Architectural Photoreproductions: A Manual for Identification and Care* (New Castle, Del. and Bronx, N.Y.: Oak Knoll Press and New York Botanical Gardens, 1999).

237 Peterson and Peterson, *Archives & Manuscripts: Law*, 89–90.

238 "Statement on the Reproduction of Manuscripts and Archives for Reference Use," *American Archivist* 39 (July 1976): 411.

239 Steven Puglia, "Reformatting and Copying Architectural Records," *Architectural Records Conference Report* (May 2000) at http://www.ccaha.org/arch_records.php. See also, "Preservation Photocopying in Libraries and Archives," *Restaurator* 8 (1987).

240 National Archives and Records Administration, "Research Room," at http://www.archives.gov/research_room/obtain_copies/self_service.html. In the Cartographic and Architectural Research Room at College Park, use of oversize electrostatic copiers is restricted to NARA staff, but researchers may arrange same-day, cash-and-carry copying of a limited number of items at $2.70 per foot per item.

241 Ibid., at http://www.archives.gov/research_room/obtain_copies/scanning.html. A useful summary of scanners is Stephen Chapman, "Book Scanners and Cradles: Links to Products and Reviews," RLG *DigiNews* 6 (15 August 2002), on-line at http://www.rlg.org/legacy/preserv/diginews/diginews6-4.html#chapman.

242 Ibid., at http://www.archives.gov/research_room/media_formats/visit_motion_picture_room.html#intro.

243 "Statement on the Reproduction of Manuscripts and Archives for Reference Use," *American Archivist* 39 (July 1976): 411.

244 "Archives: Reference Photocopying," *Conserve o gram* 19/7 (July 1993), on-line at http://www.cr.nps.gov/museum/publications/conserveogram/19-07.pdf.

245 Ritzenthaler, *Preserving Archives and Manuscripts*, 125–28.

246 Kelsey Osborn, "Current Methods of Reproducing Architectural Plans," 1996; Kissel and Vigneau, "Architectural Photoreproductions."

247 Spriggs, "Access to Oversize Records."

248 Nancy E. Elkington, RLG *Preservation Microfilming Handbook* (Mountain View, Calif.: Research Libraries Group, 1992) and RLG *Archives Microfilming Manual*

(Mountain View, Calif.: Research Libraries Group, 1994). See also Lisa L. Fox, *Preservation Microfilming: A Guide for Librarians and Archivists* (Chicago: American Library Association, 1996). More information can be had through American National Standards Institute (ANSI), 1430 Broadway, New York, NY, 10018, and the Association for Information and Image Management (AIIM) 1100 Wayne Ave, Silver Spring, MD, 20910.

249 In addition to Sung, see Ritzenthaler, et al., "Managing a Photographic Copying Service," *Archives and Manuscripts: Administration of Photographic Collections* (Chicago: Society of American Archivists, 1984), 141–52.

250 Spriggs, "Access to Oversize Records."

251 Christopher Ann Paton, "Preservation Re-Recording of Audio Recordings in Archives: Problems, Priorities, Technologies, and Recommendations," *American Archivist* 61 (Spring 1998): 188–219.

252 Visit ARSC at http://www.arsc-audio.org/.

253 The *National Recording Preservation Act of 2000*, Public Law 106-474, HR 4846. Visit the National Recording Preservation Board on-line at http://www.loc.gov/rr/record/nrpb/.

254 Association of Moving Image Archivists, at http://www.amianet.org/.

255 Stephen Chapman and Anne R. Kenney, "Digital Conversion of Research Library Materials: A Case for Full Informational Capture," *D-Lib Magazine* (October 1996), on-line at http://www.dlib.org/dlib/october96/cornell/10chapman.html. See also Bertrand Lavédrine, *A Guide to the Preventive Conservation of Photograph Collections* (Los Angeles, Calif.: Getty Trust, 2003).

256 Norman Paskin, "On Making and Identifying a 'Copy,'" *D-Lib Magazine* 9 (January 2003), on-line at http://www.dlib.org/dlib/january03/paskin/01paskin.html; Steven Puglia, "Technical Primer," in Maxine K. Sitts, ed., *Handbook for Digital Projects: A Management Tool for Preservation and Access* (Andover, Mass.: Northeast Document Conservation Center, 2000), on-line at http://www.nedcc.org/digital/dman.pdf.

257 Teresa Grose Beamsley, "Securing Digital Image Assets in Museums and Libraries: A Risk Management Approach," *Library Trends* 48 (Fall 1999): 359–78.

258 *Copyright Act of 1976*, Public Law 94-553, 90 Stat. 2541, U.S. Code, Title 17. For more information on copyright see the U.S. Copyright Office home page, "Copyright," at www.copyright.gov/.

259 I am most grateful to William J. Maher for his careful, helpful, and encouraging reading of this topic. He clarified several major issues. Jessica Litman, "The Demonization of Piracy," describes this shift in the assumptions underlying copyright. Her paper, given in Toronto, 6 April 2000, can be found at http://www.law.wayne.edu/litman/papers/demon.pdf.

260 Michael S. Shapiro, "Not Control, Progress," *Museum News* (September/October 1997), 37.

261 Title 17 does not cover sound recordings made before 15 February 1972.

262 Peter Hirtle maintains a very useful chart summarizing these provisions especially for archivists, *When Works Pass into the Public Domain in the United States: Copyright Term for Archivists*, posted on-line by the Cornell Institute for Digital Collections at http://www.copyright.cornell.edu/training/Hirtle_Public_Domain.htm.

263 Peter Hirtle, "Recent Changes to the Copyright Law: Copyright Term Extension," *Archival Outlook* (January/February 1999): 1–4.

264 A summary of the DMCA by the Copyright Office is found at http://www.loc.gov/copyright/legislation/dmca.pdf.

265 Library of Congress, Circular 21, "Reproduction of Copyrighted Works by Educators and Librarians" is the most authoritative guide, but does not speak clearly to the concerns of archivists dealing with unpublished materials. See it on-line at http://www.loc.gov/copyright/circs/circ21.pdf.

266 Christine Steiner, "The Double Edged Sword: Museums and the Fair Use Doctrine," Museum News (September/October 1997): 32; William Maher, letter to author, May 2003.

267 Note House of Representatives Report 94-1476 at page 78. See Melville B. Nimmer and David Nimmer, *Nimmer on Copyright* (New York: Matthew Bender and Lexis Publishing, 1978), § 8.03 [B], who say "Nonetheless, a library may engage in reproduction of even the non-exempted works to the extent that such reproduction finds shelter in the fair use doctrine."

268 The required notice is found in 37 *Code of Federal Regulations* 201. 14.

269 Brewster Kahle, Rick Prelinger, and Mary E. Jackson, "Public Access to Digital Material," *D-Lib Magazine* 7 (October 2001), on-line at http://www.dlib.org/dlib/october01/kahle/10kahle.html.

270 See for example, Linda M. Matthews, "Copyright and the Duplication of Personal Papers in Archival Repositories," *Library Trends* (Fall 1983): 223–40; Peterson and Peterson, *Archives and Manuscripts: Law,* chapter 6; Alex Ladenson, "Legal Clinic: Questions and Answers on Copyright," SAA *Newsletter* (May 1979): 8–9.

271 "Statement by Copyright Task Force, Society of American Archivists," in U. S. Copyright Office, *Library Reproduction of Copyrighted Works (17 U.S. Code 108): Report of the Register of Copyrights to the Congress* (Washington, D.C.: Library of Congress, 1983), appendix iv, part 2: 89–96. The opinion of the Registrar of Copyright is found throughout *Library Reproduction of Copyrighted Works,* particularly 105–6, 121–24, and 329–31.

272 Michael Crawford, "Copyright, Unpublished Manuscript Records, and the Archivist," *American Archivist* 46 (Spring 1983): 141; Carolyn A. Wallace, "Archivists and the New Copyright Law," *Georgia Archive* 6 (1978): 1–17.

273 *Harper & Row v. the Nation,* 471 U.S. 555 (1985); *J. D. Salinger v. Random House, Inc.,* 811 F.2d 90 (1987).

274 "Fair Use of Unpublished Works," Public Law 106, *U.S. Statutes at Large* 3145 (1992).

275 Kenneth D. Crews, "Fair Use of Unpublished Works: Burdens of Proof and the Integrity of Copyright," *Arizona State Law Journal* 31 (1999): 1–93; Dwayne K. Butler and Kenneth D. Crews, "Copyright Protection and Technological Reform of Library Services: Digital Change, Practical Applications, and Congressional Action," in *Libraries, Museums, and Archives: Legal Issues and Ethical Challenges in the New Information Era* (Lanham, Md.: Scarecrow Press, 2002): 275–94. See also, William Maher, "Current Issues in Copyright Law and Archival Administration," *Archival Issues* 26 (2001): 63–75.

276　Heather Briston, "Digital Rights Management and Archivists," *Archival Outlook* (July/August 2003): 14. Relevant Web sites are Berkeley Center for Law and Technology, et al., The Law and Technology of DRM Conference, 27 February 2003 at www.law.berkeley.edu/institutes/bclt/drm; and Association of Research Libraries, "Digital Rights Management," at http://www.arl.org/info/frn/copy/DRM.html.

277　Steiner, "The Double Edged Sword," 49.

278　See, for example, the rights and permissions page for the Bancroft Library at the University of California-Berkeley at http://bancroft.berkeley.edu/reference/permissions.html.

279　Library of Congress, Circular 22, "How to Investigate the Copyright Status of a Work," at http://www.copyright.gov/circs/circ22.pdf.

280　Frank G. Burke, *Research and the Manuscript Tradition* (Lanham, Md.: Scarecrow Press and Society of American Archivists, 1997): 211.

281　Richard A. Cameron, "The Concept of a National Records Program and Its Continued Relevance for a New Century," *American Archivist* 63 (Spring/Summer 2000): 43–89.

282　The Association for Documentary Editing is found at http://etext.lib.virginia.edu/ade/. A useful handbook of theory and practice is Michael E. Stevens and Steven B. Burg, *Editing Historical Documents: A Handbook of Practice* (Walnut Creek, Calif.: AltaMira Press, 1997). A list of documentary publications is found at http://etext.lib.virginia.edu/ade/editions.html.

283　David Chesnutt, "The Model Editions Partnership: Historical Editions in the Digital Age," *D-Lib Magazine* (November 1995) at http://www.dlib.org/dlib/november95/11chesnutt.html; and "The Model Editions Partnership: 'Smart Text' and Beyond," *D-Lib Magazine* (July/August 1997) at http://www.dlib.org/dlib/july97/07chesnutt.html.

284　Similarly, archivists defined the DTD for finding aids in the Encoded Archival Description.

285　"Nine of the experimental mini-editions are based on full-text searchable document transcriptions; two are based on document images; and one is based on both images and text," University of South Carolina, "Model Editions Partnership" Web site at http://adh.sc.edu/.

286　Model Editions Partnership Reference Manual, "Tag Set Documentation," on-line at http://adh.sc.edu/meptsdv1.html.

287　See the Research Center's Web site at http://bailey.uvm.edu/specialcollections/gpmorc.html.

288　Elizabeth H. Dow with David R. Chestnutt, William E. Underwood, Helen R. Tibbo, Mary-Jo Kline, and Charlene N. Bickford, "The Burlington Agenda: Research Issues in Intellectual Access to Electronically Published Historical Documents," *American Archivist* 64 (Fall/Winter 2001): 292–307. Also available on-line at http://etext.uvm.edu/bagenda/.

289　See the EDOCS Web site at http://history.furman.edu/edocs/.

290　See the Web site at http://memory.loc.gov/amhome.html; Caroline R. Arms, "Historical Collections for the National Digital Library Lessons and Challenges at the Library of Congress," *D-Lib Magazine* (April 1996 and May 1996) at http://www.dlib.org/dlib/april96/loc/04c-arms.html: Anne J. Gilliland-Swetland, "An Exploration of K–12 User Needs for Digital Primary Source Materials," *American Archivist* 61 (1998): 136–57; Caroline R. Arms, "Getting the Picture: Observation from the Library of Congress on Providing Online Access to Pictorial Images," *Library Trends* 48 (Fall 1999): 379.

291 See the Statue of Liberty-Ellis Island Foundation Web site at http://www.ellisisland.org/.

292 Behrnd-Klodt, "Lawyers, Archivists and Librarians," 122.

293 Gail Farr, *Archives and Manuscripts: Exhibits* (Chicago: Society of American Archivists, 1980), discusses all aspects of exhibits including loaning for exhibits.

294 Ritzenthaler, *Preserving Archives and Manuscripts*, 123.

295 Timothy L. Ericson and Joshua P. Ranger, "'The Next Great Idea': Loaning Archival Collections," *Archivaria* 47 (Spring 1999): 85–113.

296 National Park Service, *Museum Handbook,* vol.2, chapter 5, "Outgoing Loans," on-line at http://www.cr.nps.gov/museum/publications/MHII/mh2ch5.pdf.

297 American Association of Museums, Registrars Committee, *Standard Facility Report,* 2nd ed. (1998).

298 Repositories wishing to loan original materials for research or exhibition may consult the RBMS "Guidelines for the Loan of Rare and Unique Materials," *C&RL News* 54 (May 1993): 267–69, or the "Guidelines for Borrowing Special Collections Materials for Exhibition," *C&RL News* 51 (May 1990): 430–34. Repositories wishing to participate in the interlibrary loan of materials may consult as a model the "Additional Guidelines for Access to Archives, Manuscripts, and Special Collections," chapter 8, of the RLF *Shared Resources Manual,* 3rd ed. (Stanford, Calif.: Research Libraries Groups, 1987). The chapter is reprinted in *Rare Books & Manuscripts Librarianship* 3 (Fall 1988): 126–30.

9. Managing Reference Services and Evaluating the Use of Archives

299 Janice E. Ruth, "Educating the Reference Archivist," *American Archivist* 51 (Summer 1988): 266–76; and Hugh Taylor, *Archival Services and the Concept of the User* (Paris: UNESCO, 1984); Terry Eastwood, "Public Service Education for Archivists," in *Reference Services for Archives and Manuscripts,* edited by Laura B. Cohen (New York: Haworth Press, 1997), 27–38; American Library Association, *Professional Competencies for Reference and User Services Librarians,* 2003; Stuart Strachan, "How Good Are We?: Sketching the Parameters of Service Evaluation," *Archifacts* (April 1996): 50–54.

300 Library literature is helpful on this topic. See, for example, Rhea Joyce Rubin, "Anger in the Library: Defusing Angry Patrons at the Reference Desk (and Elsewhere)," *Reference Librarian* 31 (1990): 39–51.

301 Page Putnam Miller, *Developing a Premier National Institution: A Report from the User Community to the National Archives* (Washington, D.C.: National Coordinating Committee for the Promotion of History, 1989), 23–35.

302 Donna Baker, "Frameworks Revisited: Comprehensive User Agreement System

of the Manuscript Department of the University of North Carolina at Chapel Hill" (master's thesis, University of North Carolina at Chapel Hill, 2001), cited in Helen Tibbo, "Learning to Love our Users: A Challenge to the Profession and a Model for Practice," paper delivered at the Midwest Archives Conference, 2002.

303 Online Registration Form at http://web.si.umich.edu/expo/#W2003.

304 Bruce Dearstyne, "What Is the Use of Archives? A Challenge for the Profession," *American Archivist* 50 (Winter 1987): 76–87.

305 Richard J. Cox, "Researching Archival Reference as an Information Function: Observations on Needs and Opportunities," *RQ* (Spring 1992): 387–39.

306 Conway, "Facts and Frameworks," 393–407.

307 Society of American Archivists Task Force on Standard Reporting Practice, "Final Report," *SAA Newsletter* (November 1983): 13–16; Task Force on Institutional Evaluation, *Archives Assessment and Planning Workbook* (Chicago: Society of American Archivists, 1989); National Association of Government Archivists and Records Administrators, *Program Reporting Guidelines for Government Records Programs*, 1987.

308 Ailes and Watt, "Survey of Visitors," 182.

309 Interview with Nancy Bartlett, 2 July 1997.

310 Conway, "Facts and Frameworks," 404. See also, Judy Diamond, *Practical Evaluation Guide: Tools for Museums and Other Informal Educational Settings* (American Association for State and Local History and AltaMira Press, 1999).

311 David Bearman, "User Presentation Language," *Archives and Museum Informatics* 3 (Winter 1989–90): 3–7.

312 Found on-line at Academy of Certified Archivists http://www.certifiedarchivists.org/html/RoleDelineation.html.

313 American Library Association, *Professional Competencies for Reference and User Services Librarians,* at http://www.ala.org/ala/rusa/rusaprotools/referenceguide/professional.htm.

314 American Library Association, *Guidelines for Behavioral Performance of Reference and Information Services Professionals,* at www.ala.org/ala/rusa/rusaprotools/referenceguide/guidelinesbehavioral.htm.

315 IFLA Digital Reference Guidelines found on-line at http://www.ifla.org/VII/s36/pubs/drg03.htm.

316 http://www.vrd.org/facets-06-03.shtml.

317 Diane G. Schwartz and Dottie Eakin, "Reference Service Standards, Performance Criteria, and Evaluation," *Journal of Academic Librarianship* 12 (1986): 4–8; Jane P. Kleiner, "Ensuring Quality Reference Desk Service: The Introduction of a Peer Process," *RQ* 30 (Spring 1991): 349–61.

318 Ailes and Watt, "Survey of Visitors."

319 *Archives Planning and Assessment Workbook* (Chicago: Society of American Archivists, 1989). Section 9, "Access Policies and Reference Services," is reproduced in appendix 4 of this book.

320 Dearstyne, "What Is the Use of Archives?" 80.

321 Examples of such studies include Fredric Miller, "Use, Appraisal, and Research: A Case Study of Social History," *American Archivist* 49 (Fall 1986): 371–92; Jacqueline Goggin, "The Indirect Approach: A Study of Scholarly Users of Black and Women's Organizational Records in the Library of Congress Manuscripts Division," *Midwestern Archivist* 11 (Summer 1986); Diane Beattie, "An Archival User Study: Researchers in the Field of Women's History," *Archivaria* 29 (Winter 1989–90).

322 Tibbo, "Learning to Love Our Users."

323 Ailes and Watt, "A Survey of Visitors," 178.

Index

Boldface indicates figures and tables.

(AAD) Access to Archival Databases
System, 206
Academy of Certified Archivists, 265
Access. *See also* Equality of access; Privacy
access concepts, **151,** 151–155
definitions, 149–151
types of, 22–24
Access points, **91.**
Access policies
ALA-SAA Joint Statement on Access
to Original Materials, 313–315
Checklist for Access Policies and
Reference Services, 318–322
historical manuscripts tradition vs.
public archives tradition, 20
history of, 19–22
writing of, 162–172, **163**
Access restrictions. *See* Restrictions on
access
Access to Archival Databases (AAD)
System, 206
Access to information. *See* Equality of
access
ADE (Association for Documentary
Editing), 239
Administrative dimensions of reference
interaction, 131–132
Administrative histories in inventories,
107

Administrative use of archives
extensive research, 105
and loans of materials, 243
in parent organization, 18, 44
Advocacy for needs of users, 258
Age limits in access policy, 165
ALA-SAA Joint Statement on Access to
Original Materials, 313–315
American Experience series, 46
American Library Directory, 94
American Memory site, 56
AMIA (Association of Moving Image
Archivists), 224
Anniversaries and celebrations
as outreach, 144
support for, 44, 45, 59–60
Annual report of repository, 142
Archival and Manuscript Control
(MARC AMC), 91
Archives. *See also* Historical manu-
scripts; Organizational archives
as buildings, 15
as collections of documents, 14–15
definitions, 9–16, **14,** 36
uses of, 16–19
vs. records, 36
ArchivesUSA, 93, 103
Archivists
as archives users, 45
attitudes, 22

changing role of, 4, 5–7
as mediators, 111, 118
qualifications for, 254
as researchers, 160
Arrangement, 76–83
ARSC (Association for Recorded Sound
Collections), 224
*Articles Describing Archives and
Manuscript Collections in the United
States,* 94
Association for Documentary Editing
(ADE), 239
Association for Recorded Sound
Collections (ARSC), 224
Association of Moving Image Archivists
(AMIA), 224
Audiovisual materials
copying and copyright, 233–234
copying of, 212–213, 215, 224–225
directories to, 95
equipment for use, 179–180
intellectual access to, 88–89

Barcoding, 204
Bentley Historical Library, 5–6, 50, 98,
140, 264
Berrypicking model of information
retrieval, 61–63, **62**
Bibliographic databases
and dissemination of information, 138
effect on archives, 2
and intellectual access, 101–102
Bibliographic instruction. *See*
Information literacy programs
Biographical notes in inventories, 107
Body language. *See* Nonverbal commu-
nication
Bridging tools, 89
Brochures, 95–96, 137. *See also* Handouts
Browsing as information seeking, 66–67
Buckley Amendment, 157
Burlington Agenda, 240
Burnout, 132, 251

Call slips, 199, 201–202
Card catalogs, 5–6

Career ladders, 254
Case files and privacy, 158, 161
Celebrations. *See* Anniversaries and cel-
ebrations
Chain of custody, 78
Chairs, 178, 184
Checklist for Access Policies and
Reference Services, 318–322
Citation guidelines
in access policies, 169–171, **170–171**
and permission to publish, 238
Class assignments, 51–53
Classification, security, 156–157
Clerical staff. *See* Support staff
Collections
definition, 83
description of, 88
Communication patterns
as component of records systems, 11
oral communication, 64
Community colleges, promotion to, 56
Conferences as means of promoting
archives, 49, 145
Confidentiality, 153, 158
Conflicts of interest, 160
Constituencies. *See* User communities
Content-based descriptive systems,
87–88
Continuing education, 253
Continuing interaction
and administrative details, 132
intellectual dimensions of, 119
interpersonal dimensions of, 128–130
Copying, 210–225
issues, 23
policies, 133, 212–219
procedures, 219–221
Statement on the Reproduction of
Manuscripts and Archives, 316–317
types of copies, 221–225
types of requests, 210–212
Copying technology, 14–15
Copyright Act of 1976, 228
Copyright issues
in access policies, 169, 172
on copy forms, 220
and copying, 23, 218, 225–239
ownership rights, 226–227

permission to publish, 236
term of copyright, 228–232, **229–231**
Copyright notice, 233–234, **234**
Corporate archives. *See* Organizational
 archives
Court records, uses of, **38–39**
Creators of records
 descriptive aids to, 90
 networking with, 145
 providing information about, 106–108
Credit lines for photographs, 170
Curatorial organization of reference
 services, 250
Customer-driven services. *See*
 Researcher services

DAMRUS *(Directory of Archives and
 Manuscript Repositories in the United
 States)*, 93, 103
Demanding or difficult users, 130, 132,
 253
Description, 83–92
 content-based, 87–88
 definition, 84
 dissemination of on Web, 138
 effect on reference interaction, **116,**
  117, 204
 electronic resources, 90–92
 and hierarchy of control, 84–85
 history, 76, 85–86
 provenance-based, 86–87
 and quick reference tools, 108
 and security concerns, 180
Difficult or demanding users, 130, 132,
 253
Digital copies, 225, 240–242
Digital Millennium Copyright Act
 (DMCA), 228
Digital Reference Service Guidelines, 265
Digital reference services, 142–143
Digitization, 11, 241–242
Directional devices, 187–188
Directories to repositories, 93–95, 108
*Directory of Archives and Manuscript
 Repositories in the United States*
 (DAMRUS), 93, 103
*Directory of Historical Organizations in
 the United States and Canada*, 94

*Directory of Special Libraries and
 Information Centers*, 95
Direct uses of archives, 37, **38–40**
Disabled users, access for, 139–140, 176
Discovery, legal, 165
DMCA *(Digital Millennium Copyright
 Act)*, 228
Documentary films as dissemination of
 information, 46–47
Documents
 as artifacts, 40, 50
 as component of records systems, 11
 definition, 10–11
 in hierarchy of control, 81
 as information sources, 65–67
 outgoing, copies of, 14
Document type definitions (DTD), 240
Donor restrictions, 158–159
 in access policies, 164–165, 165–166
 copyrights and permission to publish, 227, 237–238
 and permission to use records, 160
DTD (document type definitions), 240
Dusty materials, 186

EAD (Encoded Archival Description)
 administrative histories in, 107
 for finding aids on Web, 141
 overview, 91–92
Economics of information, 73
Electronic access systems, 92
Electronic records, access to, 205–207
Electronic reference services, 142–143
Electronic resources
 description, 90–92
 as information sources, 67–68
 and user communities, 143
Elevator speeches, 144
E-mail inquiries, 134–138, 266
Emergency plans, 184, 187
Encoded Archival Description. *See* EAD
 (Encoded Archival Description)
Entertainment as use of archive, **39**
Environmental issues, **39,** 46
Equality of access
 in access policy, 164
 ethical norms, 160
 practical concerns, 154–155

and public archives tradition, 19–20

Ethics, 29–30, 159–160

Evaluation of archive use, 258–266

Evaluation of employees, 265, 327–330, 331–333

Evidential value of records, 35

Exhibitions

    copying for, 211

    loans for, 243–244, 245

    on-line, 142

Exit interview

    administrative details, 132

    interpersonal dimensions, 129–130

    uses of, 120

Extrinsic motivation for users, 41

Facets of Quality for Digital Reference, 265

Facsimile documents

    searchable digitized copies, 241–242

    as substitutes for original, 165

    in user education, 54–55

Fair use, 232–234, 235, 256

Family Educational Rights and Privacy Act (FERPA), 157

Fees

    in access policies, 168–169

    copying, 215–216, 221

    for intermediate copies, 214

    for permission to publish, 238

FERPA (Family Educational Rights and Privacy Act), 157

File unit in hierarchy of control, 81–82

Filing structure

    and evidentiary value of records, 35

    and original order, 79

    as primary mode of retrieval, 13

Films. *See* Audiovisual materials; Moving images

Filum, definition, 82

Finding aids. *See also* Description

    in access policies, 166–167

    effect on reference interaction, **116,** 117, 204

    and facilitation of research, 25–26, 109

    incorporating discoveries of researchers, 137, 160

    on Internet, 49, 105, 141

location in reading room, 178–179

    as outreach tools, 145

Fire emergencies, 184

FOIA (Freedom of Information Act), 21, 156

Follow-up activities. *See* Exit interview

Footage 91, 95

Footage.net, 95

Footnote chasing, 49, 66–67

Forms

    copy orders, 219–220, 256

    follow-up questionnaire, **267**

    for inquiries, 136, 255–256

    management of, 204, 255–256

    permission to publish, 236

    registration of users, 193–196, **194–195,** 255

    telephone reference, **137**

    tracking requests, **257**

Fragile materials, copying of, 222. *See also* Preservation

Freedom of Information Act (FOIA), 21, 156

Freedom of information laws, 21, 156

Freelance researchers, 106

Frequency of registration, 193

Frequently asked questions

    and e-mail inquiries, 136

    and tracking requests, 257–258

    on Web, 142

Functional organization of reference services, 251–252

Furnishings and equipment, 177–178

    and handling materials, 185

    and security, 181

Genealogists, 58–59

Governmental archives, 18

    access policies, 150

    history of, 19–20

    privacy laws, 155–156

    restrictions on access, 21

Graduate students as researchers, 51–52

Guidelines for Behavioral Performance of Reference and Information Services Professionals, 265

Guides to inventories, 86, 98–99

Guide to Archives and Manuscript Collections in the United States, 94
Guide to Federal Records in the National Archives of the United States, 98

Handling of materials, 180–185, 202–203
Handouts. *See also* Brochures
    on copying, 219
    on policies and procedures, 189
Hierarchy of control, 80–83, **81,** 84–85
Historical library, definition, 15
Historical manuscripts, definition, 12. *See also* Manuscript repositories
Historical manuscripts tradition
    evolution of, 20
Historical societies
    history, 20
Historic preservation, **39,** 46
Hobbyists and private collectors, 60
Holdings, 49, 97–103
Holdings, information from, 103–106
Hours, schedule of, 41, 187
Human dimensions. *See* Interpersonal dynamics

ICPSR (Inter-University Consortium for Political and Social Research), 205
Illustrations and examples as use of archives, 44
ILS (integrated library systems), 102
Imposed queries. *See* Third-party inquiries
Indexes to collections, 88, 89
Index to American Photographic Collections, 95
Index to Personal Names in the National Union Catalog of Manuscript Collections, 99
Indirect uses of archives, 37–40, 47
Informational value of records, 35
Information family tree, **17**
Information flow in organizations, **63,** 65–66
Information literacy programs, 53. *See also* User education

Information retrieval, models of, **62**
Information seeking, 61–72, **63**
    in archives, 71–72
    and changes in technology, 4
    from documents, 65–67
    from electronic resources, 67–68
    in organizations, 68–71
    from people, 64–65
Information systems. *See* Records and record systems
Infrastructure maintenance, 44
Initial interview. *See also* Continuing interaction
    and administrative details, 131–132
    human dimensions, 122–126
    intellectual dimensions, 113
    response to, 126–128
Inquiry tracking, **257,** 257–258
Institutional archives. *See* Organizational archives
Institutional memory as descriptive aid, 87
Instruction in use of archives. *See* User education
Integrated library systems (ILS), 102
Integrity, measurement of, 260
Intellectual access, 75–110. *See also* Arrangement; Description
    in access policies, 166–168
    and arrangement of records, 22
Intellectual dimensions
    reference interview, 113–120
    and staff qualifications, 253–254, 331–333
Intended use
    in access policies, 169
    and types of information, 41
Interlibrary loan, 244
Intermediate copies, 213–214, 224, 225
Internet. *See also* Web
    access to electronic records, 205–206
    directories to repositories, 93–95
    finding aids, 49, 105, 141
Interpersonal dynamics, 120–130
    and parent organization, 144
    in phone reference, 133–134

and staff qualifications, 252–253, 327–330

Inter-University Consortium for Political and Social Research (ICPSR), 205

Intranets, 143

Intrinsic motivation for users, 41

Intrinsic value of records, 35–36

Intuition in reference process, 118

Inventories as descriptive aid
history, 86–87
information about creators, 107

Invisible colleges, 49, 70

Item-level description, 88

Iteration in reference process, 119

Knowledge systems. *See* Records and record systems

Large-format materials
copying of, 221
handling of, 178

Layout and design of archive, 128, 176, 178, 180

Least Effort, Principle of, 4, 65, 67–68

Legal issues, 155–158
access policies, 21, 22
and changing technologies, 4–5
copying for evidence, 211
discovery and subpoenaed records, 165
donor restrictions, 158–159
Family Educational and Privacy Rights Act, 157
freedom of information laws, 21, 156
privacy laws, 155–156
security classification, 156–157
and staff of parent organization, 44

Legislative records, uses of, **38**

Leisure users, 57–60

Libraries
as information sources, 66–67
as term for archive, 15
vs. archives, 15, 121, 125–126

Library of Congress
Encoded Archival Description (EAD), 91–92
prohibited items in reading room, **198**
registration policy, 192

Lighting in reading room, 177, 185

Listening, 126

Loan of materials
in access policies, 172
policies and procedures, 242–246

Local historians as users, 59–60

Local history, 59–60

Location of initial interview, 128

Log of users, 196, 256

Mail inquiries, 134–138

Manuscript repositories
access policies, 150
content-based descriptive systems, 87–88
donor restrictions, 158–159
history of, 20
query resolution in, 117–118
referrals, 109

MARC AMC format, 91

Massachusetts Institute of Technology Archives, 45

Master copies. *See* Intermediate copies

Measurement of usage, 37, 258–266

Microforms, 212, 222–223

Minnesota Historical Society, 56

Mission of parent institution
and evaluation of significance of use, 268
as guide for reference services, 19
and unskilled user education, 53

Model Editions Partnership, 240

Motion pictures. *See* Moving images

Moving images. *See also* Audiovisual materials
copies, 224–225
directories to repositories, 95

Multiplier effect, 40

National Archives and Records
Administration
Access to Archival Databases System,
206
audiovisual copies, 224
citation guidelines, **170–171**
curriculum aids, 56
description in, 86
fees, 216
Guide to Federal Records, 98
mission, 18
presidential libraries, 15
records management, 256
research use of, 72
and security classification, 157
self-service copying, 214–215
National Association of Government
Archivists and Records
Administrators, 93
National Historical Publications and
Records Commission (NHPRC),
93, 239
National History Day, 56–57
*National Inventory of Documentary
Sources* (NIDS), 102, 103
*National Union Catalog of Manuscript
Collections* (NUCMC), 99–103, **101,**
103, 109
New York State Archives, 38–39
NHPRC (National Historical
Publications and Records
Commission), 93, 239
NIDS *(National Inventory of
Documentary Sources),* 102, 103
Nonverbal communication, 64–65, 121–122
Note taking, rules for, 203
NUCMC *(National Union Catalog of
Manuscript Collections),* 99–103, **101,**
109

OCLC, 102. *See also* Bibliographic databases
Online Archive of California, 103
On-line reference services, 142–143. *See
also* Internet; Web; Web sites for
repositories

OPACs (on-line public access catalogs),
102
Open meeting laws, 21
Organizational activities as filing struc-
ture, 79–80
Organizational archives, 12–13, 21, 117
Organizational charts as information
sources, 70
Orientation sessions, 55
Original order
and disturbed order, 181
in everyday life, 76–77
Outreach, 143–147
Outside organizations, networking in, 145
Oversize materials. *See* Large-format
materials
Ownership of copyright, 226–227

Parallel research, 172
Paraprofessionals. *See* Support staff
Parent organization
networking in, 144
outreach to, 144
research for, 105
staff of as users, 43–45
Parties and celebrations as outreach, 144
People as information sources, 64, 69
Performance evaluations
of repository, 265–266
of staff, 265, 327–330, 331–333
Performances, copying for, 211
Personal belongings in reading room,
197–199, **198**
Personal networks in information *seek-
*ing, 72
Personal records
arrangement of, 82
on computers, 67
definition, 12
as information sources, 65–66
privacy of, 156
sharing with colleagues, 70
Phone reference, 133–134, **137,** 188
Photocopying, 221–222. *See also* Copying
Photographic copying, 223–224

Photographs. *See also* Audiovisual materials
  citations for, 170
  copying, 215, 223–224
  handling of, 186
  publication of, 239
Physical access, 175–208
  in access policies, 23–24, 168
  for nonusers of archives, 165
  and restricted materials, 161
Picture Researcher's Handbook, 95
Pile management, 82
Place as principle of arrangement, 76–77
Planning, 255, 259
Policies and procedures.
  copying, 212–219
  excessive requests from users, 130
  and facilitation of research, 26
  on information from holdings, 106
  loan of materials, 242–246
  as management responsibility, 255
  permission to publish, 236–239
  Reference Procedures Manual sample contents, 323–326
  in reference process, 119
  for remote users, 133
  Statement on the Reproduction of Manuscripts and Archives, 316–317
  statements for users, **188,** 188–189
Preservation
  and copying, 23, 211–212, 217, 233
  and physical access, 185–187
  protection of materials while in use, 180–185, 202–203
  and rough handling by scholars, 49
Privacy
  definitions, 152–153
  in institutional records, 158
  legislation, 155–156
  and repository staff, 172
  of user information, 196–197
Professional Competencies for Reference and User Services Librarians, 265
Professional users, 46–47

Promotion of archives
  in parent organization, 44–45
  to scholars, 49
Provenance
  definition, 78
  and disturbed order, 181
  and electronic searching, 92
  in everyday life, 76–77
  as a retrieval mode, 66
  values of, 78–80
Provenance-based descriptive systems
  history, 86–87
  on intranet, 143
Public archives, 18
Public archives tradition, 19–20, 21
Publication
  by archive, 238–240
  copying for, 210–211
  requests for permission, 236–239
Public programs, 55, 97, 145–147
Public relations. *See* Outreach
Public service, staff attitude toward, 252–253
Published materials in archives, 16
Pull slips, 199, 201–202

Quality, measurement of, 259–265, **261,** 266
Quantitative measurements, 259, **262**
Query abstraction, 114–115
Query refinement. *See* Continuing interaction
Query resolution, 115–119
Question negotiation. *See* Reference interactions
QuestionPoint, 142

Reading room
  design of, 176–180
  managing materials in, 199–202
  personal belongings in, 197–199
"Ready, 'Net, Go! Archival Internet Resources," 93
Record groups, 82–83

Recording technologies
    effect on archives, 1–5
    and filing structures, 13
    in orientation sessions, 55
    variety of, 11
Records and record systems
    definition, 11–13
    restrictions on, 161–162, 165–166
    structure of, 78
Records management as management
    responsibility, 255–256
Records retention and destruction, 34, 158
Records *vs.* archives, 36
Recreational users, 57–60
Redaction, 161
Reference interactions, **113**. *See also*
    Reference interview
    factual vs. interpretive, 42
    handouts, **125**
    initial interview 113–128
    human dimension, 120–130
    mail and e-mail inquiries, 134–135
    and registration interview, 193
Reference interview
    exit interview, 120
    human dimension, 120–130
    initial interview, 113–128
    intellectual dimensions, 113–120
    query abstraction, 114–115
    query refinement, 119
    query resolution, 115–119
Reference process, 111–147, **112, 114, 116**
    administrative dimensions, 131–132
    human dimensions, 120–130
    intellectual dimensions, **112**, 112–119
    outreach, 143–147
    query abstraction, 114–115
    query resolution, 115–120
    remote users, 132–138
    on Web, 138–143
Reference services
    and access policy, 149–151
    Checklist for Access Policies and
        Reference Services, 318–322
    evaluation of, 259, 265–266
    levels of, 19, 167–168
    management of, 254–258
    organizational models of, 249–254
    scope of, **23,** 24–28, **25**

    vs. research, 43, 104–105
    work space for, 178, 180
Reference tools and secondary sources
    directories to repositories, 93–95
    guides to holdings, 98–103
    instruction in, 42
    location in reading room, 179
    in reference interview, 126
Referrals
    to other institutions, 108–109
    within parent organization, 108
Reformatting. *See* Preservation: and
    copying
Registers, 89. *See also* Inventories as
    descriptive aid
Registration of users
    automated, 204
    demographic analysis of, 263
    forms, 193–196, **194–195**
    and physical access, 189, 192–197
Remote users
    copying for, 218–219
    management of records, 256
    reference interactions with, 132–138
    statistics on, 264
Repositories, information about, 92–97.
    See also Holdings
"Repositories of Primary Sources," 93
Reproduction. *See* Copying
Research
    copying for, 210
    interpretive research, 48
    loans for, 244
    models for scholarly research, 48
    as purpose for archives, 41
    reference support for, 42–43
    by users outside the organization, 19
    vs. reference services, 42, 104–105
Researcher services. *See also* Reference
    services
    definition, 24
    facilitating research, 25, 25–26
    levels of, 19, 167–168
Research Libraries Group, 101–102
Research methodology, 48
Research room. *See* Reading room
Response time for e-mail queries, 135–136
Restrictions on access, 160–162. *See also*
    Donor restrictions

in access policy, 165–166
in governmental archives, 21
and scholars, 48
Retrieving materials, 200–201
Returning materials, 201–202
Right to know, 154
RLIN, 102. *See also* Bibliographic data-
bases
*Role Delineation Statement for
Professional Archivists,* 265
Rotating reference services, 250–251

Safety concerns, 184
Scanners, 215
Scanning for digital copies, 225
Scheduling of staff, 256–258
Scholars. *See also* Research
research support for, 47–49
resistance to asking questions, 123–124
Schools, uses of archives in, **39**
Search room. *See* Reading room
Search strategy, 115–119
Secondary school users, 50–53
Security, 180–185
and intimidation of users, 122, 131, 185
in loans for exhibitions, 245
of materials in transit, 213
personal belongings in reading
room, 197–199, **198**
and retention of call slips, 201
security checklist, **182–183**
Self-service copying, 214–215
Seminars as promotion of archive, 49
Series
arrangement and search strategy,
115–116
in hierarchy of control, 82
Signage, 128, 176–177, 187–188
Society of American Archivists (SAA)
and access traditions, 21–22
directories on web site, 94
*Sonny Bono Copyright Term Extension
Act,* 228

Space configuration. *See* Layout and
design of archive
Staff
and copy requests, 217
handling of materials, **186**
health and safety of, 184
and models of reference services,
250–252
performance evaluations, 265,
327–330, 331–333
qualifications of, 252–253
Staff directories as information
sources, 70
Staff of other organizations
as users, 46–47
Staff of parent organization
as users, 43–45
Standards
ALA-SAA Joint Statement on Access
to Original Materials, 313–315
for description, 85, 90–91
Reference Archivists, 327–330
Statement on the Reproduction of
Manuscripts and Archives for
Reference Service, 316–317
Statistics on use
automation of, 204
call slips, 201
and copy order forms, 220
measures of, 260–265
from registration information, 192,
193–196
Storage space, off-site, 200
Storage space, secure, 180
Stores and sales, on-line, 142
Students
privacy of records, 157
as users, 50–53, 52
Subject access in provenance-based sys-
tems, 89–90
Subject Collections, 94
*Subject Directory of Special Libraries and
Information Centers,* 95
Subject surveys, 99
Subpoenaed records, 165
Sunshine laws, 21
Supervision of users, 180

Support staff
administrative duties, 253
delegation of administrative details, 132
paraprofessionals, 58–59, 254
role in reference process, 119

Teachers, college and university, 53–56, 145
Teachers, K-12, 56–57
Teaching American History Grant Program, 56
Technologies, recording. *See* Recording technologies
Telephone reference, 133–134, **137,** 188
Term papers, assistance with, 51–53
Thieves and vandals
apprehending and prosecuting, 184
most users not, 122, 131, 185
motivation of, 181
Third-party inquiries, 115, 127–128
Timelessness of filing structures, 80
Time management, 256–258
Time required for remote reference, 137–138
Tours of facilities, 144
Turnover of employees, 254

University of Idaho, **190–191**
University of North Carolina, 72
University of Oklahoma Libraries, 72
University of Virginia, 56
Unprocessed collections in access policy, 166
Unpublished works and copyright, 232, 234–235
Usage information may not always be statistical.
Usage information. *See* Statistics on use
User communities. *See also* Users
in access policy, 164–165
conflict between needs of, 19
and electronic resources, 143
and equality of access, 154–155
levels of service, 19, 167–168
potential users, 264–265
and registration information, 192

User education
and courses in research methodology, 48
genealogists, 58–59
for general public, 57
need for, 42–43
on preservation, 185
in reference process, 118–119
and students, 53
User needs
and evaluation of quality, 260–265
and Web site design, 140
Users. *See also* User communities
characterization of, 38
follow-up questionnaire, **267**
individual needs of, 40–43
as information seekers, 61–63
and refinement of descriptive aids, 85
resistance to asking questions, 123–124
screening of, 160–161
and security regulations, 184–185
studies of, 268–270
Uses of information
in query negotiation, 127
in reference interaction, 114–115
Uses of records
direct uses, 37
indirect uses, 37–38
primary uses, 34
secondary uses, **34,** 35–36

Value of use, measurement of, 259, 260, 266–268
Vendors, use of for copying, 212–213
Vertical file and information about creators, 108
Videos. *See* Audiovisual materials
Virtual reference services, 142–143, 264
Vital records, uses of, **39**
Volunteers
genealogists as, 59
for referrals to researchers, 106
Vulnerability in initial interview, 122

Web. *See also* Internet
effect on archives, 2

references services on, 138–143
Web sites for repositories, 96–97, **97**
    design of, 140–142
    and frequent queries, 107
    policies and procedures on, 189,
        190–191
Withdrawal flags, 200, 203
Working files, 65
Worldwide Moving Image Sourcebook, 95

About the Author

Mary Jo Pugh is Supervisory Archivist at San Francisco Maritime National Historical Park. She was Reference Archivist at the Bentley Historical Library, University of Michigan, taught archival administration at the University of Michigan and the University of California, Berkeley, and has consulted for business and organization archives. A long-time member of the Society of American Archivists (SAA), she has served on committees and task forces and was elected to serve on the governing Council and the Nominating Committee. In 1983 she received SAA's Fellows' Ernst Posner Award for an outstanding essay published in the *American Archivist* and in 1992 was made a Fellow of SAA. She was also elected as President of the Michigan Archival Association and to the Board of Regents of the Academy of Certified Archivists.